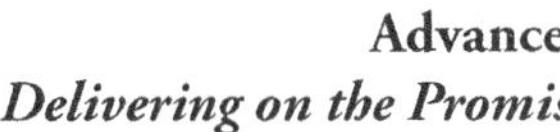
Advance

Delivering on the Promi

"Universities are waking up to their *kuleana*. Institutional leaders, including those of us in educational development, need to read, reflect on, and discuss the chapters of this book with the aim of centering equity in HIPs—of (re)assessing and (re)imagining HIPs, and creating new entry points for historically marginalized and excluded students. It's time to be equity-minded educators and, as Shaun Harper writes, this means strategically moving some students to the front of the line."—***Fay Yokomizo Akindes***, *Director, Office of Professional and Instructional Development (OPID), University of Wisconsin System*

"Our ability to give students a valuable college experience requires us to provide the instruction, programs, services, and connections that will prepare them for their myriad future goals. High-impact practices, when delivered equitably and effectively across an institution, can ensure students are ready for the complex challenges that await them. This collection of discussions from national experts is a perfect guide for institutions that seek a robust strategy for providing the high-impact practices that students need and deserve."—***Amelia Parnell***, *Vice President for Research and Policy, NASPA–Student Affairs Administrators in Higher Education*

"Whether one is an enthusiastic advocate of high-impact practices or in the 'I'd like more evidence, please' camp, *Delivering on the Promise of High-Impact Practices* is the book to read now. Taking an equity-focused approach to interpreting research on HIPs, this book answers—and asks—questions about how these practices might be done with fidelity and at scale to improve educational outcomes for all students. It sets an agenda for the third decade of HIP implementation and assessment."—***Kristen A. Renn***, *Mildred B. Erickson Distinguished Chair and Professor of Higher Education, and Associate Dean of Undergraduate Studies for Student Success Research, Michigan State University*

"Thoughtful. Timely. Courageous. This book addresses many of the critical issues that higher ed leaders must address, including the need to scale up HIPs and the equity imperative. Moreover, this book provides much-needed clarity on the evolution of high-impact practices while highlighting measurement and evaluation as critical steps for implementation." —***Michael T. Stephenson***, *Provost and Senior Vice President for Academic Affairs, Sam Houston State University*

DELIVERING ON THE PROMISE OF HIGH-IMPACT PRACTICES

DELIVERING ON THE PROMISE OF HIGH-IMPACT PRACTICES

Research and Models for Achieving Equity, Fidelity, Impact, and Scale

Edited by John Zilvinskis, Jillian Kinzie, Jerry Daday, Ken O'Donnell, and Carleen Vande Zande

Afterword by George D. Kuh

Epilogue by Shaun Harper

NEW YORK AND LONDON

First published in 2022 by Stylus Publishing, LLC.

Published in 2023 by Routledge
605 Third Avenue, New York, NY 10017
4 Park Square, Milton Park, Abingdon, Oxon OX14 4RN

Routledge is an imprint of the Taylor & Francis Group, an informa business.

Library of Congress Cataloging-in-Publication-Data

Names: Zilvinskis, John, editor. | Kinzie, Jillian (Jillian L.), editor. | Daday, Jerry, editor. | O'Donnell, Ken (College administrator), editor. | Vande Zande, Carleen, editor. | Kuh, George D., writer of foreword. | Harper, Shaun, writer of afterword.
Title: Delivering on the promise of high-impact practices : research and models for achieving equity, fidelity, impact, and scale / edited by John Zilvinskis, Jillian Kinzie, Jerry Daday, Ken O'Donnell, Carleen Vande Zande ; afterword by George D. Kuh; epilogue by Shaun Harper.
Description: First edition. | Sterling, Virginia : Stylus, 2022. | Includes bibliographical references and index.
Identifiers: LCCN 2022029262
ISBN 9781642673616 (paperback) | ISBN 9781642673609 (cloth)
Subjects: LCSH: College student development programs--United States. | College
teaching--United States. | Holistic education--United States. | Experiential learning--United States. | Transformative learning--United States. | Dropouts--Prevention. | Education, Higher--Aims and objectives--United States.
Classification: LCC LB2343.4 .D44 2022 (print) | LCC LB2343.4 (ebook) | DDC 378.1/980973--dc23/eng/20220815
LC record available at https://lccn.loc.gov/2022029262

ISBN: 9781642673609 (hbk)
ISBN: 9781642673616 (pbk)
ISBN: 9781003444022 (ebk)

DOI: 10.4324/9781003444022

We dedicate this book to the scholars who study HIPs, to the educators who design, teach, and mentor students in HIPs, and to the institutional leaders who enthusiastically support them, and finally, to the students who engage deeply in experiential learning.

To view full versions of all figures and tables, see:

https://www.routledge.com/9781642673616

CONTENTS

ACKNOWLEDGMENTS xi

INTRODUCTION
When Done Well—14 Years of Chasing an Admonition 1
John Zilvinskis, Jillian Kinzie, Jerry Daday, Ken O'Donnell, and Carleen Vande Zande

PART ONE: ADVANCING EQUITY

1 DESIGNING EQUITY-CENTERED HIGH-IMPACT PRACTICES 17
Ashley Finley, Tia McNair, and Alma Clayton-Pedersen

2 MAPPING THE CONNECTIONS OF VALIDATION AND HIGH-IMPACT PRACTICES 30
Adrianna Kezar, Ronald E. Hallett, Joseph A. Kitchen, and Rosemary J. Perez

3 METHODOLOGICAL CHALLENGES OF STUDYING HIGH-IMPACT PRACTICES FOR MINORITIZED POPULATIONS 40
Cindy Ann Kilgo

4 PROMOTING EQUITY BY DESIGN
Stacking High-Impact Practices for Faculty and Students in a First-Year Experience Program 50
Denise Bartell and Caroline Boswell

5 INTENTIONALLY DESIGNING LEARNING COMMUNITIES TO ADVANCE AUTHENTIC ACCESS AND EQUITY
Key Communities 62
Heather Novak, Taé Nosaka, and Ryan P. Barone

PART TWO: ASSURING FIDELITY

6 A DESIGN APPROACH TO UNDERGRADUATE RESEARCH FOR 1ST-YEAR STUDENTS 81
William Loker and Thia Wolf

7 THEMED LEARNING COMMUNITIES AND SERVICE-LEARNING LEVERAGED FOR STUDENT SUCCESS 92
Michele J. Hansen and Thomas W. Hahn

8 DATA COLLECTION IN COURSE-BASED UNDERGRADUATE RESEARCH EXPERIENCES
Best Practices and Lessons Learned 102
Sara Z. Evans and Jocelyn Evans

9 INTERNSHIPS FOR ALL?
How Inequitable Access to Internships Hinders the Promise and Potential of High-Impact Practices and Work-Based Learning 113
Matthew T. Hora

10 LIVING UP TO THE CAPSTONE PROMISE
Improving Quality, Equity, and Outcomes in Culminating Experiences 124
Caroline J. Ketcham, Anthony G. Weaver, Jessie L. Moore, and Peter Felten

11 IDENTITY AND COMMUNITY AMONG FIRST-GENERATION STUDENTS
High-Impact Practices and Communicating Belonging Throughout Department Design 135
Adrienne Viramontes and Theresa Castor

PART THREE: ACHIEVING SCALE

12 HIGH-IMPACT PRACTICES AND EQUITY
Pathways to Student Success in General Education Courses at a Large Urban Community College 151
Dallas M. Dolan, Jennifer Kilbourne, Monica Walker, and Glenda Breaux

13 DOCUMENTING HIGH-IMPACT PRACTICES IN INSTITUTIONAL DATA 164
Pam Bowers and Lara Ducate

14 REQUIRED EXPERIENTIAL LEARNING
Cultural Change and Commitment to Student Success 175
Jon C. Neidy, Kelly McConnaughay, and Jennifer Gruening Burge

15 INCREASING STUDENT ACCESS AND LEARNING IN EMPLOYMENT AND INTERNSHIP EXPERIENCES 188
Joe O'Shea, Myrna Hoover, and James Hunt

16 HIGH-IMPACT PRACTICES IN THE CURRICULUM
Implementing and Assessing a High-Impact Practice Course Designation Program 199
Bradley Wilson, Brian Danielson, Jason Hilton, and Kevin McCarthy

17 USING ASSESSMENT DATA TO EXPAND ACCESS TO HIGH-IMPACT PRACTICES FOR EVERY STUDENT 209
Kimberly Yousey-Elsener and Kirsten Pagan

18 TRACKING HIGH-IMPACT PRACTICE PARTICIPATION AND STUDENT SUCCESS WITH FIDELITY ACROSS A COMMUNITY COLLEGE SYSTEM 219
Heidi Leming

PART FOUR: ASSESSING OUTCOMES

19 HIGH-IMPACT PRACTICE CONNECTIONS AS CATALYSTS FOR EQUITABLE RETENTION 237
Meena C. Naik, Adam N. Wear, Scott Peecksen, Regina Branton, and Mike Simmons

20 MEASUREMENT AND EVALUATION OF HIGH-IMPACT PRACTICES WITHIN A CENTRALIZED MODEL 249
Rasha M. Qudisat and Frederick H. White

21 USING PROPENSITY SCORE MATCHING TO ASSESS HIGH-IMPACT PRACTICES OUTCOMES 262
Angela Byrd, Heather A. Haeger, Wendy Lin, A. Sonia Ninon, and Steven S. Graunke

AFTERWORD 273
The HIPs Just Keep Coming!
George D. Kuh

EPILOGUE 285
Shaun Harper

EDITORS AND CONTRIBUTORS 291

VOLUME INDEX TABLE 303

INDEX 305

ACKNOWLEDGMENTS

The idea for this book came about in the lobby of the Hyatt Place Hotel on the campus of Western Kentucky University in February of 2019. It was the last day of the second HIPs in the States conference, the first hosted by California State University Dominguez Hills in the spring of 2018. We attended wonderful sessions at both conferences, illuminating efforts to create, deliver, and scale high-quality high-impact practices (HIPs) in specific programs, units, or institutions. We sought to elevate the solid scholarship and assessment work that was being conducted about HIPs, with the goal of putting equity-minded questions at the center of this work, providing examples that might inspire others in the field to tackle similar questions, employing rigorous methods and valid data, and ensuring wider dissemination of this important work. The role of HIPs anchored in and integrated with student success strategies is evident in the contributors' research presented in this book. Interrogating HIPs through methodologically well-constructed research provides the foundation for more evidence-based practices that will reach more students and inform faculty, student success staff, and administrators to develop comprehensive and informed student services and experiences. This book is a part of that sharing process for the second decade of HIPs research and practice.

Putting together this book was a fun, collaborative, and collective effort, and as editors, we could not have completed our work without the help and contributions of many individuals. First, we want to offer our deepest and most sincere thanks to the 59 contributors who worked with us on the 21 chapters and the afterword and epilogue to this volume. These authors wrote and submitted their initial drafts by the fall of 2020 and worked with us in a very collaborative and constructive way through the difficult 2020–2021 academic year on several rounds of edits and revisions. All of these contributors have done and are continuing to do important work in the field related to equity, fidelity, scaling, and assessment, and we are honored to have the opportunity to elevate and disseminate the important work they are doing for students and their colleagues on their campuses and for the field of HIPs.

We would like to offer our sincere thanks to John von Knorring and his team at Stylus Publishing for seeing the promise and possibilities that this book could bring to the field and for being a constant support through this review and publishing process.

We know that student employment, when structured properly, can serve as a HIP. We embraced this idea and recruited several students from our home institutions to help us in compiling this book. Zach Wilson and Mack Ottens at Binghamton University organized submissions by the authors and provided general administrative support to this project. Anna Comer and Amelia Shull at Indiana University–Purdue University Indianapolis (IUPUI) checked the references and citations within each chapter, and where appropriate, offered suggested edits for APA compliance. Morgan Allen, also from IUPUI, conducted some qualitative analyses that helped to shape the structure of the volume. A special and heartfelt thanks to all of these students for helping us pull this volume together.

We would like to thank Christian Rogers, an associate professor of computer graphics technology and a senior faculty fellow in the Institute for Engaged Learning at IUPUI, for guiding us through an extensive design thinking exercise, which helped us in finalizing the ordering of the chapters in this volume.

Lastly, we would like to thank our families and colleagues for their support over the past 18 months as we put this volume together. Each of us works within higher education, and our direct supervisors and colleagues have been very supportive of our work on this effort, and for that, we are very grateful. And, on the home front, we would like to thank our families for their encouragement and support on this wonderful journey.

John Zilvinskis, Binghamton University
Jillian Kinzie, Indiana University
Jerry Daday, Indiana University–Purdue University Indianapolis (IUPUI)
Ken O'Donnell, California State University Dominguez Hills
Carleen Vande Zande, University of Wisconsin System

INTRODUCTION

When Done Well—14 Years of Chasing an Admonition

John Zilvinskis, Jillian Kinzie, Jerry Daday, Ken O'Donnell, and Carleen Vande Zande

The Association for American Colleges & Universities (AAC&U) publication by George Kuh (2008), *High-Impact Educational Practices: What They Are, Who Has Access to Them, and Why They Matter*, reintroduced higher education to the transformative power of enriching experiential education. The idea of "High-Impact Practices" has since had an outsized influence in higher education. Using data from the National Survey of Student Engagement (NSSE), Kuh showed that enriching learning experiences such as learning communities, service-learning, undergraduate research, internships, and senior culminating experiences were positively associated with student engagement, deep and integrated learning, and personal and educational gains for all students—particularly for historically underserved students, including first-generation students and racially minoritized populations. These practices earned the label *high-impact* because of their association with transformative learning and correlation with high levels of engagement, student retention, and GPA, and in particular, their benefits to historically underserved students (Finley & McNair, 2013; Kuh, 2008; NSSE, 2021).

Although many of these educational strategies have existed within higher education for decades, such as service-learning or study abroad, the term *high-impact practices* (HIPs) grouped them for the first time, attracting fresh attention to their similarities and importance. Findings about HIP gains for student learning and success amounted to a call to action for many in higher education. Compelled by national attention on graduation rates and closing completion rate gaps, public colleges and universities especially viewed HIPs as part of a comprehensive strategy to engage and retain their students. State governments, philanthropies, and organizations like Complete College America added to the urgency. At the same time, independent colleges and universities deepened their own long-standing historical commitment to HIPs, as a way to recruit students and advance the promotion of special, personalized learning opportunities.

The combination of educators' commitment to individual HIPs, positive research about their benefits for learning and completion, and broad interest across higher education sectors has highlighted the value of HIPs on at least three fronts: (a) providing educators with a way to meet increased requirements to support students and retain them through degree completion; (b) promoting deep, integrated, applied, and engaged learning, effectively increasing graduation rates without sacrificing academic rigor or career readiness; and (c) offering a shared language for experiential learning, valued by individual educators and a way to connect otherwise disparate practices.

Delivering on the Promise of HIPs

Much of this potential remains unrealized. Despite a great deal of enthusiasm for HIPs and a deep existing knowledge base, scholarship on the implementation and efficacy of HIPs remains halting and beset by challenges. Much of what gives these practices their high impact seems local, personal, and idiosyncratic. For example, a summer research experience that immerses a few students in a faculty marine research project may not work for a whole class, or at other institutions. In addition, HIPs often defy the familiar tools of administration—uniform, credit-bearing, countable courses; modular class schedules; and impressive economies of scale—making them hard to track or assess. Meanwhile, college and university leaders expect a lot from HIPs: They want this nomenclature to help them identify evidence-based practices that promote student success, aid in recruitment and retention, promote equity and access for traditionally underserved student populations, and provide high-quality and relevant educational experiences that prepare lifelong learners and successful professionals. All these opportunities raise a question: *How can colleges and universities deliver on the promises of equity, fidelity, impact, and scale of HIPs?*

Kuh himself saw this coming, warning educators in the original publication and ever since that we can expect these benefits from HIPs, but only "when done well." The checklist of named practices is tempting, but misleading. It skips over the knotty questions of equity, scale, and fidelity that continue to vex the field. As he continued to explain his work over the years, you could hear him adding italics to the phrase *when done well.* This book collects multiple responses to his caution, asking what we mean by *done well,* how we know when it happens, and who benefits. Here too, most of the work is still ahead of us. Although HIPs' association with desirable student outcomes makes them popular to implement, in practice, research shows HIPs are not reaching all student populations equally (Finley & McNair, 2013; Kuh, 2008; NSSE, 2021). Yet the pressure to scale raises worries about quality and consistency. Can colleges and universities really dedicate sufficient resources to achieve scale and ensure that every HIP offering is high quality? Or are HIPs effective educational innovations precisely because they are selective and special?

We cannot afford another 14 years of study to figure this out. In recent years urgent attention in the field has rightly turned to equity, to the role of experiential learning in taking on racial and socioeconomic disparities, closing gaps in attainment, and leveling up (AAC&U, 2015, 2018). The focus is increasingly on participation rates, as foreshadowed in Kuh's (2008) conclusion: "Sadly, some groups of historically underserved students are less likely to participate in high-impact activities—those first in their families to attend college and African-American students in particular" (p. 17). It is hard to read that conclusion without feeling a certain moral imperative, no less urgent all these years later. As an update to this concern, NSSE results show year after year lower participation rates for historically underrepresented student populations, and annual results continue to document uneven access to HIPs by institutional type (NSSE, 2021).

Critical scholarship on equity in HIPs raises more pointed concerns about implicit bias that may lead faculty and other educators to select or recommend their White students for certain HIPs, such as internships or undergraduate research (Patton et al., 2015), and calls for race-conscious student engagement practices to increase equity (Harper, 2009). In recent research examining students' experience in HIPs, Kinzie et al. (2021) adopted Yosso's (2005) community cultural wealth framework to spotlight the expertise of racially minoritized students and lift up what makes HIPs valued by students of color. Equity in HIPs is definitely about eliminating participation rate gaps. But it is also about recentering these experiences around students of color and ensuring that HIPs are culturally relevant.

Not that we needed one, but this is another sign the field is outgrowing the checklist of 10-then-11 named practices. The list, promulgated by AAC&U, includes: first-year seminars and experiences, common intellectual experiences, learning communities, writing-intensive courses, collaborative assignments and projects, undergraduate research, diversity/global learning, service-learning, internships, capstone courses/projects, and e-portfolios.

This list had the initial virtue of grouping disparate educational strategies for the first time, highlighting their commonalities. But it was too tempting, too reductive. Patton et al. (2015) have shown us that it is also regressive. High impact for one population may not be high impact for another, and different learners grow differently. Identifying the strategies that close gaps and drive engagement is hard work, and it happens one campus at a time.

To this end, Kinzie et al. (2021) have called attention to the quality of implementation, arguing that it matters more than the *high-impact* label. Finley (2019) cautioned that the popularity of HIPs and the push for institutions to tag and tout their HIPs can result in casual adoption, or a rush to implement without attending to all the qualities that make them so effective and transformative. In addition, the label *high-impact* is itself loaded, practically assuming efficacy. As Finley (2019) asked, "With a name like that, what is left to assess?" (p. 4). HIP proponents, scholars, and the institutions seeking the positive outcomes of HIPs are right to want to insist that HIPs be implemented with fidelity, and their impact monitored and tracked. This requires empirical studies with bold research questions, using the best methodologies to explore the most valid and reliable institutional and primary data sources available. And it requires an open mind.

Once these local, powerful practices are identified, assuring full and equitable participation in HIPs means being unambiguous about what counts. It means looking some well-intentioned colleagues in the eye and saying, "What you're doing may be effective, but it's not what the rest of us mean by undergraduate research, and so we're not going to let you call it that." For example, faculty may work hard to develop a comprehensive undergraduate research experience, but if this opportunity only favors students who are already privileged in higher education—that is not acceptable. Without such self-discipline, HIPs cannot be made consistent and explicit; they will remain buried in the hidden curriculum, available mostly to those with the social and cultural capital, money, and college-going savvy to seek them out, and opt in.

Once made explicit and attuned to the local culture, the final thing that HIPs want to be is *more widespread.* Put another way, experiences this educationally beneficial should be part of all undergraduate programs, not just a luxury for students who figure it out or have the resources to be involved. The "HIPs for All" goal suggests making them a requirement, or at the very least, building them into the undergraduate experience so they are inescapable. For example, several institutions have integrated HIPs into the general education curriculum, whereas others integrate HIPs into the academic major. Building HIPs into the curriculum makes them accessible, or at least harder to miss, even for students who work off campus, commute from a distance, or care for others at home. Plainly, colleges and universities and systems that adopt the curricular approach have seen that optional is too often inequitable.

What Does This Book Contribute?

The goal of *Delivering on the Promise of High-Impact Practices* is to provide examples from around the country of the ways educators are advancing equity, promoting fidelity, achieving scale, and strengthening assessment of their own local HIPs.

This volume brings together the best current scholarship, methodologies, and evidence-based practices within the HIPs field. The editors solicited contributions from researchers and practitioners who have made presentations at AAC&U conferences, from national grant projects such as the National Association of System Heads (NASH) Equity Minded HIPs project, and at the annual HIPs in the States conference. The chapters illustrate new approaches to faculty professional development, culture and coalition building, research and assessment, and continuous improvement that can help institutions understand and extend practices with a demonstrated high impact. Our goal is to elevate the quality of HIPs research within the scholarly literature, and to encourage faculty, staff, and administrative leaders to employ premier methods and data analysis to understand which of their practices are most effective, and for whom. By documenting sound HIP scholarship and administration, we want to encourage HIP proponents and academic leaders to tackle the big, pressing challenges of the field, including equity and access for traditionally underserved students, fidelity and quality of implementation, expanding capacity, and tracking and assessing these experiences.

Importantly, this book showcases the talent of committed faculty, student affairs educators, and administrative leaders who have demonstrated the effectiveness of their HIP initiatives. Their contributions are practical and accessible, and offer insight and inspiration for campuses striving to deliver on the promise of HIPs.

Where This Book Is Coming From

The editors of *Delivering on the Promise of High-Impact Practices* are unabashed proponents of HIPs, but we are also disturbed (and maybe a little excited) by the current messiness of the field: It remains new, raw, and emerging. Scholarship and HIPs administration on individual campuses are similarly uneven. This long into the hoopla we are overdue for a backlash, and in many ways, it is deserved. Too often the leaders of individual programs approach documentation and assessment defensively, stacking the deck to protect their budgets. Students and researchers may be unclear about the qualities and boundaries of the practices they are asked to weigh in on. And administrators are often readier to espouse these practices than take the time to understand them or provide appropriate support. These different shortcomings muddy the findings and discredit the research base. Although this book draws inspiration from our collective love of HIPs, as scholars, educators, and administrators in higher education, we also know there is still a lot of underbrush to be cleared—and much still to learn, share, and act on.

A strength of the field is that it brings together practitioners from a range of backgrounds, and the five of us are no exception. Our different backgrounds and shared commitment to HIPs scholarship prompted our search for the best HIP research and implementation in higher education. By attending sessions at the AAC&U Annual Conference, the NASH Taking Student Success to Scale (TS3) initiative, and the HIPs in the States conferences, we found exciting and innovative examples of educators, practitioners, and researchers striving to collect evidence about these forms of applied and experiential learning. We wanted to make this research available to a wider audience, reaching beyond the conference attendees, accelerating and strengthening the field's development. From the colleagues we had met this way, we extended invitations to the contributors of 15 of the chapters in this book. The other six chapters were selected from 55 submissions following our national call for proposals. You will find assembled here not just a wide range of educators, professions, and institution types, but also of hopes for HIPs themselves. The work is still young, the field wide open.

How This Book Is Organized

This volume contains 21 chapters grouped into four sections: "Advancing Equity," "Assuring Fidelity," "Achieving Scale," and "Assessing Outcomes." For many years these have been key to living up to the phrase "when done well." In that sense, we could have guessed these would be our four sections before collecting the first chapter.

But along the way we learned something important about these dimensions of HIPs: They are utterly interdependent. That is, we will not deliver on the promise of HIPs, least of all their potential for driving equity, without simultaneously attending to questions of fidelity, scale, and assessment. Figure I.1 illustrates the overlap and centers attention to equity.

Figure I.1. Four dimensions to deliver on the promise of HIPs.

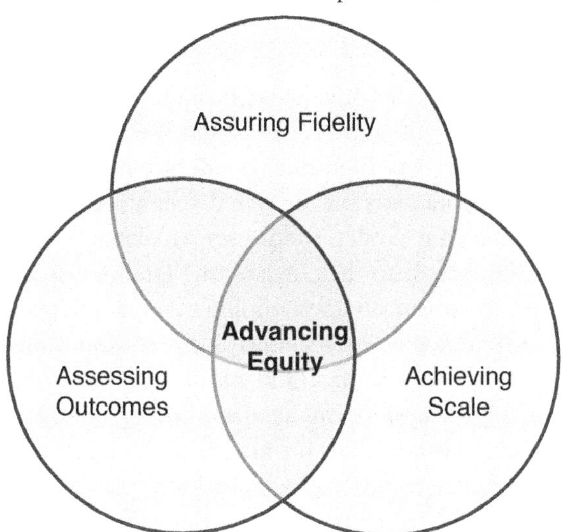

These four broad dimensions emerged in part from the guidance we provided to chapter contributors, articulated in the form of a rubric that prioritized

1. promoting equity and access for traditionally underserved student populations and answering a central research problem related to either fidelity and quality, tracking, equity and access, or scaling;
2. summarizing relevant literature that provides a clear context for what is already known about practice in HIPs;
3. describing how the work provides evidence-based pedagogies and practices that promote student success by identifying and presenting data to support equity findings for underrepresented populations; and
4. ensuring quality in research design, methodologies employed, valid and reliable datasets, and how data are used to increase the quality of HIPs and reduce inequities of participation in HIPs.

We are providing that rubric as an appendix to this introduction, because it may be a useful resource for institutions interested in studying their own, local HIPs, and to guide their formal HIP evaluation efforts.

Given the importance of equity in student success and the benefits of HIP participation for historically underserved students (AAC&U, 2015, 2018; Finley & McNair, 2013; Kuh, 2008), we asked all contributors to discuss the role of equity and equitable access within their chapters. Although you can read these chapters in any order, we recommend beginning with the opening section on equity and keeping these chapters in mind as you read the others.

Anchoring the theme of "Advancing Equity" are five chapters discussing equity and equity mindedness. The second section, "Assuring Fidelity," includes chapters that reflect high-quality, intentional, and evidence-based efforts to ensure that practices are delivered reliably and consistently. The third section, "Achieving Scale," addresses challenges of moving HIPs beyond niche experiences into the curriculum. The final section, "Assessing Outcomes," explores advanced methodological approaches to isolate the impact of a given practice while accounting for confounding factors. This section is meant to show how data and results can be used in practice to inform and create high-impact, evidence-based pedagogies. Each section has its own introduction and questions for further discussion.

There are two other things you should know about this book, which frankly we struggled with as editors. First, at the suggestion of our contributors we created an index to help readers find chapters that align with their HIP interests. Having created it, we almost did not include it: The index risks perpetuating the same, reductive categories of HIPs, student populations, and institution types that so much of this work is straining to leave behind. With the contributors to this book, we keep rediscovering that what really matters for human development is the messy intersectionality of identities, contexts, and educational strategies—sources of power and connectedness that epitomize good learning, but that are severed by brute categorization. This truth is the bane of researchers and administrators alike, but we cannot avoid complexity just because it is hard. So we hope you will take the index for what it is: a user-friendly on-ramp, but nothing more; the first word rather than the last.

Second, the field's past due reckoning with equity and race has raised important questions of language. We encouraged our contributors to address the value of HIPs for historically underserved and marginalized student populations, and few needed the reminder. Most of us are excited by HIPs precisely because they provide intellectual richness with the possibility of social justice. Similarly, most contributors are careful with their use of English. Out of respect for their personal experiences and convictions, we have kept their preferred phrasing to describe students' social identities such as ethnicity, race, socioeconomic status, and so on, even when that meant including contested terms. We agreed that keeping their original diction was more important than editorial consistency.

It is fitting that George Kuh, the scholar who inspired HIPs, closes out the volume in the Afterword. Finally, the equity theme is elevated to its next level with the rousing call to action in the Epilogue from Shaun Harper. This last contribution calls out what is still needed to illuminate and eliminate racism in HIPs, and to achieve HIP equity goals by creating sustainable practices and cultures of inclusion and respect.

Who Should Read This Book?

We developed this book aware it would have a certain built-in audience: advocates of HIPs, educators who teach and coordinate HIPs, scholars and institutional research professionals who want to study the effectiveness and influence of HIPs, campus-based professional development coordinators, and postsecondary leaders and policymakers who are interested in advancing HIPs in undergraduate education. These audiences often find each other through national membership organizations and communities of practice, such as HIPs in the States, NASH TS3, the AAC&U and their annual HIPs Summer Institute, NSSE, and the annual Indiana University–Purdue University Indianapolis (IUPUI) Assessment Institute.

On individual campuses, administration leaders, including provosts, deans, directors, and directors of centers for teaching and learning, should find this a helpful resource. So should the frontline faculty and student affairs professionals who understand the power of engagement by design, and want help making their work more visible and intentional. Finally, the volume's emphasis on equity and research will appeal to HIP scholars and respond to the broad call to deepen the HIP evidence base and strengthen equity in undergraduate education.

However, we cannot stop with the already initiated. To fully deliver on the promise of HIPs, we need more help. As we take this book to publication, we hope the scholarship it assembles will make a compelling case to newcomers, people who may have missed the attention lavished on HIPs so far or who, on the contrary, are turned off by it. To the newcomers and skeptics we offer an especially warm welcome. Diverse points of view accelerate learning, and higher education still has much to learn about our most engaging practices—how to promote them, to know where they are happening, and above all, how to bring them to the students who most stand to benefit.

Finally, all of the editors of this volume have heard Tia McNair (hear her voice in chapter 1) describe a vision for HIPs that promotes and leverages the assets of the pluralistic student bodies on our campuses, and the examples in this text provide inroads to better achieve this vision. The examples in this text highlight the ways educators have strengthened HIPs along the values described previously (equity, fidelity, scale, and assessment), but even these examples are not perfect. Although these chapters illustrate how educators can do better to deliver on the promise of HIPs, our field still has a lot more work to do to achieve that promise.

References

Association of American Colleges & Universities. (2015). *Committing to equity and inclusive excellence: A campus guide for self-study and planning.* https://www.aacu.org/sites/default/files/CommittingtoEquityInclusiveExcellence.pdf

Association of American Colleges & Universities. (2018). *A vision for equity—Results from AAC&U's project committing to equity and inclusive excellence: A campus guide for self-study and planning.* https://www.aacu.org/publications/vision-equity

Finley, A. (2019, November). *A comprehensive approach to assessment of high-impact practices* (Occasional Paper No. 41). University of Illinois and Indiana University, National Institute for Learning Outcomes Assessment (NILOA). https://www.learningoutcomesassessment.org/wp-content/uploads/2019/11/Occasional-Paper-41.pdf

Finley, A., & McNair, T. (2013). *Assessing underserved students' engagement in high-impact practices.* Association of American Colleges & Universities. https://www.aacu.org/assessinghips/report

Harper, S. R. (2009). Race-conscious student engagement practices and the equitable distribution of enriching educational experiences. *Liberal Education, 95*(4), 38–45.

Kinzie, J., Silberstein, S., McCormick, A. C., Gonyea, R. M., & Dugan, B. (2021). Centering racially minoritized student voices in high-impact practices. *Change: The Magazine for Higher Learning, 53*(4) 6–14. https://doi.org/10.1080/00091383.2021.1930976

Kuh, G. D. (2008). *High-impact educational practices: What they are, who has access to them, and why they matter.* Association of American Colleges & Universities.

National Survey of Student Engagement. (2021). *Engagement insights: Survey findings on the quality of undergraduate education.* Indiana University Center for Postsecondary Research. https://nsse.indiana.edu/research/annual-results/hips/index.html

Patton, L. D., Harper, S. R., & Harris, J. (2015). Using critical race theory to (re)interpret widely-studied topics related to students in U.S. higher education. In A. M. Martínez Alemán, E. M. Bensimon, & B. Pusser (Eds.), *Critical approaches to the study of higher education* (pp. 193–219). Johns Hopkins University Press.

Yosso, T. J. (2005). Whose culture has capital? A critical race theory discussion of community cultural wealth. *Race Ethnicity and Education, 8*(1), 69–91. https://doi.org/10.1080/1361332052000341006

APPENDIX

Rubric for Delivering on the Promise of HIPs

Table I.1 is a rubric provided to contributors and may be a useful resource for institutions interested in studying their own, local HIPs, and to guide their formal HIP evaluation efforts.

TABLE I.1
Chapter Expectations Rubric

HIP Chapter Attribute	*Clear Evidence Presented*	*Suggestions/ Additions*
Addresses a central implementation question: • fidelity and quality • tracking/assessment • equity and access • scaling		
Summary of relevant literature: Provides a succinct summary of the most relevant literature that offers a clear context for what is already known about your practice in HIPs.		
Evidence-based pedagogies and practices are addressed. Provides evidence of your empirical investigation of one or more HIPs, including influence on student success.		
Identifies and presents data to support equity findings on such underrepresented populations as: • first-generation students • racially and ethnically minoritized groups • low-income and transfer students		
Quality of research: • question development • methodologies employed • valid and reliable primary data sources • describes how data are used to improve practice		

(Continues)

TABLE I.1 (*Continued*)

HIP Chapter Attribute	*Clear Evidence Presented*	*Suggestions/ Additions*
Addresses use of assessment data to increase the quality of HIPs and reduce inequities of participation in HIPs. Provides comments on degree to which methodological approach addressed impact of HIPs.		

PART ONE

ADVANCING EQUITY

This book identifies four areas within higher education that require further work and advancement in order to deliver fully on the promises of high-impact practices (HIPs): equity, fidelity, scale, and assessment. Of these four priorities, we think equity is the most urgent; therefore, these chapters are in a place of prominence as the very first section of this volume. In fact, as stated in the volume introduction, the other three priorities are in service of advancing equity. We encourage you to have these equity-focused pieces in mind as you read the chapters in the other sections. Why is equity so urgent? Since the seminal Kuh (2008) publication from the

Association of American Colleges & Universities (AAC&U), we have known three things:

1. The effects of participating in high-impact practices are positive for all types of students.
2. But historically underserved students tend to benefit more from engaging in educationally purposeful activities than majority students.
3. Sadly, some groups of historically underserved students are less likely to participate in high-impact activities—those first in their families to attend college and African-American students in particular. (p. 17)

Together these three striking sentences amount to an unequivocal call to action for those working in the field: If we know something is good, and if we know the students who most stand to benefit are also the ones least likely to get it, then this inequity is on us. Unfortunately, the results from the National Survey of Student Engagement (NSSE) over time suggest that after years of sincere effort, we have done little to rebalance participation rates in these experiences. On the contrary, the students engaging in HIPs remain the ones who have enough time, money, and social capital to engage in more than minimal coursework for degree completion.

These realities leave us with several burning questions that set up the first section of this book: How do we unhide the hidden curriculum of HIP participation? How do we lower the barriers to entry, and build HIPs into the baseline expectations of college enrollment and attendance? And how do we make these experiences within reach of all students? To judge from the chapters in this first section on equity, the answer is by starting early and building a team.

If we design great educational experiences first and think about equity second, our action is already too late. The chapters in this first section clearly show that we must begin this work with equity. For example, the contributors of chapters 4 and 5 designed learning communities and first-year experiences from the ground up so that they work for all students, regardless of their means or moxie. There are also significant roles for faculty professional development and processes for collecting data at the institution level. The body of work collected and presented in this first section demonstrates that programs cannot improve equitable access to HIPs by working on their own.

Once the educational structures are conceived and alliances forged, we must assess continuously and scrupulously, watching for the reemergence of inequity. These authors show us that we must engage in close, high-touch assessment. The contributors of chapters 2 and 3 emphasize very close-up scrutiny of practices offered and populations served. Without such feedback at full strength, we risk drifting back to where we started.

Ashley Finley, Tia McNair and Alma Clayton-Pedersen are familiar to many in this field. Clayton-Pedersen created cutting-edge work on inclusive excellence when she was at AAC&U. All three were at AAC&U when the HIPs framework was created. The Finley-McNair monograph *Assessing Underserved Students' Engagement in High-Impact Practices* (2013) has remained for many of us the best and last word on the subject. That is, until now, with a new statement on designing equity-centered HIPs, which serves as the first chapter of this volume, and a call to action for all of us in the field.

Discussion Questions

- What barriers keep historically underserved students from participating in HIPs at your institution? How do you know?
- How has the implementation of HIPs increased your institutional awareness of opportunity gaps?
- How could you adjust your institutional evaluation of HIPs to include an equity lens?
- What institutional practices could be adapted to increase the efficacy of HIPs?
- How do we create HIPs that are not only equitably beneficial for all students but also leverage the assets that diverse groups bring to our campus?

References

Finley, A. P., & McNair, T. (2013). *Assessing underserved students' engagement in high-impact practices.* Association of American Colleges & Universities.

Kuh, G. D. (2008). *High-impact educational practices: What they are, who has access to them, and why they matter.* Association of American Colleges & Universities.

I

DESIGNING EQUITY-CENTERED HIGH-IMPACT PRACTICES

Ashley Finley, Tia McNair, and Alma Clayton-Pedersen

The increasing attention on high-impact practices (HIPs) across higher education has prompted an emphasis on identifying where these practices exist on campuses, gathering the evidence to justify efficacy, and beginning discussions around quality of implementation. Foundational to all of these emphases is the role of HIPs in advancing equity and student success, particularly for underserved and minoritized students (Finley & McNair, 2013). But too often a focus on equity is lost among the other considerations that go into designing HIPs. Equally problematic is that equity is often an afterthought—the piece that is included once everything else has been designed.

The advantage of taking an equity-centered approach from the beginning of the design process is the opportunity to weave in a clear understanding of what equity means and how it can be applied within every element of the HIPs design process. This approach also comes with the potential to simultaneously reflect upon and advance institutional commitments to equity and HIPs across the curriculum and cocurriculum. By encouraging administrative leaders, faculty, and student affairs professionals to consider systems of power and privilege both within and outside the academy, resulting learning experiences can better reflect the value in students' diversity and support their unique strengths and cultural legacies. Equity-centered designs also create intentional plans for implementation that address issues of access to participation and institutionalization of practices, whether in person or virtual, that entail examining policies and practices for sustaining and improving efforts over time. Finally, equity-centered designs of HIPs are committed to improvement by considering equity at multiple stages of the assessment process, from defining relevant outcomes to the quality of practice implementation, and through direct and authentic evaluation of learning.

This chapter introduces an equity-centered approach to the design of HIPs and examines design in three parts:

1. How to conceptualize the equitable, expansive, and quality design of HIPs based on the sensemaking of educators and institutional priorities for student success
2. What it means to implement equity-centered practices across the institution with an eye toward access and sustainability
3. How to approach the assessment of HIPs from an equity-centered lens

We assume equity-centered HIPs can be implemented at any institution, whether 2-year or 4-year, public or private. We also assume that although more resources are always better, these practices primarily require the human resources of time, communication, commitment, and patience. And, finally, we assume that equity-centered HIPs are applicable within a range of learning environments—face-to-face, virtual, or hybrid.

Equity in Design

Taking an equity-centered approach to the design of HIPs across modalities requires intentionality and reflection. The design process is dependent on educators' sensemaking related to student success, which is influenced by their own lived experiences, values, and perceptions. Bensimon (2007) stated,

> Practitioners in higher education, over time and through a variety of experiences, have developed implicit theories about students: why they succeed, why they fail, and, what, if anything, they can do to reverse failure. . . . Practitioners for the most part are likely not aware of what knowledge or experiences constitute their sense-making and how the judgments they make about a phenomenon such as student success or failure are shaped by that sense-making. (p. 446)

The growing diversity of the postsecondary student population and the misalignment of faculty representation from similar demographic backgrounds (American Council on Education, 2020) necessitates efforts to build capacity among educators to expand their funds of knowledge and sensemaking to understand not only who their students are and will be, but how to center equity and equity-mindedness in the design of HIPs to create expansive learning environments.

Acknowledging that the definitions of *equity* and *equity-mindedness* vary across institutions and among educators, for the purposes of this chapter, as stated in *From Equity Talk to Equity Walk: Expanding Practitioner Knowledge for Racial Justice in Higher Education* (McNair et al., 2020), we define *equity* as a form of corrective justice (McPherson, 2015); as an antiracist effort to confront racism embedded in institutional structures, policies, and practices (Pollock, 2009); and as a lens for seeing how whiteness is privileged as the norm for educational design and definitions of student success. Further, we examine the design, implementation, and assessment of HIPs as *equity-minded practitioners*, a term coined by Estela Bensimon (2007), who are race-conscious and "willing to assess [our] own racialized assumptions . . . and take responsibility for the success of historically underserved and minoritized student groups" (p. 20). In doing so, we acknowledge that the design of HIPs cannot be based on the dominant perspective of whiteness as the norm and the standard of student engagement and success (Patton et al., 2015). The designs have to be based on equity-minded sensemaking, which includes both qualitative and quantitative data that value the process for understanding the experiences of minoritized students and asking why certain educational strategies are not working as intended for certain students (McNair et al., 2020).

Efforts to examine equity and quality of HIPs should prioritize the process through which educators design learning experiences. As stated, educators enter into the design process with various funds of knowledge on equity, equity-mindedness, and student success. For this reason, it is important that educators utilize a framework for design that values the diversity of the student population at an institution. Given our definition of *equity* and the use of equity-mindedness as principles for designing HIPs, we offer Tara Yosso's cultural wealth model as an example of a design framework that can be utilized in correlation with the quality design elements of HIPs (Kuh et al., 2013). Yosso (2005) wrote:

> The main goals of identifying and documenting cultural wealth are to transform education and empower. . . . These forms of capital draw on the knowledges Students of Color bring with them from their homes and communities into the classroom. . . . Community cultural wealth involves a commitment to conduct research, teach and develop schools that serve a larger purpose of struggling toward social and racial justice. (p. 82)

The six forms of cultural capital include aspirational (maintaining hopes and dreams, even when facing barriers), linguistic (intellectual and social skills attained through communication experiences in multiple languages), familial (community well-being, sense of community history), social capital (networks of people and community resources), navigational (abilities to navigate through social institutions), and resistance (lived experiences fostered through efforts to secure equal rights; Yosso, 2005; Yosso & Garcia, 2007). These six forms of cultural capital are essential to incorporate in the HIP design process.

Understanding how to incorporate these six forms of cultural capital in the HIPs design process begins with inquiry and data collection that will help educators build higher levels of understandings of students' lived experiences from an asset-based approach. For example, educators engaging in equity-minded sensemaking may incorporate what they learn from the inquiry and data collection processes into the design of HIPs by asking the following questions in relationship to the quality elements of HIP design:

1. How do the performance expectations that are set acknowledge the cultural capital of students, rather than privilege some students' goals and outcomes as the standard of excellence for student success?
2. How do the interactions with faculty and peers about substantive matters acknowledge and reflect the ways that students employ their cultural capital?
3. What are ways that the design of HIPs promote experiences with diversity that incorporate students' cultural capital?
4. How are HIPs that are designed to encourage relevance of learning through real-world applications valuing and utilizing students' lived experiences, interests, and cultural capital?

Equity-minded approaches to the design process for HIPs require an assessment of educators' funds of knowledge and sensemaking, clarity in equity language and goals, an understanding of who students are and expect to become, and a framework for design and inquiry that values the assets that students bring to the learning environment.

In addition, educators need to avoid common obstacles that hinder the achievement of racial equity in education, including claiming not to see race as a factor in educational design and adopting the myth of universalism in which program design claims to be race-neutral but actually privileges whiteness as the normalized frame for design, implementation, and assessment (McNair et al., 2020). Avoiding these obstacles means programs are designed such that they decenter whiteness, and value and embed the experiences of marginalized and racially minoritized students in the design process. If these equity considerations are at the forefront of the design of HIPs, implementation and assessment efforts also will reflect a more equity-centered approach and equitable outcomes.

Equity in HIP Implementation

Institutionalizing HIPs with a focus on equity requires the alignment of organizational structures, policies, practices, and resources to broaden access to HIPs, particularly among students who have not previously had access. A guiding framework referred to as "RIBS" helps institutionalize the implementation of HIPs and the elements of the process that may accelerate broadening equitable access to them: Raise awareness, Increase knowledge, Build capacity, and Sustain efforts toward making excellence inclusive (Clayton-Pedersen & Dungy, 2007; Clayton-Pedersen et al., 2007). Just as ribs play a vital supporting and protecting role in our skeletal structure, the RIBS framework suggests there are critical actions within institutional structures to help support and protect equitable HIPs and learning outcomes.

Raise Awareness of Existing HIPs

Equitable implementation of HIPs should begin with forming interdisciplinary and cross-stakeholder (e.g., student life, support staff, and faculty) teams working together to identify HIPs already offered, who has access to them, and any barriers that restrict students' access, particularly among marginalized and underserved students. Approaches to offering HIPs vary, but too often the criteria for participation create barriers to access—some are readily apparent, whereas others may be more obscure. For example, some campuses limit participation in undergraduate research to juniors and seniors only, and/or having a minimum GPA. These restrictions assume that 1st-year students and sophomores of all backgrounds are not equipped to undertake even a basic research project or that those with GPAs below a subjective threshold will not succeed.

These restrictions may also include cost of participation and lack of structural supports for faculty development that promote teaching strategies shown to enhance student learning outcomes. Raising awareness must be supported with campus-specific data about who has access to HIPs and disaggregated along various dimensions such as gender, race/ethnicity, age, and previous educational experience, to name a few. For example, Elon University's commitment to HIPs is shown by its nine HIP offerings throughout the curriculum, required for all students. As campus administrators seek to broaden awareness of HIPs, they should ask:

1. What institutional barriers exist that prevent us from embedding HIPs into the general education curriculum or into majors?
2. How can the obstacles students face in accessing HIPs be assessed and removed?

Increase Knowledge About Why HIPs Matter

Success in HIPs implementation is in large part dependent upon faculty and student affairs understanding *how* HIPs stimulate deeper learning. Faculty and staff should be given the time to explore the research and evidence that demonstrate the ways in which HIPs stimulate students' interest in exploring subjects more deeply and improving learning and overall success outcomes, such as retention and graduation. Similarly, strategies to broadly introduce or expand existing HIP offerings require examination of which HIPs will work best in a given context. Through the creation of communities of practice, attending conferences, and developing common resource hubs, faculty and staff can examine which HIPs fit best within the context of disciplines and campus culture to determine which practices should be introduced and which others might be expanded.

Increasing knowledge also suggests finding ways to stimulate faculty and staff thinking with regard to experimentation with HIPs. Such encouragement may also lay a foundation for improving and broadening HIPs offerings once established. By offering incentives for faculty, staff, and students to provide honest feedback on efficacy, practices can evolve, grow, and innovate. As faculty and staff seek to increase understanding of HIPs, they should ask:

1. How can we work collaboratively to increase our knowledge and understanding of the connecting points across our disciplines and units?
2. What is needed—in terms of resources, support, and assurance from leadership—for us to scale and innovate?

Build Capacity to Make HIPs Pervasive

Building capacity for institutionalizing the equitable implementation of HIPs can take a number of forms on campuses, but effective professional development must be at the core of these efforts. In order to assist faculty and staff in understanding barriers to student success and engagement, professional development must be proactive, practical, and inclusive. Programming should tackle issues like implicit biases, discrimination, students' cognitive development, and the learning process itself. These discussions take careful curation and continued engagement of participants over time. For example, rather than one-off workshops, professional development programming might be seen as delivering an entire curriculum centered on instilling a culture of teaching and learning excellence among faculty and staff (Eynon & Iuzzini, 2020). Such an approach would be aimed at supporting faculty and staff learning through a diverse set of topics, forming learning communities to create space for deeper engagement, and careful documentation of benchmarks and milestones that indicate achievement in advancing equitable access and success in HIPs. As instructional designers, faculty, and staff seek to build capacity for HIPs, they should ask:

1. How can we develop a curriculum of professional development for faculty, staff, and administrators that will spark ongoing dialogue, reflection, and action to promote equitable, high-quality HIPs implementation?
2. How can we assess the influence professional development has on student learning outcomes?

Sustain Efforts for Institutionalizing Equitable HIPs Implementation

Campus leaders at all levels play an important role in sustaining the examination, implementation, assessment, and improvement of HIPs. They do this through supporting those who are innovative HIPs designers and also those who are effective HIPs implementers and assessors. Efforts can also be sustained through identifying essential collaborative engagements across the institution. This requires creating bridges across administrative, departmental, and academic silos such that student success *and* organizational success can be mutually reinforcing. Examples of such alignment can be found in the Office of Diversity, Equity and Community Engagement (ODECE) at the University of Colorado Boulder, which has linked its strategic plan with those of other academic and functional units, including the new Center for Teaching and Learning, to support a broad commitment to advancing equity through HIPs. Similarly, Bolton et al. (2017) described their catalytic work in transforming the curriculum by aligning key performance indicators through an equity lens and using appropriate tools to create an "inclusive and student-ready culture" across functional areas (p. 9). Finally, leaders can reflect on multiple areas for institutional alignment of processes and practices through application of the RIBS rubric (Clayton-Pedersen et al., 2007). As campus leaders seek to sustain efforts to institutionalize HIPs, they should ask:

1. How can we support increasing faculty knowledge and experimentation with HIPs and build capacity by rewarding their time investment in ways that are meaningful to them?
2. What administrative structures can best facilitate the broad engagement of a critical mass of the campus constituency to make a real difference in its effort to provide equitable access to HIPs?

Equity in Assessment

Because assessment, along with equity, can often be an afterthought, building both of these elements in from the beginning of the HIP design process can feel daunting. But considering both together serves to both maximize time and efficacy of the overall assessment plan. In a nutshell, an equity-centered assessment process requires conceptualizing assessment as more than a single activity but one that is instead envisioned as relevant at multiple stages of design and implementation processes. At the same time, each assessment "touchpoint" should be guided from the perspective that students succeed not as a homogenous whole, but rather as a uniquely diverse assembling of cultural backgrounds, strengths, and assets upon which to draw. An equity-centered approach also suggests the expectation that results will be used to inform targeted improvement that addresses the diversity of the student population and such that existing practices can be tailored to support the potential of all students.

The breadth of this approach is best illustrated by the use of a logic model. Because the use of logic models to develop a comprehensive assessment plan for equity and HIPs has been addressed at length elsewhere (Finley, 2019), the remainder of this chapter focuses on three significant elements of an equity-centered assessment design for HIPs. Each of these elements (i.e., vision and outcomes, quality of practice, and authentic assessment of students' work) appears within a logic model framework, although they can also be considered outside of that structure. What follows can provide a useful starting point at the early stages of assessment development that holds equity at its core.

Vision and Outcomes

A common refrain for assessment plans is that they should begin with outcomes. Although that is true, plans should actually begin a step ahead of outcomes. This is even more critical when taking an equity-centered lens. The starting point for assessing equity-centered HIPs demands the articulation of a vision for the practices that conceptualizes why equity matters for the future of the institution, for students' lives, and for standards of educational excellence. Although the vision statement itself is not assessed, all other elements of the assessment process should be able to be traced back to the vision as a kind of guiding north star. Specifically, the outcomes chosen to operationalize the effects of HIPs on students' learning and development should, themselves, have echoes in the vision. If, for example, the vision for HIPs articulates an expectation for "supporting students' intellectual, personal, and social development," the associated outcomes should span these areas with a nod to outcomes such as critical thinking or written communication, resilience or sense of purpose, and civic agency or global perspective-taking.

Quality of Practice

The foundation for assessing outcomes depends on the quality of implementation of the practices themselves. Because quality of implementation is often assumed rather than intentionally assessed, it can be the Achilles' heel of outcomes results. Without implementation of the aspects of HIPs that actually make them high impact, hypothesized effects on outcomes can fall apart or, at the very least, are far less assured.

A number of qualities of HIPs have been identified (see Finley & McNair, 2016; Kuh et al., 2013). But for the sake of simplicity, these quality dimensions could be reduced to a core few, not because they are the most important but because they tend to represent categories under which the other quality dimensions can be encapsulated. These categories are reflection, interaction, and intentionality (see Clayton-Pedersen & Finley, 2011). For example, HIPs should consistently invite students to reflect often and in structured ways. In part this reflection should be motivated by consistent feedback from the instructor and from peers, and in ways that invite students to respond productively. Feedback is often assumed to be one-directional and transactional, where comments represent an endpoint rather than the start of a dialogue. The category of "interaction" encapsulates the social qualities of HIPs that underscore the effectiveness of learning in a communal space and as an associative activity. Such practices, therefore, include engagement among faculty and peers, and interactions among people with different perspectives and cultural backgrounds. Intentionality suggests qualities of HIPs—such as high expectations, real-world applications, and demonstrations of competence—are unlikely to occur by happenstance or to emerge "organically" within the learning environment. HIPs take careful planning, structure, and implementation.

For each of these categories of quality—reflection, interaction, intentionality—assessment can take the form of a rubric used to guide classroom observation and/or faculty self-assessment. Students can also be asked to evaluate their experience based on those components, as the National Survey of Student Engagement (NSSE) has started to do with their HIP Quality assessment tool (Kinzie et al., 2021). Any form of assessment, however, should examine how qualities of HIPs have been implemented in ways that attend to the needs and supports of all students. For example, intentional structured reflection that is attentive to equity should not only be frequent; it should also indicate the ways in which students from all backgrounds have been invited into the reflection process through the lens of their cultural capital, drawing upon the strengths of background, upbringing, and the questions that inform their worldview.

Authentic and Asset-Based

There has been a steady and transformative movement toward the direct assessment of students' development of broad skills (e.g., critical thinking, written communication, and ethical reasoning) that builds upon the direct assessment of students' mastery of content knowledge. This movement has been largely guided by campus and faculty deployment of Association for American Colleges & Universities VALUE rubrics to specify the dimensions and markers of these skills. As with the long tradition of faculty assessment of content knowledge, the assessment of skills similarly utilizes authentic classroom-based assignments. Just as assignments are designed to elicit students' application and understanding of relevant disciplinary or course-specific material, authentic assessment of skills is similarly contingent on assignments designed to address a particular broad learning outcome, such as critical thinking. The focus on assignment design for direct, authentic assessment also provides an important layer for simultaneously designing for equity. For example, equity-centered signature assignments, in addition to being tailored toward outcomes, also promote a student-driven inquiry process that supports and empowers each student to ask and answer their own question(s) and approach problem-solving from their unique vantage point.

Additionally, rubrics structured as developmental tools, such as the VALUE rubrics, provide a basis for assessing students' performance at a point in time and also their trajectory toward greater levels of cognitive development. From an equity standpoint, these tools are an asset-based guide for providing students with feedback and for telling an institutional story about student learning across the curriculum (and potentially the cocurriculum). The multidimensional nature of rubrics enables equal attention to be given to areas of strength, as might be given to opportunities for improvement. The ability to emphasize where students have excelled provides a nuance that is often missing from rote procedures simply aimed at disaggregating data.

Conclusion

Although HIPs have been widely regarded as a strategy for boosting equity in student outcomes, far less attention has been given to inserting equity into the design process. Yet the imperative for equity in design is just as important as seeking equity in outcomes. In fact, one could argue, the latter only happens with attention to the former. By weaving in equity-centered thinking at the beginning of programmatic design, rather than as an afterthought, the benefits of HIPs go beyond just deepening students' learning and development. The connection of equity throughout implementation encourages a process that is inclusive of the learning and professional development across the multiple stakeholders—faculty, staff, and administrators—who play a critical role in delivering high-quality HIPs.

Valuing the learning of stakeholders as much as the learning of students is a paradigm shift for campuses. It suggests an ecosystem of support, collaboration, and sustainability of efforts that goes well beyond any one high-impact experience or initiative. To fully explore what it means to adopt a mindset where cultural capital is valued and one that engages and celebrates students' unique strengths is to invite the kind of holistic model of implementation outlined in the RIBS framework. And to move from implementation to improvement is to consider how equity is assessed at multiple stages of the design process. Thus, each section of this chapter is intended to fit together as pieces of a new paradigm—a paradigm that views learning as a shared responsibility and a common goal; that acknowledges systemic inequities, particularly across racial differences, are pervasive and endemic; and that supports the belief that transformation is a collective opportunity. At their very best, equity-centered designs of HIPs do more than provide new lenses and standards for student success. These designs reshape the lenses through which stakeholders view institutional success, as well.

References

American Council on Education. (2020). *Race and ethnicity in higher education: 2020 supplement release.* https://www.acenet.edu/Events/Pages/Race-and-Ethnicity-in-Higher-Education-2020.aspx#:~:text=EventsCurrently%20selected-,Race%20and%20Ethnicity%20in%20Higher%20Education%3A%202020%20Supplement,November%2010%2C%202020

Bensimon, E. M. (2007). The underestimated significance of practitioner knowledge in the scholarship on student success. *The Review of Higher Education, 30*(4), 411–469. https://doi.org/10.1353/rhe.2007.0032

Bolton, K. J., Felton J., Fine, R., Gavin, M., Jackson, J., & Morse, A. (2017). Committing to equity: A catalyst for institutional transformation. *Peer Review, 19*(2), 9–10. https://www.aacu.org/peerreview/2017/Spring/Bolton

Clayton-Pedersen, A. R., & Dungy, G. (2007). Developing effective collaborations. In J. H. Cook & C. A. Lewis (Eds.), *Student and academic affairs collaboration: The divine comity* (pp. 63–76). National Association of Student Personnel Administrators (NASPA). https://www.naspa.org/book/student-and-academic-affairs-collaboration-the-divine-comity

Clayton-Pedersen, A. R., & Finley, A. (2011). Dimensions of high intensity, high-impact practices. In J. E. Brownell & L. E. Swaner (Eds.), *Five high-impact practices: Research on outcomes, completion, and quality* (pp. 53–57). Association of American Colleges & Universities. https://www.aacu.org/publication/five-high-impact-practices-research-on-learning-outcomes-completion-and-quality

Clayton-Pedersen, A. R., Parker, S., Smith, D. G., Moreno, J., & Teraguchi, D. H. (2007). *Making a real difference with diversity: A guide for institutional change.* Association of American Colleges & Universities. https://secure.aacu.org/AACU/Pubexcerpts/RealDiff.html

Eynon, B., & Iuzzini, J. (2020). *ATD Teaching and Learning Toolkit: A research-based guide to building a culture of teaching and learning excellence.* Achieving the Dream. https://www.achievingthedream.org/press_release/18251/achieving-the-dream-releases-atd-teaching-learning-toolkit

Finley, A. (2019, November). *A comprehensive approach to assessment of high-impact practices* (Occasional Paper No. 41). University of Illinois and Indiana University, National Institute for Learning Outcomes Assessment (NILOA). https://www.aacu.org/sites/default/files/files/publications/accu_niloa_hips_pub_2019.pdf

Finley, A. P., & McNair, T. (2013). *Assessing underserved students' engagement in high-impact practices.* Association of American Colleges & Universities. https://www.aacu.org/sites/default/files/files/assessinghips/AssessingHIPS_TGGrantReport.pdf

Finley, A. P., & McNair, T. (2016). The intersection of life and learning: What cultural wealth and liberal education mean for whole student development. In B. Barnett & P. Felten (Eds.), *Intersectionality in action: A guide for faculty and campus leaders for creating inclusive classrooms and institutions* (pp. 147–158). Stylus.

Kinzie, J., McCormick, A. C., Gonyea, R. M., Dugan, B., & Silberstein, S. (2021, March 3). *Getting beyond the label: Three takes on quality in high-impact practices.* https://www.aacu.org/blog/getting-beyond-label-three-takes-quality-high-impact-practices

Kuh, G. D., O'Donnell, K., & Reed, S. (2013). *Ensuring quality and taking high-impact practices to scale.* Association of American Colleges & Universities. https://www.aacu.org/publications-research/publications/ensuring-quality-and-taking-high-impact-practices-scale

McNair, T. B., Bensimon, E. M., & Malcom-Piqueux, L. E. (2020). *From equity talk to equity walk: Expanding practitioner knowledge for racial justice in higher education.* Wiley.

McPherson, L. K. (2015). Righting historical injustice in higher education. In H. Brighouse & M. McPherson (Eds.), *The aims of higher education: Problems of morality and justice* (pp. 113–134). University of Chicago Press. https://doi.org/10.7208/chicago/9780226259512.003.0007

Patton, L. D., Harper, S. R., & Harris, J. C. (2015). Using critical race theory to (re) interpret widely-studied topics in U.S. higher education. In A. Martinez-Aleman, E. M. Bensimon, & B. Pusser (Eds.), *Critical approaches to the study of higher education* (pp. 193–219). Johns Hopkins University Press.

Pollock, M. (2009). *Colormute: Race talk dilemmas in an American school.* Princeton University Press.

Yosso, T. J. (2005). Whose culture has capital? A critical race theory discussion of community cultural wealth. *Race Ethnicity and Education, 8*(1), 69–91. https://doi.org/10.1080/1361332052000341006

Yosso, T., & García, D. (2007). "This is no slum!": A critical race theory analysis of community cultural wealth in culture clash's Chavez Ravine. *Aztlan: A Journal of Chicano Studies, 32*(1), 145–179. https://www.researchgate.net/publication/242722692_This_Is_No_Slum_A_Critical_Race_Theory_Analysis_of_Community_Cultural_Wealth_in_Culture_Clash's_Chavez_Ravine/link/603c7dda299bf1cc26fbda56/download

2

MAPPING THE CONNECTIONS OF VALIDATION AND HIGH-IMPACT PRACTICES

Adrianna Kezar, Ronald E. Hallett, Joseph A. Kitchen, and Rosemary J. Perez

> *It's kind of a community between students and the faculty that really care about your success and really want to see you do well and provide those opportunities for you to do well.*

> *She was like I want to get to know you. And for like an instructor who doesn't have a commonality with me to be in community, to sit there and say I see something in you and I want you to be able to enlarge that potential as much as possible and kind of emphasize certain things that I don't see in myself, was huge, and I don't think it happens very often. Instructors kind of wanting to be personable with you, especially of a different race.*

These are quotations from students in our study of a large-scale comprehensive college transition program (CCTP) serving low-income, first-generation, and racially minoritized (i.e., t-promise) students. We use the term *at-promise,* which was coined in the K–12 literature to combat the deficit thinking of *at-risk* typically associated with these populations, and instead connotes asset-based terminology. The way these students spoke about their experiences in CCTP high-impact practices (HIPs)—specifically, shared courses, proactive advising, the first-year seminar, and particularly their validating interactions with instructors and staff—was not common in their experiences outside the program. Research suggests that HIPs are even more important for at-promise populations and are pivotal to their persistence (McCormick et al., 2017; Ribera et al., 2017). Yet, although scholars have written about how these populations are often least likely to participate in HIPs, there has been little exploration about how HIPs can best support them when they do (Finley & McNair, 2013). This chapter explores the importance of *how* the HIPs get implemented in terms of their impact on at-promise student success. Our study of the CCTP identified the importance of instructors and staff providing validation as they executed the HIPs in shaping the way that students interacted and whether they felt supported in their engagement in HIPs. Validation, described in detail in the following sections, is the process of faculty and staff taking an asset-based approach to working with students, being proactive and taking responsibility for student success, and working with students holistically, acknowledging how their life experiences shape their academic success.

This chapter reviews validation theory and suggests ways it can and should be incorporated into HIPs. More specifically, we summarize findings from our study about HIPs implemented with validation and provide recommendations about how campuses can help instructors and staff implement HIPs in a validating way that is especially important for at-promise students. The quality and nature of HIPs is often overlooked; this chapter fills this important knowledge gap and, in fact, recommends that validation be considered an additional key element for quality implementation of HIPs.

The Thompson Scholars Learning Community Program and Study

The Thompson Scholars Learning Community (TSLC) is a CCTP in the University of Nebraska system. TSLC began in 2008 and its goal is to improve at-promise student success in Nebraska. TSLC is housed in academic affairs, guided by multiple staff, and ranges in size from 200–600 1st- and 2nd-year students for a total of 1,400 in first and second years of college. Program support includes a 5-year scholarship, shared academic courses, proactive advising, and peer mentors, as well as academic, social, and career support provided by staff advisors (Hallett et al., 2019).

This chapter elaborates findings from a project examining whether, how, and why TSLC promotes at-promise student success (Cole et al., 2018). The study included longitudinal surveys conducted with two cohorts of TSLC participants for 4 years, over 900 one-on-one interviews with TSLC participants, and case study data collection (e.g., program observations, interviews with instructors and staff in the program).

Quantitative findings from the project demonstrated increases in critical measures of student success, including at-promise students' belonging, mattering, and career self-efficacy (Kezar et al., 2020; Melguizo et al., 2020). In order to better understand how and why the program promotes these outcomes, qualitative researchers explored key aspects of the program linked to students' success. One of our key findings was that it was not any particular TSLC element (or HIP) that led to the outcomes, but the validating way they were implemented. The program did not intentionally design validating HIPs, but that was the result of intentionally considering the needs of at-promise students and we document this new approach in our research. In the next four sections, we elaborate the validation practices implemented in the CCTP that explain success for at-promise students who participated in the program.

Implementing Validation Into HIPs

Validation is a strengths-based and proactive process initiated by in- and out-of-class institutional agents that affirms, supports, and empowers at-promise students in holistic ways that allow them to realize and (re)learn their innate potential for success (Rendón, 1994; Rendón & Muñoz, 2011). A strengths-based approach is an overarching idea that includes asset-based approaches that center on students' cultures and other characteristics (e.g., personality, identities, skills, talents, and experiences). At-promise students may come to college with experiences and perspectives that are not reflective of the dominant norms associated with White, middle-class life that undergird higher education. Consequently, some may be unaware of their potential whereas others are fully aware of their abilities but may not have the opportunity or support to realize them due to structural and societal barriers. Validation is the proactive process of helping students who may be unaware of their capacities to realize their potential while also enabling those who know their potential to fully reach it within a higher education system that may not be set up to affirm them.

According to Rendón (1994), validating experiences should be intentionally incorporated into the structures of higher education rather than left to individual institutional agents. However, most postsecondary institutions have found it difficult to achieve this goal given the entrenched traditions within the structure of higher education. College transition and support programs often serve as supplemental support structures for at-promise students, providing additional tools and resources designed to assist in navigating postsecondary institutions. Many studies have shown how programs like TRIO, a federal outreach program based on a "trio" of three student services designed to identify and provide resources for individuals from disadvantaged backgrounds, often provide a safe haven where at-promise students feel validated despite an unaccommodating overall institutional structure. Our study shows the ways that traditional formats such as learning communities (shared courses), proactive advising, and first-year seminars can provide a similar sort of validation that students often find in particular niches.

We imagine that many educators reading this chapter would say, of course, we (I) take a validating approach to offering HIPs. One could argue that a first-year seminar is a proactive approach to counter potential student difficulties. Many first-year seminars offer assessments that try to identify students' strengths. We are not arguing that HIPs have been devoid of any validating aspects. What we are suggesting is that validation is not necessarily baked into every experience and for every student. What we offer is a recipe for ensuring that validation is much more systematically a part of HIPs.

Implementing Validation Into Shared Academic Courses

Shared academic courses (SAC) are a novel loose-cohort structure that follows a learning community format. SACs are limited to TSLC students, but there is no integration or thematic link across courses. The loose-cohort structure comes from not requiring courses being taken together, yet they often have several courses together. Courses often fulfill students' general education requirements or represent introductory courses and have low enrollment caps. SACs are overseen by a faculty coordinator at each campus, who serves as a bridge between TSLC staff and SAC instructors who teach these courses. Having a faculty coordinator who works closely with the staff and instructors helps with validation as the coordinator can communicate issues important for the students' success to SAC instructors.

Our study of the SACs revealed several important validation practices. First, faculty coordinators identified and chose specific instructors and departments that demonstrated validating approaches to teaching, such as knowing students personally, making themselves accessible before and after class, and fostering peer support in class. In addition, the faculty coordinator who oversaw SACs met with each instructor to socialize them to the norms for teaching these courses, especially as they began teaching. In doing so, the faculty coordinator shared the SAC teaching philosophy (strengths-based, proactive, and affirming). In the words of one faculty coordinator, "making sure you know students' names, getting to know students personally by having a meeting with them at the beginning of the course, understanding the students' background in the communities they come from, drawing out their assets and strengths, and letting them know you're available and ways to reach you." One faculty coordinator also shared a tip sheet that talked about good instructional practices (active, collaborative, experiential learning) and humanistic pedagogy (also grounded in validation). He went on to talk about the responsibility of instructors to follow up with students if they do not show up at class, submit assignments that seem off, or are quiet in class.

As a result of these norms, students reported that instructors were regularly proactive, initiating conversations and connecting them to resources. Being available and accessible to students is a form of proactive support. An example of proactive support was noted by one student regarding a time she ran into some issues with her class schedule and came into her TSLC instructor's office in a panic, sharing how "she was willing to just drop everything and work on my problem. And she looked at my degree audit, and she mapped out my classes. And we made sure that it wasn't going to mess anything up, and I was able to drop the class, which was fantastic."

When instructors took time to engage their students in conversations that transcended academics and involved aspects of their personal lives, students were more likely to open up about their concerns and assets or resources they might draw upon (Museus & Neville, 2012). A student's comment illustrates how the personal care shown in shared courses made her feel validated:

> I did definitely feel like [my instructor] cared about how I was doing in and outside of class a lot. She took a lot of interest in making sure of my well-being, like emotionally and everything is all right, and making sure that I had everything gathered together like I'm not going to go crazy or anything, like overwhelmed with work and school and all that. I think just checking in to make sure that I'm on the right path. It was definitely a, "We care about you as a student, and we care about you as an individual," not just, like, "Oh, your grades are good. Perfect. You're done."

Many students similarly commented on how instructors expressed concern that extended beyond the classroom, which felt validating.

One SAC used autobiographical writing, which students found very validating. Students were encouraged to write autobiographical essays in their writing course and these stories were then shared within the course. Instructors set up the expectation that peers affirmed students' stories as they were shared, and they themselves provided validating feedback. Being validated by others led participants to increasingly believe in their abilities to be knowers and creators of knowledge. In addition to reviewing them in class, at the end of the term students presented their autobiographical stories to a public audience. The public reading is a significant event in the program that brings students, instructors, and staff together to listen and support students selected to share their powerful stories chronicling personal struggles, traumas, and triumphs. This space is filled with encouragement and validation from members of the program community.

Implementing Validation Into Proactive Advising

Proactive advising is a mode of holistic advising support that places the responsibility on educators to reach out and support students early and consistently (Kitchen et al., 2020). This approach involves building relationships with students to support their personal and academic success and to identify and connect students to learning opportunities for achieving success. The goal is to identify challenges related to students' success early on, to strategize with time to connect them to support to address those challenges, or to identify opportunities to enhance the success of students that might otherwise go missed without proactive outreach (Kitchen et al., 2020). In the past, proactive advising has been framed as a way to reach out and address student "problems" before they worsen—like using an advising system to "red flag" students who are doing poorly. However, our study suggests proactive advising can be a strengths-based and validating approach that promotes student success (Kitchen et al., 2020). Our research pointed out the importance of ensuring that proactive advising is not only proactive and holistic; at-promise students benefit when it is also asset- and strengths-based and affirms that they are capable of achieving success.

There were several structures that helped ensure that this type of validation was present within TSLC proactive advising. To be validating in proactive advising, the program (usually initiated by the program director) established norms that reinforced the importance of staff advisors, instructors, and peer mentors building relationships with students, getting to know the students' history and background, being proactive and reaching out to the students and connecting them to support early on, and creating a sense of comfort among students discussing which experiences in college may be affecting their success—both academic and personal (i.e., holistically). This is communicated as a norm across educators involved in the proactive advising process and as part of the program, including the director of the program, staff advisors, peer mentors, and instructors.

Moreover, it is a norm in the program's proactive advising to take an asset- and strengths-based perspective, and to recognize that these students are capable of success when the right support is in place and institutional barriers are removed. The TSLC recruits educators who believe in, or who are socialized into, the idea that the students are not the problem. Instead it is the institution that is not set up for students to be successful. It is an expectation in program advising that educators will work with students proactively to identify plans and opportunities for meeting each student's college goals—guided by the belief and expectation that this is a possibility for each and every student. A key part of this norm is that all students have the opportunity to participate in proactive advising, which is therefore not experienced as deficit-oriented by students (i.e., only the failing students have to do it), because everyone has the opportunity. Indeed, many students noted that they initially thought proactive advising meetings meant they were doing something wrong or were in trouble—but the validating approach and language that the educators adopted put their minds at ease, made them feel like someone was looking out for them, cared about them, and believed that they could be successful.

As a final note on the proactive advising process—the TSLC program implements elements of their validating proactive advising in a variety of capacities to support students' success, including academic, social, personal, and major/career advice and support. Much of the past proactive advising literature was hyperfocused on promoting academic success of students (e.g., increased GPA) and typically would involve a couple of timed academic check-ins during the semester. The TSLC has recognized there are several facets to students' ultimate success in college and graduation; thus, they take a more inclusive approach to proactive advising with multiple opportunities to engage students actively in validating advising experiences across academic, personal, and major/career domains. As a result, there are lessons that could be learned from this validating advising process relevant to educators working across multiple functional areas in college (e.g., major/career advising, academic advising, counseling).

Implementing Validation Into First-Year Seminar

First-year seminars (FYSs) are a proactive response by institutions to support students early on. The TSLC FYSs involved staff members providing college transition knowledge, college success skills (e.g., time management, studying), and other content aimed at easing transition. Yet having a FYS in place does not mean that students all experience them as validating. In fact, similar to proactive advising, students often experience them as deficit-oriented, undermining their confidence. Our study identified several practices that helped ensure the FYS was validating, including a validating self-exploration and strengths-based orientation, rituals that support holistic engagement, check-in activities, storytelling, and the integration of peer mentors as coteachers.

The FYS includes a variety of strengths-based assessment tools and identity assignments (e.g., helping students to better understand what it means to be first generation or racially minoritized) that enable FYS educators to better understand the students and respond to their identified needs. Staff commented on how beneficial it was when students used these opportunities for self-reflection to report back to them challenges they faced. Students appreciated the inventories and self-assessments that helped them identify their strengths and activities that allowed students to share information about their history and personal life. Students felt that when staff knew them better, they were more able to support them in ways that were validating. For instance, one campus used Gallup's Strengths Finder measure as one way for students to consider their assets. The staff helped students explore their results and used this tool to identify opportunities for growth based on what they were good at without focusing on deficits. The assessment was only the beginning of the strengths-based orientation and a way to introduce the validating approach that they would take to working with students. As one staff member explained, "They all have assets and the program is here to help them capitalize on them."

The FYS classes integrated a number of community-building activities to take the pulse of how students were doing, such as "highs and lows," which allowed students to talk about their lives holistically. When students could share how they got a new job, completed an assignment, had a family member who was ill, or struggled to find friends, these sorts of opportunities allowed the FYS educators to validate the students' lived experience holistically, and to understand and engage in the connection between students' personal lives and their academics. Sharing collectively about the accomplishments and struggles of others was consistently noted by students as validating and affirming of themselves.

Students also described how having peer leaders who assisted with the class was validating, as they saw someone who was not that much older than them playing such a central role in knowledge construction and lesson planning. Peer leaders were integrated into the delivery of the course and provided instruction, increasing students' feeling that they were also capable learners. In addition, students were assigned a peer mentor outside of the FYS experience and the peer mentors being present in the class was helpful in connecting mentors to their academic learning and course assignments so that they could not only serve as a mentor about the college transition but also specifically about their coursework and the skills they were learning there.

Quality, Scale, Assessment, and Equity

Validation is all about the quality of a HIP. We recognize that the field has been articulating the important qualities that define well-executed HIPs. In this chapter we have proposed that validation be added as an additional key element, particularly for institutions that are working with and want to support the success of at-promise students. Our study shows that the eight key elements (see chapter 12), including high expectations, self-reflection, and real-world application, are likely not enough to ensure success.

As campuses consider implementation of validation, we provide a few important closing points for consideration. Validation is scalable with virtually no additional resources. Educators can be socialized to and trained in validating approaches. For example, faculty coordinators in the program provided sessions about the characteristics of students, ways to be validating and strengths-based, tip sheets that could be used later during the semester, and observation opportunities with faculty that had already mastered a validating approach. Our experience studying TSLC is that instructors and staff leaders served as role models and socialized others into the norms of validation, making the practice extremely scalable. In today's resource-poor institutions coming out of a global pandemic, solutions that are cost neutral and scalable will be in high demand. One of the challenging aspects of validation is that it does not easily lend itself to measurement or assessment. Our study used the Higher Education Research Institute (HERI) measure of validation (Hurtado et al., 2011). This measure focuses exclusively on academic validation related to instructors. As a result, we developed measures of validation related to staff activities and practices in areas such as advising that complement the measures of validation created by HERI.

Integrating validating approaches within HIPs relates to equity because it influences academic and psychosocial outcomes that address equity gaps in success. At-promise students typically do not feel they belong or matter on campus and this has negatively shaped their academic performance. Validation is a lever or mechanism that leads to belonging and mattering. Another issue related to equity is that the strengths-based approach to validation used in this program encompasses asset-based notions that honor students' cultural backgrounds as often identified by constructs of community cultural wealth. Educators were encouraged to honor and draw on students' cultural backgrounds. We encourage practitioners that work with diverse students to integrate a community cultural wealth perspective. Connecting HIPs to a validating approach is a highly effective practice for serving at-promise students. This chapter helps to provide a vision for practitioners to purposefully and intentionally structure validation into their HIPs. We also hope to inspire more research on the way validation can be integrated meaningfully into HIPs.

References

Cole, D., Kitchen, J. A., & Kezar, A. (2018). Examining a comprehensive college transition program: An account of iterative mixed-methods longitudinal survey design. *Research in Higher Education*, *60*, 392–413. https://doi.org/10.1007/s11162-018-9515-1

Finley, A. P., & McNair, T. (2013). *Assessing underserved students' engagement in high-impact practices.* Association of American Colleges & Universities. https://www.aacu.org/assessinghips/report

Hallett, R. E., Kezar, A., Perez, R. J., & Kitchen, J. A. (2019). A typology of college transition and support programs: Situating a 2-year comprehensive college transition program within college access. *American Behavioral Scientist, 64*(3), 230–252. https://doi.org/10.1177/0002764219869410

Hurtado, S., Cuellar, M., & Wann, C. G. (2011). Quantitative measures of students' sense of validation: Advancing the study of diverse learning environments. *Enrollment Management Journal.* https://www.heri.ucla.edu/ford/downloads/Students_Sense_of_Validation.pdf

Kezar, A., Kitchen, J. A., Estes, H., Hallett, R., & Perez, R. (2020). Tailoring programs to best support low-income, first-generation, and racially minoritized college student success. *Journal of College Student Retention: Research, Theory & Practice, 87*(1), 1–26. https://doi.org/10.1177/1521025120971580

Kitchen, J. A., Cole, D., Rivera, G., & Hallett, R. (2020). The impact of a college transition program proactive advising intervention on self-efficacy. *Journal of Student Affairs Research and Practice, 58*(1), 29–43. https://doi.org/10.1080/19496591.2020.1717963

McCormick, A. C., Kinzie, J., & Gonyea, R. M. (2017, November 11). *High-impact practices: Is the impact positive or negative for students of color?* [Paper presentation]. Association for the Study of Higher Education Annual Meeting, Houston, TX, United States.

Melguizo, T., Martorell, P., Swanson, E., & Kezar, A. (2020). *Increasing student success: Understanding the impact of a comprehensive college transition program.* Pullias Center for Higher Education. https://pullias.usc.edu/download/increasing-student-success-understanding-the-impact-of-a-comprehensive-college-transition-program/

Museus, S. D., & Neville, K. M. (2012). Delineating the ways that key institutional agents provide racial minority students with access to social capital in college. *Journal of College Student Development, 53*(3), 436–452. https://doi.org/10.1353/csd.2012.0042

Rendón, L. I. (1994). Validating culturally diverse students: Toward a new model of learning and student development. *Innovative Higher Education, 19*(1), 33–51. https://doi.org/10.1007/BF01191156

Rendón, L. I., & Muñoz, S. M. (2011). Revisiting validation theory: Theoretical foundations, applications, and extensions. *Enrollment Management Journal, 2,* 12–33. https://doi.org/10.1007/BF01191156

Ribera, A. K., Miller, A. L., & Dumford, A. D. (2017). Sense of peer belonging and institutional acceptance in the first year: The role of high-impact practices. *Journal of College Student Development, 58*(4), 545–563. https://doi.org/10.1353/csd.2017.0042

3

METHODOLOGICAL CHALLENGES OF STUDYING HIGH-IMPACT PRACTICES FOR MINORITIZED POPULATIONS

Cindy Ann Kilgo

Scholars have proposed high-impact practices (HIPs) as beneficial for college students (Kilgo et al., 2015; Kuh, 2008). As a result, these practices have been incorporated into many institutions. Not all studies, however, have illustrated overarching positive effects from participation in HIPs. Wolniak and Engberg (2019) found that although early career earnings were increased for students who participated in internships or study abroad, none of the HIPs predicted job satisfaction. Similarly, Culver and Bowman (2020) found that first-year seminars did not have a significant relationship to many college outcomes beyond the 1st year. Their study, however, did find that first-year seminars had a positive relationship with grades and satisfaction for Black students. Given that a closer examination by subgroup yielded differential effects provides reason for pause into the widespread application of HIPs. Culver and Bowman stated, "Researchers and practitioners should shift their focus from examining—or simply assuming—the effectiveness of first-year seminars overall to understanding what kinds of seminars are most effective for different types of incoming students" (p. 190). In other words, although HIPs have been incorporated into higher education in a widespread manner, we still lack information on how these practices influence different subpopulations of students.

Part of the dilemma about the influence of HIPs and student subpopulations relates to the overall lack of consideration of the role of the environment in the ways that HIPs influence students' learning and development. This stems partially from the use of large-scale majoritized samples (Kilgo, 2020). In other words, there are small numbers of students who hold minoritized identities within many large-scale, national datasets. Some of this stems from the lack of inclusive demographic data across many large-scale, national datasets. The presence of more inclusive demographic categories has improved over time, but as a practice it is still not fully integrated across higher education research (Garvey, 2019). Similarly at the institution level, the lack of inclusive student records system data is evident (Kilgo, 2020). Many institutions collect sex rather than gender information, or conflate the two. Further, very few institutions gather data on sexual orientation. These factors challenge our capacity to fully investigate the experiences of and outcomes from participation in HIPs by minoritized student populations.

In summary, although many studies do suggest HIPs have powerful effects for students, not much is known about the ways these practices influence students who hold minoritized identities. Within the higher education research world, often students who hold minoritized identities comprise a smaller faction of the available data. Additionally, given the lack of consideration of the role of the environment or climate in the implementation of these practices, a lot is unknown about their utility for promoting success among minoritized student populations. Within this chapter, I highlight three studies that I coauthored investigating the role of HIPs for minoritized student populations. I outline the datasets, analyses, and findings of these three studies. At the end of the chapter, I discuss ways that campuses and higher education scholars can work toward collecting data to fully interrogate the role of these practices.

Featured Datasets

For this chapter, I chose to highlight three studies that investigate the role of HIPs for minoritized student populations. These three studies use data from two large-scale, quantitative datasets: the Wabash National Study of Liberal Arts Education (WNS) and the National Study of Lesbian, Gay, Bisexual, Transgender, and Queer Student Success (LGBTQSS). There are a few notable differences between these two datasets. First, the WNS focused on the experiences of undergraduate students enrolled at liberal arts colleges; however, the overall sample included regional and research universities, community colleges, and a few minority-serving institutions. The WNS was a longitudinal study comprising three cohorts and was collected from 2006 to 2012. Each cohort was sampled in the fall semester of their 1st year, the spring semester of their 2nd year, and the spring semester of their 4th year of college. A total of 52 institutions participated across the three cohorts, with a few institutions participating in multiple cohorts.

The LGBTQSS focused specifically on the experiences of LGBTQ+ students. The LGBTQSS sample included both undergraduate and graduate students. The dataset did not include institutional-level data, however, so the typology of institutions comprising the entire dataset is unknown. It was a cross-sectional study, with data collected over a 4-week period around a midwestern LGBTQ+ and allies student conference. The studies highlighted in this chapter relate to the experiences of students minoritized by two social identities—race and sexual orientation—as well as one other identifying factor—academic performance. I briefly describe the studies in the following, focusing on the purpose and research questions guiding each study, analytic decisions, and findings.

Diversity Interactions by Race

In this study, we focused on the HIP of diversity/global learning (Kilgo, Linley, & Bennett, 2019). Of the Association for American Colleges & Universities' (AAC&U) HIPs, diversity/global learning is quite broad. Kuh (2008) stated, "these studies [diversity/global learning]—which may address U.S. diversity, world cultures, or both—often explore 'difficult differences' such as racial, ethnic, and gender inequality, or continuing struggles around the globe for human rights, freedom, and power" (p. 10). We used positive and negative diversity interactions as our independent variables of interest. We operationalized these variables as the frequency of interactions with peers who hold different social identities. For example, an item of the three-item scale of positive diversity interactions included "how often participant had meaningful and honest discussions about issues related to social justice with diverse students attending this college." An example of the five-item negative diversity interactions scale included "how often participant had guarded, cautious interactions with diverse students while attending this college." These concepts vary slightly from the classroom-based or facilitated outside-of-class experience that AAC&U described, yet Watt et al. (2017) noted that, "in addition to those traditional [AAC&U] high-impact practices, researchers have delineated some strategies that specifically intend to support development in the area of diversity experiences," with one being informal interactions outside of structured or facilitated experiences (p. 500).

We used psychological well-being as the dependent variable (Kilgo, Linley, & Bennett, 2019). We conducted single-group analyses, wherein we ran four separate analytic models by racial groups: Black, Asian, Latinx, and white. Single-group analyses allowed us to investigate the effects of diversity interactions within each group, rather than comparing groups (Carter & Hurtado, 2007). We found that negative diversity interactions negatively influenced the psychological well-being of all four groups, yet positive diversity interactions only significantly positively influenced the psychological well-being of white students (Kilgo, Linley, & Bennett, 2019). This finding illustrates a differential effect of interactions with diverse peers for students who hold minoritized racial identities and ultimately calls into question at whose expense these interactions take place.

Intersection of Identity and Environment for LGBQ+ Students

In this study, we investigated lesbian, gay, bisexual, and queer (LGBQ+) students' participation in five HIPs (undergraduate research, internship, study abroad, learning community, and senior capstone experience) on their academic development (Kilgo, Linley, & Bennett, 2019). We used the five HIPs as our independent variables of interest. Our dependent variable was academic development, a five-item scale assessing students' perceived intellectual development. Additionally, we examined if three environmental factors played a role in mediating any influence the HIPs had on students' academic development: student–instructor relations, overall student support, and how socially accepted students felt by their peers. We found that only undergraduate research significantly predicted students' academic development within their sample. Further, when examining if the environmental factors played a role in mediating that effect, we found that student–instructor relations was significant. In other words, although participation in undergraduate research was significantly and positively related to LGBQ+ students' academic development, the effect was mediated by perceptions of student–instructor relations (Kilgo, Linley, & Bennett, 2019). This finding magnifies the role of environment in the utility of participation in HIPs for students who hold minoritized sexual identities.

Internships for Students With Lower Grade Point Averages

In the final study highlighted in this chapter, we examined the role of internships on self-reported end-of-4th-year grade point average (GPA) by both demographic and institutional factors (Parker et al., 2016). Our analyses portrayed positive benefits for students' end-of-4th-year GPA based on participation in internships, while controlling for GPA at the end of their 1st year along with several covariates. When examining the conditional or interaction effects by varying demographic and institutional factors, however, we found no significant differences by race or institution type; however, we did find that students who had lower end-of-1st-year GPAs and participated in an internship had greater gains than their peers who also participated in internships with higher end-of-1st-year GPAs. This finding signifies the increased positive impact that internships may hold for students who have lower end-of-1st-year GPAs, which calls into importance the ways internships are offered to students.

Evidence of Data-Supported Equity

Across all three studies, the reality of findings is that they are mixed regarding equity. First, diversity interactions only positively impacted white students' psychological well-being (Kilgo, Linley, & Bennett, 2019). Second, undergraduate research participation positively influenced LGBQ+ students' academic development, but that effect was mediated by their interactions with instructors (Kilgo, Linley, Renn, et al., 2019). Finally, internship participation led to increased gains in GPA, a finding that was amplified for students who had lower GPAs at the end of their 1st year of college (Parker et al., 2016). These findings complicate the evidence of equity within HIPs. Although participation led to positive effects—at least for undergraduate research and internships—a lack of data surrounding the ways these practices were implemented is a major limitation in understanding minoritized students' experiences with HIPs. Instead, these findings point to the importance of examining the implementation of these practices in gleaning positive effects for students who hold minoritized identities.

One framework of interest to this topic is Museus's (2014) culturally engaging campus environments (CECE) model, which includes nine indicators for cultural relevance and responsiveness. Museus et al. (2020) applied the CECE model to HIPs and they identified five elements that practioners can incorporate in creating culturally relevant HIPs: (a) culturally familiar spaces, (b) space to engage deeper with community, (c) opportunities to give back to community, (d) collaboration across cultures, and (e) antideficit approaches. The researchers also noted that culturally relevant HIPs are already occurring on campuses.

For all three of the studies highlighted in this chapter, however, there are not variables examining these indicators. As a result, there is not a clear picture of how these indicators might influence students' development from participation in HIPs and particularly how that might differ based on a student's social identities. What at least two of these studies do illustrate; however, is that the role of the environment is critical in a student's positive experience or gains with HIPs.

Quality of Research

For all three studies highlighted in this chapter, secondary data was employed from large-scale quantitative studies. Both datasets, however, had limitations that did not allow the authors to fully consider the role of the environment or the quality of implementation of the HIPs. Critical quantitative research methods can be used to alleviate challenges when researching and assessing the impact of HIPs.

When working with minoritized populations within large-scale datasets, a few notable challenges are a lack of data for specific groups, small sample sizes for groups that do exist, and overall aggregation of groups. Furthermore, the need for inclusive demographic indicators is critical and scholars must not only include expansive demographic questions but also be intentional in the categories offered. For example, sex and gender are often conflated in higher education surveys (Kilgo, 2020). Further, when HIPs were first identified, demographic information for students minoritized based on gender or sexual identities was not included. These demographic indicators are now more common in higher education surveys, but still not present across all surveys (Garvey, 2019).

Despite having demographic indicators, some student populations are still poorly represented in samples. For example, within the WNS data used for the study on diversity interactions, the low sample sizes for students with minoritized racial identities (Black students = 552, Asian students = 365, and Latinx students = 328) necessitated the use of single-group analyses (Kilgo, Linley, & Bennett, 2019). Single-group analyses were conceptualized as helpful when studying minoritized student populations, to avoid norming or referencing the majoritized group within analyses (Carter & Hurtado, 2007). Single-group analyses were particularly useful in the Kilgo, Linley, & Bennett (2019) study because the group sample sizes were disproportionately skewed with significantly more white students in the original sample, which could have led to a concealing or *white-washing* of any effects of HIPs on minoritized student groups. Additionally, given what we know about the experiences that minoritized student populations have on college campuses, it is important to investigate these experiences within a group rather than only comparatively with the majoritized group. Single-group analysis is one way to achieve that goal.

Finally, a third challenge is the aggregation of subpopulations of students. Aggregating students is a common practice within higher education research, particularly when small sample sizes exist. It is important to consider the ways this aggregation masks variation and negates the opportunity to interpret findings. One example of this is when scholars aggregate students holding minoritized racial identities into one group—Students of Color. Given the wide array of experiences students have across racial groups, examining Students of Color as one group is limiting. This aggregation, however, even occurs in surveys that attempt to have more options. For example, Asian American is often a single racial demographic option, yet it represents a multitude of cultures. Having expanded demographic options is critical to gaining more insight into the different experiences students have based on their social identities. Further, including interaction or moderating effects is important in identifying practices that are beneficial in differing ways across demographic groups. A lack of consideration of these solutions can lead to the majority group erasing the effects that may differ if the researcher examined interaction effects.

Overall Implementation

In summary, one central question emerges regarding the implementation of HIPs for minoritized student populations: *What is "high impact" for minoritized college students?* This question is not meant to diminish the value of HIPs, but rather to keep minoritized students' experiences central in future investigations. Specifically, this question is formed by the existing research on HIPs and necessitates both sample and methodological considerations.

When HIPs were first put forth by AAC&U, no national datasets existed that included sexual identity or gender identity beyond a binary—in fact, most included only sex or conflated sex and gender (Kilgo, 2020). Garvey (2019) identified that no federally managed datasets included questions on sexual orientation. Garvey (2019) also noted that although several national surveys have added sexual orientation in the last half decade, the response items vary and in some cases preference "heterosexual" by it being listed first in the string of response items. Further, racial groups are often excluded or not sufficiently expansive (Allen et al., 2019). Ultimately, the emergence of HIPs led to large-scale implementation of these practices on college campuses, including performance-based funding for the number of students participating in HIPs (Zumeta & Li, 2016). Indeed, these practices have been shown to be effective for student learning and development across a host of outcomes (Kilgo et al., 2015; Kuh, 2008). An important caveat, however, is that these practices by and large emerged as "high impact" based on majoritized samples. In other words, minoritized students' experiences were not fully examined, because students were not able to share some of their identities (gender beyond a binary, sexuality due to lack of inclusion on demographic survey) and the fact that Students of Color were aggregated into one group compared to white peers. Moving forward, researchers can lean on two important components in designing their investigations and assessments of HIPs: sample and methodological considerations.

First, I want to reiterate my earlier point that higher education research needs to include expansive and inclusive demographic categories. It is not sufficient to limit the categories provided to students. The survey itself can affirm a student's identity by merely including expansive options, so that students can select the identity that best describes theirs. This is becoming more of a discussed topic related to student record systems and gender identity beyond a binary. As of September 2020, the Campus Pride Trans Policy Clearinghouse noted that only 60 institutions allow students to change their gender identity on their student record without evidence of medical intervention (Campus Pride, n.d.). Frankly, institutions are not doing enough to capture students' identities within their student record system. Because of this, institutions cannot adequately assess differences in outcomes for trans or gender nonbinary students (among other minoritized subpopulations). Institutions need to provide more inclusive options for student records systems, and ultimately this change needs to occur where most student records systems are inputting data from—the admissions applications (Linley & Kilgo, 2018). Institutions also need to allow students to change or update their student record system at any point that the student needs to. This not only provides an affirmation to students' identities by allowing the student to represent themselves accurately, but it also allows the institution to consider the experiences that students holding minoritized identities have—including those experiences with HIPs.

Second, the types of methods being used should be expanded. Although the research forming the creation of HIPs is mostly quantitative, qualitative methods should not be overlooked as a path to truly investigate what is high impact for minoritized student populations. This is even more pressing given the exclusion of some minoritized identities when HIPs were first put forward. Using quantitative methods, we can examine what effects certain practices have on student learning and development and we can even investigate if those practices are mediated by environmental factors or moderated by identity. For example, if an institution has inclusive and expanded gender options, administrators can evaluate what role participation in HIPs has on time to graduation, grades, and any other outcome an institution has data for.

What we cannot find through quantitative methods alone is the ways these practices are being facilitated and promoted to students. For example, how are faculty members affirming a student's identities in conversations and communication? How do students perceive the climate of the lab or interactions with the faculty member? Why do students decide not to participate in certain HIPs on their campus and is their decision based on their identities and the climate? Who and how frequently are students holding minoritized identities being encouraged to participate in HIPs? Examining all these questions with multiple methodological approaches while leaning on qualitative research to explore the meaning that minoritized students make of their experiences with HIPs and other collegiate experiences is critical.

In conclusion, this chapter is meant to boost the research surrounding HIPs for minoritized students. In some ways, my critiques can seem to be downplaying the role of HIPs on student learning and development. My intention in writing this chapter, rather, is for researchers and practitioners to (re)consider the ways they are emphasizing specific practices on their campus. Until sufficient research has occurred that points to the experiences and practices that are most influential for minoritized students, we cannot fully know how to best serve these student populations. HIPs have validity and importance, but the foundation for these practices lacks in truly understanding the ways these practices influence students who hold minoritized identities and whether other practices are, in fact, high impact. Until research answers those questions, the emphasis on AAC&U's HIPs should be facilitated carefully.

References

Allen, W., Jones, C., & McLewis, C. (2019). The problematic nature of racial and ethnic categories in higher education. In L. L. Espinosa, J. M. Turk, M. Taylor, & H. M. Chessman (Eds.), *Race and ethnicity in higher education: A status report* (pp. 13–19). American Council on Education.

Campus Pride. (n.d.). *Colleges and universities that allow students to change name and gender on campus records.* https://www.campuspride.org/tpc/records/

Carter, D. F., & Hurtado, S. (2007). Bridging key research dilemmas: Quantitative research using a critical eye. In F. K. Stage (Ed.), *Using Quantitative Data to Answer Critical Questions* (New Directions For Institutional Research, no. 133, pp. 25–35). Jossey-Bass.

Culver, K. C., & Bowman, N. A. (2020). Is what glitters really gold? A quasi-experimental study of first-year seminars and college student success. *Research in Higher Education, 61*, 167–196. https://doi.org/10.1007/s11162-019-09558-8

Garvey, J. C. (2019). Queer quantitative query: Sexual orientation in higher education surveys. *Journal of College Student Development, 60*(4), 495–501. https://doi.org/10.1353/csd.2019.0042

Kilgo, C. A. (2020). *Supporting success for LGBTQ+ students: Tools for inclusive campus practice.* National Resource Center for The First-Year Experience and Students in Transition.

Kilgo, C. A., Linley, J. L., & Bennett, L. M. (2019). Critically examining the relationship between peer diversity interactions and psychological well-being. *Journal of Student Affairs Research and Practice, 56*(1), 63–77. https://doi.org/10.1080/19496591.2018.1490305

Kilgo, C. A., Linley, J. L., Renn, K. A., & Woodford, M. R. (2019). High-impact for whom? The influence of environment and identity on lesbian, gay, bisexual, and queer college students' participation in high-impact practices. *Journal of College Student Development, 60*(4), 421–436. https://doi.org/10.1353/csd.2019.0038

Kilgo, C. A., Sheets, J. K. E., & Pascarella, E. T. (2015). The link between high-impact practices and student learning: Some longitudinal evidence. *Higher Education, 69*(4), 509–525. https://doi.org/10.1007/s10734-014-9788-z

Kuh, G. D. (2008). *High-impact educational practices: What they are, who has access to them, and why they matter.* Association of American Colleges & Universities.

Linley, J. L., & Kilgo, C. A. (2018). Expanding agency: Centering gender identity in college and university student record systems. *Journal of College Student Development, 59*(3), 359–365. https://doi.org/10.1353/csd.2018.0032

Museus, S. D. (2014). The culturally engaging campus environments (CECE) model: A new theory of success among racially diverse college student populations. In M. B. Palmer (Ed.), *Higher education handbook of theory and research* (pp. 189–227). Springer.

Museus, S., Chang, T.-H., & Zilvinskis, J. (2020). Merging cultural diversity and academic quality to (re)envision 21st century college campuses: The promise and power of culturally relevant high-impact practices in promoting racial equity in higher education. In C. Spencer Platt, A. Hilton, C. Newman, & B. Hinnant-Crawford (Eds.), *Multiculturalism in higher education: Increasing access and improving equity in the 21st century* (pp. 12–19). Information Age.

Parker, E. T., Kilgo, C. A., Sheets, J. K. E., & Pascarella, E. T. (2016). The differential effects of internship participation on end-of-fourth-year GPA by demographic and institutional characteristics. *Journal of College Student Development, 57*(1), 104–109. https://doi.org/10.1353/csd.2016.0012

Watt, S., Kilgo, C. A., & Jacobson, W. (2017). Designing programs for engaging difference. In J. H. Schuh, S. R. Jones, & V. Torres (Eds.), *Student services: A handbook for the profession* (pp. 499–513). Jossey-Bass.

Wolniak, G. C., & Engberg, M. E. (2019). Do "high-impact" college experiences affect early career outcomes? *The Review of Higher Education, 42*(3), 825–858. https://doi.org/10.1353/rhe.2019.0021

Zumeta, W., & Li, A. Y. (2016). *Assessing the underpinnings of performance funding 2.0: Will this dog hunt?* TIAA Institute. https://www.tiaainstitute.org/sites/default/files/presentations/2017-02/ti_assessing_the_underpinnings_of_performance_funding_2.pdf

4

PROMOTING EQUITY BY DESIGN

Stacking High-Impact Practices for Faculty and Students in a First-Year Experience Program

Denise Bartell and Caroline Boswell

Our chapter examines the ways in which a high-impact approach to faculty development promotes instructors' understanding of culturally relevant pedagogy (CRP) and an asset mindset in a high-impact 1st-year program. Previous research on UW-Green Bay's Gateways to Phoenix Success (GPS) program has shown it significantly improves educational outcomes for the students who participate (Bartell et al., 2020) and provides GPS instructors "high-impact faculty development" that promotes equity-minded approaches to teaching and transfer of learning beyond GPS (Bartell & Boswell, 2019, p. 27). This study expands upon previous work by utilizing an innovative mixed methodology combining qualitative interviews on the impact of GPS participation on instructors' teaching philosophy and practices with quantitative longitudinal data on GPS student outcomes. We explore the ways in which promoting high-impact engagement with the theory and practice of CRP supports the development of equity-oriented instructors, and how this orientation may moderate the impact of high-impact practices (HIPs) for racially marginalized students (Kuh et al., 2013).

The Role of CRP and an Asset-Based Mindset

GPS asks instructors to reflect on their relationship to the three elements of CRP: academic success, cultural competence, and sociopolitical consciousness (Ladson-Billings, 1995, 2014). Ladson-Billings's work aligns with several other scholars whose research suggests that faculty–student interaction is central to the success of students who enter college with experiences and assets that differ from those historically valued in the academy (Bensimon, 2007; Pendakur, 2016; Rendon, 1994). CRP provides instructors a framework for interrogating their relationship to structural inequities in higher education and considering how their courses and pedagogies may confirm or confront them. Instructors who practice cultural competence or cultural humility reflect on and question their own biases and privileges and consider how these may influence their instructional practice. Instructors who seek sociopolitical consciousness consider how external and internal structures produce systemic inequities, not only in the classroom and college but also within their communities and politics. In this chapter, we refer to the three elements of CRP as comprising an "equity orientation" for GPS instructors.

GPS also asks instructors to cultivate an asset-based mindset about student ability. A recent large-scale study found that instructors who held a more fixed, and thus deficit-based, mindset about student ability had larger racial equity gaps in course grades. Students reported more negative experiences and lower motivation to succeed in these courses (Canning et al., 2019). The mindset was a stronger predictor of student achievement than any other instructor characteristic studied, including age, gender, amount of teaching experience, or race/ethnicity. Instructors who hold a more fixed mindset likely convey, in their engagement with students, the belief that some do not possess the innate ability necessary to succeed, which demotivates students and suppresses performance, especially for students from historically marginalized groups who are particularly susceptible to issues such as stereotype threat (Rattan et al., 2012). A deficit mindset may also be linked to poorer performance for historically marginalized students due to the tendency for instructors to attribute perceived deficits of marginalized students to stereotypes such as lack of cultural emphasis on education, lack of motivation or commitment, or the inability to overcome academic underpreparation (Bensimon, 2005).

High-Impact Faculty Development in GPS

GPS brings together stakeholders, including faculty, in an embedded professional development experience designed to empower agents of change. The equity-oriented design of GPS relies on instructors with a complex understanding of theories and practices that support social justice education. The program engages faculty and students in dialogue about how the system of higher education has been designed to marginalize certain groups in order to maintain the power of others (Anderson, 2016; Armstrong & Hamilton, 2015). Faculty work together to deconstruct dominant narratives about how and why students succeed in college and construct an experience for themselves and for their students that seeks to accomplish equity. Because the development of instructors is embedded in the larger design of the program, faculty participate in the collective construction of key HIPs for the GPS program as they learn, allowing them the opportunity to engage substantively with their peer instructors as they expend significant effort on this challenging, authentic work (Kuh et al., 2013). These key HIPs feature work to sustain instructor change even after their activities together are through. As such, GPS can serve not just as a community of practice but a community of transformation for the instructors who participate, with the potential to change the culture of the institution (Kezar et al., 2015).

GPS integrates a set of HIPs for 1st-year students, organized around the big ideas of citizenship, social justice, and education as a public good.[1] Faculty mentor students in a learning community where they lead a series of courses for a small group of 25 students, supported by a peer mentor and academic advisor. Instructors' engagement with GPS students begins via virtual summer communication, followed by an orientation where instructors, peer mentors, and students come together to engage in a miniparticipatory action research project exploring the purpose of college from a social justice lens. This work carries into their 21st Century Citizen course, where issues of citizenship, social justice, and education are examined and applied to students' college, personal, professional, and civic goals. Instructors also support engagement in a first-year seminar that builds navigational capital into a discussion-based, writing-intensive interdisciplinary course. The following semester, faculty work with their GPS cohort in a Capstone course, where students design and implement a service project around core GPS themes. The program culminates with a campus-wide event where students share their learning publicly and the projects of all GPS cohorts are recognized by campus and community leaders.

Core to GPS is the faculty–student relationship. Throughout their 1st year, faculty meet monthly with GPS students, forming deep connections that often last beyond college. Faculty work to understand the unique assets and goals of each student and connect them with resources that enhance success. They scaffold access to HIPs by building students' navigational capital, working with students to develop résumés and hone professional skills, and acting as advocates connecting students to opportunities often only available to students whose privilege allows them access to the hidden curriculum of college.

To support this work, GPS faculty join peer mentors and advisors in a community of transformation. The community reads and engages in ongoing dialogue on scholarship intended to promote a critical understanding of the systemic nature of barriers to equity and student success that are at the core of culturally relevant and asset-based teaching, including the corrosive and pervasive nature of meritocratic illusions about higher education (Astin, 2016), the personal and societal costs of social inequity (Wilkinson & Pickett, 2010), and the impact of systemic bias on the cognitive bandwidth of students (Verschelden, 2017). Moving between theory and practice, they interrogate institutional data around equity gaps and explore pedagogical practices designed to support equity, including ways to maximize transparency in academic expectations (Winkelmes, 2013), provide effective and frequent feedback using the Wise model (Yeager et al., 2014), and foster a growth mindset and adoption of learning techniques to support persistence in the face of academic challenge (McGuire, 2015).

Collective reading of these texts promotes instructors' understanding of CRP and the importance of an asset-based mindset. But it also informs shared construction of GPS program activities. Instructors apply their learning on promoting academic success by working together to ensure that all assignments meet the key criteria for transparency, including constructing rubrics for all graded elements and highlighting resources available to support student success. They work together to design culturally relevant and responsive learning activities that address the core GPS themes of citizenship, social justice, and education. For example, for the 21st Century Citizen class, instructors codesign a lesson on financial wellness that roots discussions about navigating the complex world of college financing in data on federal and state deinvestment in financial aid and rising economic inequality in the United States. As they complete this work, instructors are encouraged to interrogate their assumptions about why students make the financial decisions they do, supporting the development of cultural competence and sociopolitical consciousness elements of CRP. Each week, instructors discuss ways to support the individual needs of their students, provide vital support for processing the affective intensity of the GPS experience, and are encouraged to critically examine the ways in which their biases and assumptions influence their engagement with students and their pedagogical choices.

Methodology and Results

We solicited participation from 16 GPS faculty who had taught in the program between 2013 and 2017. Ten faculty agreed to the interviews, which were recorded and transcribed with permission. Most were White, over half identified as female, and a few were first-generation college students. The faculty came from a mix of disciplines in the humanities, arts, and social sciences. Interview questions addressed faculty perceptions of UW-Green Bay students prior to their participation in GPS and after; whether GPS influenced their awareness of issues of equity in education for underrepresented students; whether GPS influenced the extent to which they considered issues of equity in teaching; and whether GPS influenced their engagement with issues of equity at the departmental, institutional, or community level.

Instructor Equity Orientation

Our study coded interviews for language that reflected the understanding of the three elements of CRP: academic success, cultural competence, and sociopolitical consciousness (Ladson-Billings, 1995). Based on this coding scheme, we identified seven instructors with higher levels of equity orientation (EO). To be classified as higher EO, instructors must have addressed all three components of CRP or addressed two of three components while also not using deficit-based language. We found that all 10 instructors addressed academic success and cultural competence in their responses. For example, one instructor noted that he believed it was his responsibility "to do everything I can to help all the students who I meet succeed. Not to try to take the struggle away from them, because everyone is going to have to struggle, but to help empower them so that they can succeed in whatever form that means for them." One instructor reflected on her prior unconsciousness at length:

> Because that wasn't my path, right? And I think a lot of faculty are like that, that's not your path. Your path, you know, you succeed in high school, and then you succeed in college, and maybe it's not even that hard . . . and you expect everyone to be like you.

She went on to note that GPS "gave me more of an awareness of what students were dealing with . . . whether it was an immigration issue, or whether it was drugs, or whether it was an abuse-type situation. . . . There were so many things I wasn't aware of."

Although all instructors were able to explicate ways in which their approach to teaching had shifted due to GPS in the areas of academic success and cultural competence, only three of 10 instructors explicitly expressed sociopolitical consciousness in their interviews. It is possible that this may be the most advanced element of cultural competence because it requires an acknowledgment of the systemic nature of racial and socioeconomic inequity and an understanding that we either actively combat inequity or play a role in perpetuating injustice (Kendi, 2019). One instructor referenced how her experience with GPS "does provide or helps me keep racial justice and other types of equity issues as a lens that I want to think about policies that come out and sort of say, what does this mean for different students." She continued, noting that "if you have multiple people who see with that lens, then you have the opportunity to push back against some things that seem on their face to be neutral, but actually have dire consequences for some of our students." For instructors who embrace sociopolitical consciousness, their classes interrogate power structures and foster students' ability to become agents of social change, and they do this work beside their students. The same instructor noted GPS's potential influence on a new course she advocated for at the departmental level, in which "students are supposed to get a pretty thick understanding of the context in which K–12 and higher education happens."

Instructor Mindset

Although an asset-based mindset about student ability is at the center of CRP, we isolated mindset as a distinct category in recognition of the historic, pervasive discourse of college readiness that continues to inform how many members of the academy conceive of student success (Astin, 2016; McNair et al., 2020). Therefore, we coded interviews for language that reflects a deficit-based mindset about student capacities, describing students as "at-risk," "needy," having "baggage," being unable to "compete," or needing "hand-holding." This language implies a focus on perceived characteristics that interfere with college success as opposed to focusing on the assets students bring with them to support student success.

Deficit language also implies the underlying, fixed nature of students' perceived deficits. Some instructors explicitly engaged with the endemic discourse of college readiness. When reflecting on her GPS students, one noted that some "maybe didn't need to be in college yet, that they weren't quite ready." Another instructor who articulated all three elements of CRP within their interview also expressed explicit views about the "range" of GPS students and how some were less "bright" and less "prepared" for college. When speaking of this range, the instructor said there were

> students who were prepared for college versus students who were not prepared for college . . . so, we had some students in there who were incredibly bright; a lot of it was illustrated by the biology course they were all required to take; some took that class and just thrived others struggled so hard and I think some of them just were really a lot more prepared for college than others were, it's not just intelligence, but readiness to be in school.

Student Outcomes by Instructor Equity Orientation and Mindset

Analyses were conducted on GPS students from 2013 through 2017 and non-GPS students from those same cohorts, with 438 GPS students in the analyses of instructor equity orientation and mindset, including 76 racially minoritized (RM) students. Among GPS students, 74% (n = 326) had instructors displaying higher EO and 69% (n = 300) had instructors displaying more of an asset mindset.

Retention was higher through year 3 for RM and non-RM students with high equity-oriented instructors as compared to students with low equity-oriented instructors, as were graduation rates. In general, the positive impact of instructor equity orientation was greater for RM students, with RM students who had high equity-oriented instructors 12% more likely to be retained into year 2 and 5% more likely to graduate in 4 years than were RM students with low equity-oriented instructors, although no differences were statistically significant due to the small cell sizes in these analyses (see Table 4.1). Although having a high equity-oriented instructor seemed to largely eliminate equity gaps for GPS RM students, having an instructor with a lower equity orientation seemed to exacerbate gaps. RM students with low equity-oriented instructors were retained at lower rates than all non-GPS students and RM students who had instructors with a higher equity orientation, an effect that increased over time and maintained through graduation.

Retention through year 3 and graduation rates were generally higher for students with more asset-minded GPS instructors than deficit-minded instructors. As was the case with equity orientation, effects were stronger for RM students. RM students with asset-minded instructors were over twice as likely to graduate in 4 years as RM students with deficit-minded instructors and 10% more likely to do so than non-GPS RM students. Additionally, the 6-year graduation rate for GPS RM students with deficit-minded instructors was 10% lower than for non-GPS RM students. Once again, it appears as if having a deficit-minded instructor exacerbated equity gaps for RM students, but not for non-RM students.

Discussion and Implications

Our research suggests that the HIPs-infused community of transformation used for the professional development of GPS instructors has significant potential to support the implementation of equity-minded HIPs for students. All instructors in our sample showed significant evidence of understanding two of the three aspects of CRP: academic success and cultural competence.

TABLE 4.1
Retention and Graduation

By Instructor Equity Orientation								
	Overall GPS		*RM*		*Non-RM*		*Non-GPS*	
Outcome Variable	**High EO**	**Low EO**	**High EO**	**Low EO**	**High EO**	**Low EO**	**RM**	**Non-RM**
Retained Term 2	92%	88%	91%	90%	92%	88%	89%	90%
Retained Year 2	77%	71%	75%	63%	78%	72%	69%	75%
Retained Year 3	64%	60%	60%	47%	65%	62%	55%	61%
6-Year Graduation	55%	63%	39%	33%	58%	68%	40%	53%
4-Year Graduation	42%	51%	27%	22%	44%	55%	21%	37%
By Instructor Mindset								
	Overall GPS		*RM*		*Non-RM*		*Non-GPS*	
Outcome Variable	**Asset**	**Deficit**	**Asset**	**Deficit**	**Asset**	**Deficit**	**RM**	**Non-RM**
Retained Term 2	91%	91%	91%	91%	92%	90%	89%	90%
Retained Year 2	78%	70%	76%	65%	79%	70.4%	69%	75%
Retained Year 3	65%	60%	59%	52%	66%	62%	55%	61%
6-Year Graduation	57%	57%	41%	31%	60%	62%	40%	53%
4-Year Graduation	43%	46%	32%	15%	62%	51%	21%	37%

And the majority embraced an asset mindset about students' capacities. In addition, most instructors believed that participation in GPS had enhanced their ability to support equity of outcomes for students.

This study also provides evidence of the link between the level of instructor understanding and long-term student outcomes. Although overall outcomes were higher for students who participated in GPS, the impact was moderated by instructor equity orientation and asset mindset. RM students with GPS instructors who espoused higher levels of equity orientation and asset focus were retained at higher rates through year 3. If GPS students had an asset-focused instructor, they also graduated at a higher rate. However, having instructors with lower EO and a deficit mindset exacerbated equity gaps for RM students. These findings suggest that transformational faculty development should not merely incorporate HIPs key features, but rigorously engage faculty with critical pedagogy and reflexive practice that seeks equity of educational outcomes. This aligns with ongoing conversations on the design of quality HIPs, which center the conversation more closely on the quality of the GPS experience as opposed to the number or types of HIPs students experience.

We recommend the following considerations to those seeking to help faculty provide HIPs that enhance equity of student outcomes.

Center CRP in Faculty Development If You Are Seeking to Improve Equity of Student Outcomes Through HIPs

The results of our study suggest the positive impact of HIPs participation for historically marginalized students may be dependent on the nature of those experiences. RM GPS students with less equity-oriented instructors tended to show poorer long-term outcomes than RM students who did not participate in GPS, generally eliminating the positive impact of the HIPs themselves. This suggests we must prioritize meaningful faculty development opportunities around CRP and mindset in any institutional initiatives seeking to improve outcomes for historically marginalized students through HIPs. Such opportunities could include exercises that help faculty critically reflect on their preconceptions about students and see where these views intersect and potentially conflict with the equity goals that inform the HIPs they offer. When engaging faculty in the research supporting HIPs, consider articulating the relationship between the characteristics of HIPs and culturally relevant approaches to student learning. Begin conversations about service-learning models by engaging in dialogue about the problems inherent in the privileged server/underprivileged recipient model. In short, model the experience we wish to see for our students.

Utilize the Key Features of HIPs in Educational Development for Instructors

Our research indicates that the HIPs utilized in our GPS instructor community of transformation can promote lasting and transferable learning. Such sustained communities provoke deeper learning and engagement than one-off workshops or short-term programming. Intentionally infusing communities with the key features of HIPs enhances the impact. Consider ways to utilize existing collaborative faculty work as an opportunity to create communities of transformation—for example, a group of faculty working to redesign an existing gateway course, which likely involves instructors in the key HIPs features of time on task and substantive interaction with peers on a meaningful real-world task. Intentionally build opportunities to learn about differences, garner regular feedback on their progress, and critically reflect on their learning within the community.

Focus Specific Attention to Addressing Deficit Mindsets, Given the Particularly Entrenched Nature of These Beliefs

Our analysis of the interview data indicates that, although some instructors were able to intellectualize cultural competence or sociopolitical consciousness, they continued to engage with language or discourse that promoted the myth of meritocracy and deficit-based thinking. This suggests that programs such as GPS may have the potential to reinforce deficit-based thinking and problematic conceptions of college readiness if they do not directly address these attitudes and help instructors to critically engage with the impact of these attitudes on themselves and their students.

How you engage with these recommendations should be guided by your unique institutional contexts, but we wish to emphasize three guiding principles. Work with faculty to facilitate regular dialogue about the systemic inequities that higher education replicates and provide them space to reflect on their relationship to the structures that uphold them. Embed faculty development as a living part of the HIPs you design, providing a more authentic learning experience for faculty that mirrors what we wish to see for our students. Position the educational development of faculty and staff around HIPs as a retention initiative that has the potential to transform your institutional culture.

Notes

1. The GPS program underwent significant revisions starting in the 2018–2019 academic year, which is why our study focuses on the first 5 years of the program. Note that GPS is still an active program at UW-Green Bay.

References

Anderson, C. (2016). *White rage: The unspoken truth of our racial divide.* Bloomsbury.

Armstrong, E. A., & Hamilton, L. T. (2015). *Paying for the party: How college maintains inequity.* Harvard University Press.

Astin, A. (2016). *Are you smart enough? How colleges' obsession with smartness shortchanges students.* Stylus.

Bartell, D. S., & Boswell, C. (2019). Developing the whole teacher: Collaborative engagement as faculty development within a first-year experience program. *Journal of Faculty Development, 33*(3), 25–32. https://www.ingentaconnect.com/content/magna/jfd/2019/00000033/00000003/art00004

Bartell, D. S., Staudinger, A. K., & Voelker, D. J. (2020). Problem-focused liberal education in a first-year learning community at the University of Wisconsin-Green Bay. In W. Moner, P. Motley, & R. Pope-Ruark (Eds.), *Redesigning liberal education: Innovative design for a twenty-first century undergraduate education.* Johns Hopkins University Press.

Bensimon, E. M. (2005). Closing the achievement gap in higher education: An organizational learning perspective. In A. Kezar (Ed.), *Organizational Learning in Higher Education* (New Directions for Higher Education, no. 131, pp. 99–111). Jossey-Bass.

Bensimon, E. M. (2007). The underestimated significance of practitioner knowledge in the scholarship on student success. *The Review of Higher Education, 30*(4), 441–469. https://doi.org/10.1353/rhe.2007.0032

Canning, E. A., Muenks, K., Green, D. J., & Murphy, M. C. (2019). STEM faculty who believe ability is fixed have larger racial achievement gaps and inspire less student motivation in their classes. *Science Advances, 5*, 1–7. https://doi.org/10.1126/sciadv.aau4734

Kendi, I. (2019). *How to be an anti-racist.* Penguin Random House.

Kezar, A., Gehrke, S., & Elrod, S. (2015). Implicit theories of change as a barrier to change on college campuses: An examination of STEM reform. *Review of Higher Education, 38*(4), 479–506. https://doi.org/10.1353/rhe.2015.0026

Kuh, G. D., O'Donnell, K., & Reed, S. (2013). *Ensuring quality and taking high-impact practices to scale.* Association of American Colleges & Universities.

Ladson-Billings, G. (1995). Toward a theory of culturally relevant pedagogy. *American Educational Research Journal, 32*(3), 465–491. https://doi.org/10.3102/00028312032003465

Ladson-Billings, G. (2014). Culturally relevant pedagogy 2.0: A.k.a. the remix. *Harvard Educational Review, 84*(1), 74–84. https://doi.org/10.17763/haer.84.1.p2rj131485484751

McGuire, S. (2015). *Teach students how to learn: Strategies you can incorporate into any course to improve student metacognition, study skills, and motivation.* Stylus.

McNair, T. B., Bensimon, E. M., & Malcom-Piqueux, L. (2020). *From equity talk to equity walk: Expanding practitioner knowledge for racial justice in higher education.* Wiley.

Pendakur, V. (2016). *Closing the opportunity gap: Identity-conscious strategies for retention and student success*. Stylus.

Rattan, A., Good, C., & Dweck, C. S. (2012). "It's ok—Not everyone can be good at math": Instructors with an entity theory comfort (and demotivate) students. *Journal of Experimental Social Psychology, 48*, 731–737. https://doi.org/10.1016/j.jesp.2011.12.012

Rendon, L. I. (1994). Validating culturally diverse students: Toward a new model of learning and student development. *Innovative Higher Education, 19*(1), 33–51. https://doi.org/10.1007/BF01191156

Verschelden, C. (2017). *Bandwidth recovery: Helping students reclaim cognitive resources lost to poverty, racism, and social marginalization*. Stylus.

Wilkinson, R., & Pickett, K. (2010). *The spirit level: Why greater equality makes societies stronger*. Bloomsbury Press.

Winkelmes, M. (2013). Transparency in teaching: Faculty share data and improve students' learning. *AAC&U Liberal Education, 99*(2), 48–55.

Yeager, D. S., Purdie-Vaughns, V., Garcia, J., Apfel, N., Brzustoski, P., Master, A., Hessert, W. T., & Williams, M. E. (2014). Breaking the cycle of mistrust: Wise interventions to provide critical feedback across the racial divide. *Journal of Experimental Psychology: General, 143*, 804–824. https://doi.org/10.1037/a0033906

5

INTENTIONALLY DESIGNING LEARNING COMMUNITIES TO ADVANCE AUTHENTIC ACCESS AND EQUITY

Key Communities

Heather Novak, Taé Nosaka, and Ryan P. Barone

Since 2006, Colorado State University (CSU) has committed to leveraging its student success initiatives (SSIs) to increase deep and enriched learning in and outside of the classroom, which will facilitate continued improvement in the overall 6-year graduation rates and, most importantly, close graduation gaps for racially minoritized, first-generation, and/or Pell-eligible students compared to their peers. The Key Communities (Key), a learning community designed to honor the diverse identities and strengths of students, are a hallmark SSI program with promising graduation and persistence data for racially minoritized, low-income students and first-generation college attendees (Nosaka & Novak, 2014). We describe the theories and practices of Key, which have successfully enrolled and equitably graduated students with identities that are structurally underserved by higher education, and then discuss the equity-minded frames needed to ultimately transform the institution to serve all students.

To contextualize our work and to model explicitly engaging dynamics of privilege, power, and oppression stemming from social identities, we offer positionality statements. Heather Novak is director in the Office of Institutional Research, Planning and Effectiveness at CSU. She identifies as a White, cisgender, heterosexual female. Taé Nosaka is the associate executive director within the Student Success Division in the Provost Office at CSU where she oversees the Key Communities and Community for Excellence Scholar Programs, two student success initiatives designed to engage around 2,000 structurally underserved students with the goal of closing opportunity gaps. She identifies as a mixed-race Woman of Color (Japanese and White), cisgender, heterosexual, and a first-generation college student. Ryan Barone is the assistant vice president for student success, reporting directly to the provost and executive vice president. He identifies as a White, cisgender, heterosexual man with a learning disability, and is a first-generation college student. We regularly name, investigate, and amplify individual identities and positionalities to collectively have a more strategic and effective impact for institutional change in the service of authentic access and equity. Functionally, this means shifting deficit narratives surrounding structurally underserved students and working to realize an institutional culture that is authentically student-ready, where student cultural wealth is identified and celebrated, and where belonging is equitably felt, resulting in educational equity (McNair et al., 2016; Strayhorn, 2018; Yosso, 2005). Finally, the use of *authentic* as both a description of and qualifier for access and equity reflects an intentional resistance to the performative nature of these concepts widely used and rarely operationalized through the lens of intersectionality, social justice, or liberation. Succinctly, access and equity are only authentic if the needs of the least institutionally served students are centered and the institution is simultaneously committed to transformation.

Summary of Relevant Literature

The initial design of Key incorporated approaches, philosophies, and structures referenced in early learning community and retention literature, providing the framework of building a social community focused on academics that included frequent contact among staff, faculty, and students in and out of the classroom (Tinto, 1993). This frequent contact resulted from intentionally staffing the community so that students would have someone who connected with them individually and assisted with the transition to and through college, which brought in the work of Levitz & Noel (1989), who asserted that being attached to one person at the institution is the single most important step to establishing a connection.

Some of the earlier literature that continued to influence Key's approach and, given the identities of Key students, included Rendón et al. (2004), who suggested that the design of programs and services must center the transitional experience for students of color, which can be traumatic as many racially minoritized students enter environments that are drastically different from their home. To avoid the occurrence of negative experiences stemming from low expectations, inadequate high schools, and perceptions that students are deficient, programs must be intentional about creating an educational experience that is academically rigorous, compassionate, nurturing, empowering, liberating, and democratic. The entirety of Key's structure and messaging is intentional about creating this type of experience for students.

From the onset of Key, the goal was to provide a space designed to honor the identities and strengths of students and to foster access and equity to and through the university, particularly for students who are first generation to college, racially minoritized, and/or Pell-eligible. Given this intention, a challenge with some of the original literature that highly influenced the structure and purpose of Key is that it lacked a critical perspective related to the identities of the students participating in the community or on the responsibility of an institution to be equitable in design. Key's design and structure was influenced primarily by literature that centered whiteness in higher education and lacked authors with social identities similar to students in the community.

More recently, the faculty and staff who implement Key have critically reflected on the scholarly foundation of the program, asking themselves, *Who were the foundational scholars, and what social identities did they bring to their work? When student-focused research informed recommendations for the field of higher education, what were the demographics of these samples, and what epistemological assumptions underlay the research questions?* These questions have caused us to realize that in some ways Key upheld whiteness and assimilation by myopically quantifying success with retention and graduation rates rather than transformation or liberation as desired outcomes (Garcia, 2020). Rather than dismantling this successful program, Key is undergoing a paradigmatic shift attempting to retain desirable components while incrementally turning toward a liberating experience of educational equity. The modified conceptual framework is evolving to be a combination of institutional equity (Witham et al., 2015) and becoming a student-ready college (McNair et al., 2016), which prioritizes not just inclusion and diversity, but also equity and inclusion (Harris et al., 2015).

Ideally, Key would be unnecessary at CSU if we were truly a "student-ready" college as described by McNair et al. (2016). As we strive for this reality, where we can individualize holistic support and student learning efforts at scale in a campus culture validating diverse student identities, programs such as Key represent a concerted institutional effort to reenvision the role of a public land-grant university in the 21st century.

This vision is one where students coming from increasingly diverse backgrounds are welcomed, validated, and intellectually engaged in the pursuit of knowledge in a supportive community of learners. This is the experience for the hundreds of students in the Key Communities, and these program designs are leading the university community to realize our audacious student success aspirations.

Key Conceptual Foundations

The Key Communities are a student-centered experience focused on cultivating student learning and fostering a sense of community, while offering an environment that honors identities and individual life stories. The high-impact practices (HIPs) layered into the Key experience include curricular and cocurricular engagement, embedded feedback and support, and building community by providing first-year seminars, a shared on-campus living experience, common intellectual experiences, and a College Reading & Learning Association (CRLA) internationally certified peer mentoring program, as shown in Figure 5.1.

Through these components, the following elements of HIPs (Kuh et al., 2013) are embedded within the structure of Key:

1. *High expectations of students* communicated through the application and acceptance process, at the required Key Connect Orientation Program and through students' Key Seminar class.
2. *Interactions with faculty and peers about substantive matters* through implementation of a noncredit College and You course facilitated by Key mentors as well as attendance at signature campus events.
3. Offering a diverse living and learning experience where *students interact daily with others with experiences and backgrounds different from their own* through participation in the community and service-learning experiences that engage Key students with first-generation, racially minoritized, and Pell-eligible students in the local community.
4. *Frequent, timely, and constructive feedback* through regular meetings with Key mentors and Key faculty as well as grade feedback for all their classes at midsemester.
5. Periodic, structured opportunities to *reflect and integrate learning* through interdisciplinary Key Seminars that combine concepts, themes, and ideas across the linked courses in which students are enrolled, either through integrative assignments or cocurricular experiences.

Figure 5.1. Structure of the Key communities.

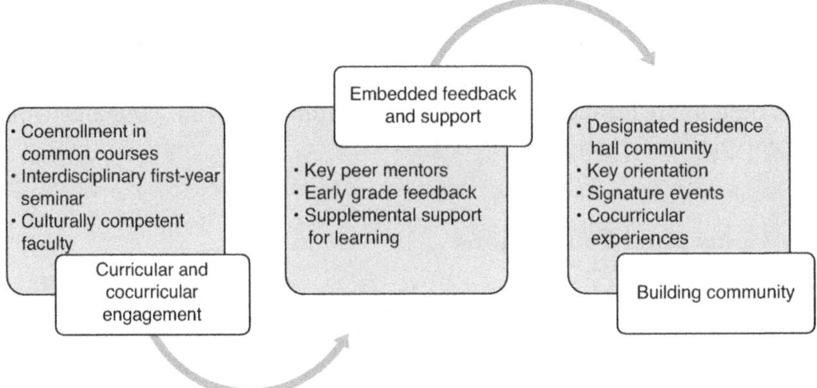

Initially Key served about 100 1st-year students and has grown to serve close to over 500 students annually. As Key continued to grow and gain recognition as a signature program, the first-come, first-serve application process created barriers to authentic access, so a comprehensive recruitment plan to reach communities underserved by higher education was implemented. The plan included visiting high schools, launching a Student Ambassador Program where students shared their experiences in Key with their home communities, and partnering with scholarship programs and student support services. Key hired a bilingual (Spanish and English), full-time recruitment and outreach coordinator to lead these efforts. Thus, the students with membership in Key each year are approximately 60% racially minoritized, 50% first generation, and 45% Pell-eligible, differing significantly from the overall demographics of CSU.

Empirical Approach to Study the Impact of Key

Propensity score matching is used to empirically access Key's impact on student success (see chapter 21 on this method). This analysis included the most recent four cohorts (dependent on outcome timeframe) of first-time, full-time (FTFT) students. The first question addressed was whether participating in Key has an impact on 1st-year measures of student progress, 2nd-year retention, or 6-year graduation rates. The second part of the inquiry explores whether participating in Key has a stronger impact on success specifically among populations that Key intentionally recruits.

Propensity scores can be utilized to estimate a causal effect when the treatment variable is not randomly assigned (Murnane & Willet, 2011; Rosenbaum & Rubin, 1983). In this study, the propensity scores are calculated with logistic regression models that predict the likelihood of participating in

Key so that non-Key students can be matched to Key students. The data for this study came from the institutions' record systems and are provided by the institutional research office.

After using propensity matching to adjust the groups to be statistically similar, the primary statistic for the first research question is the average treatment effect among the treated (ATT). ATT are the differences in success rates between the adjusted Key and non-Key students and describe the average relationship Key has with student success. The second research question uses regression models on the adjusted files to predict the probability of success by the likelihood of being in Key for Key and non-Key students after controlling for the interaction between Key status and the probability of being in Key. This allows the impact of Key to vary by a student's likelihood of being in Key to know if Key is more effective for the students intentionally served by the program.

Table 5.1 contains the logistic regression coefficients and model fit statistics for the models that predict Key participation. Three propensity score models are used in this analysis in order to obtain the probability of being Key for each outcome timeframe (fall 2010 through fall 2013 cohorts are assessed for the graduation outcome; fall 2015 through fall 2018 cohorts are assessed for the 2nd year retention outcome; and fall 2016 through fall

TABLE 5.1

Logistic Regression Coefficients,[a] Propensity to Participate in Key

Variable	*1st-Year Outcomes*	*2nd-Year Retention*	*6-Year Graduation*
High school GPA	-0.212 (0.029)*	-0.186 (0.029)*	-0.075 (0.036)*
Out of state student	-0.147 (0.029)*	-0.139 (0.029)*	-0.080 (0.036)*
Pell recipient	0.311 (0.032)*	0.353 (0.030)*	0.282 (0.033)*
Female	0.040 (0.027)	0.056 (0.027)*	0.133 (0.030)*
First generation	0.511 (0.029)*	0.392 (0.029)*	0.199 (0.033)*
Racially minoritized	0.712 (0.027)*	0.672 (0.027)*	0.749 (0.032)*
Constant	-0.887 (0.105)*	-1.023 (0.103)*	-1.539 (-0.127)*
N	18,805	19,845	17,584
Model chi-squared	2,030	1,827	1,053
Degrees freedom	6	6	6
Pseudo R^2	0.149	0.133	0.104

[a]Cells display the regression coefficient with its standard error and an asterisk to indicate when $p < .05$.

2019 cohorts for the 1st-year outcomes). The coefficients indicate that first-generation status, Pell recipient status, as well as identifying as a racially minoritized student and female are all positively associated with being in the Key community. Students paying out-of-state tuition are less likely to be in Key. Additionally, high school GPA has a negative association with the likelihood of being in Key. The students with the highest probability to be in Key are first-generation, racially minoritized, Pell Grant recipients who tended to have lower high school grade point averages.

The quality of propensity score adjustment is assessed by evaluating the Key and non-Key covariates before and after the propensity score adjustment. Table 5.2 displays the results of a series of *t*-tests that compare the representation of predicator variables by Key status both before (unmatched/unadjusted) the non-Key students are matched to Key students and after (adjusted/matched). There are statistically significant differences across all of the predictor variables among the unmatched data and the differences are negligible after matching. For example, prior to matching only 16% of non-Key students are racially minoritized, but after matching about 51% of Key and non-Key students are racially minoritized. These results indicate that the matching process created a sample of non-Key students who are similar to Key students in terms of the attributes included as predictor variables.

There are substantial limitations in the analysis presented. First, this study utilizes student success programmatic outcomes (1st-year credit completion and GPA, 2nd-year persistence, and 6-year graduation) to analytically operationalize student success. However, these are incomplete measures of student success because they do not represent the authentic equity discussed previously. Second, the analysis is limited to what is available within the institution's system of record and does not account for organizational structures or external influences (systemic racism), which limits interpretations about Key's impact on CSU student success (Garcia et al., 2019).

Propensity Score Results

Table 5.3 displays the student success outcomes for Key students and non-Key students. The outcomes among the unadjusted populations are bivariate comparisons of Key students to all other FTFT students in the relevant cohorts without accounting for any demographic or academic differences between Key students and non-Key students. The data presented in the adjusted columns limits the Key and non-Key samples to students with similar probabilities of being in Key. The difference in outcomes among the adjusted sample is the ATT statistic.

TABLE 5.2
Propensity Model Balance Assessment

	Older Cohort (FA10–FA13)						*Newer Cohorts (FA15–FA18)*					
Variable	*Unmatched*			*Matched*			*Unmatched*			*Matched*		
	Key	*Non-Key*	*t-Statistic*	*Key*	*Non-Key*	*t-Statistic*	*Key*	*Non-Key*	*t-Statistic*	*Key*	*Non-Key*	*t-Statistic*
HS GPA	3.54	3.59	–3.93*	3.54	3.55	–0.09	3.55	3.63	–7.41*	3.55	3.54	0.67
Out of state Student	17%	24%	–5.75*	17%	18%	–0.54	22%	34%	–11.98*	22%	23%	–0.80
Pell recipient	44%	21%	20.07*	44%	43%	0.25	45%	18%	29.97*	45%	44%	0.75
Female	63%	55%	5.68*	63%	62%	0.08	57%	54%	2.73*	57%	57%	–0.08
First generation	44%	24%	17.70*	44%	44%	0.17	50%	20%	31.67*	50%	49%	0.64
Racially Minoritized	51%	16%	33.73*	51%	51%	0.18	59%	22%	39.40*	59%	59%	0.60

$^{*}p < .05$.

TABLE 5.3

Overall Unadjusted and Propensity Score–Adjusted Student Success Comparisons, Key Learning Community Participants Versus Non-Key

	1st-Year GPA		*1st-Year Credits Earned*		*2nd-Year Retention*		*6-Year Graduation*	
	Unadjusted	*Adjusted*	*Unadjusted*	*Adjusted*	*Unadjusted*	*Adjusted*	*Unadjusted*	*Adjusted*
Key Participants	2.90	2.91	27.3	27.4	85.9%	85.8%	68.4%	68.4%
Non-Key	3.03	2.83	27.8	26.8	84.4%	80.4%	68.7%	64.0%
Difference[a]	−0.13 (.017)	0.08 (.023)*	−0.44 (.115)	0.63 (.167)*	1.5 (.008)	5.5 (.011)*	−0.3 (.013)	4.5 (.017)*
N for Key / Non-Key	2,225 / 16,580	2,164 / 2,164	2,225 / 16,580	2,164 / 2,164	2,170 / 17,675	2,169 / 2,169	1,477 / 16,107	1,477 / 1,477

[a]Among the adjusted data this is the average treatment effect among the treated, with standard error in parentheses.

*$p < 0.05$.

Prior to adjusting by the propensity score, Key students and non-Key students have statistically similar success outcomes. Key students graduate at a rate of 68.4%, which is similar to the non-Key rate of 68.7%. After using the propensity scores to adjust the comparison, Key students have statistically significant higher success outcomes compared to non-Key students (68.4% compared to 64%) and these differences are of a large enough magnitude to have practical importance. For instance, Key students graduate at a rate that is 4.5 percentage points higher than statistically similar non-Key, so about 66 students (4.5% of the 1,477 Key students) graduated because of Key.

The differential impact of Key on retention and graduation is assessed by graphing logistic regression models run on the matched sample that include the interaction between being in Key and the probability of being Key. Figure 5.2 displays predicted probability of retention or graduation for Key and non-Key students based on probability of being in Key. There are negligible differences in retention and graduation rates for Key and non-Key students who have a very low probability of being in Key, but there is approximately a 15 percentage point difference in retention and graduation for Key students compared to non-Key students among those most likely to

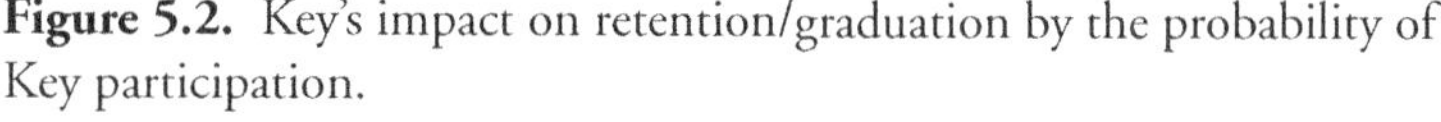

Figure 5.2. Key's impact on retention/graduation by the probability of Key participation.

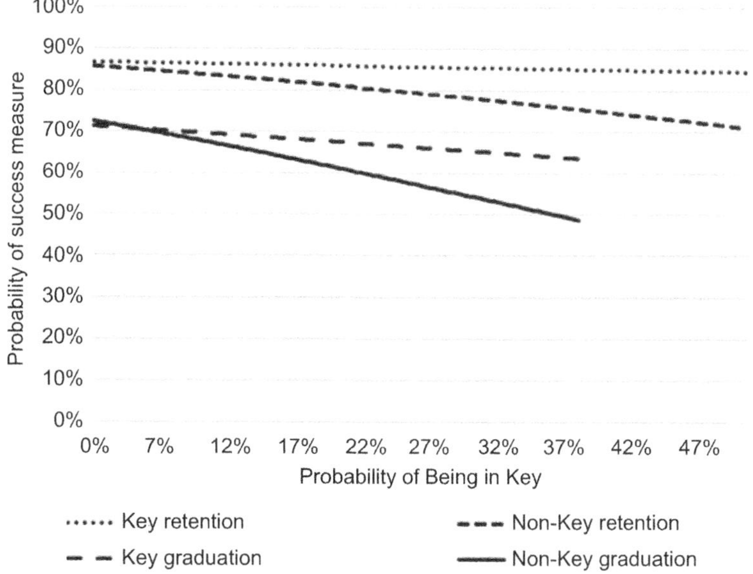

be in Key. This indicates that Key is most effective for the students that are the most likely to be in Key.

Implementation Implications and Authentic Equity

The HIP described has been conceived, tested, implemented, assessed, and scaled, demonstrating a commitment to reenvision what a public land-grant university should engage itself with in the 21st century. The Key Communities now present a challenge for the university to center students historically and currently marginalized by mainstream societal systems, including higher education. Due to Key's successes, there is a danger of privileging individual student narratives of resilience and grit, and thereby not evaluating the institutional systems, processes, and narratives that continue to manifest oppression. In other words, the success of the minoritized students served in programs like Key, despite existing institutional oppression, can function to let institutions off the hook for creating broadly equitable educational experiences; therefore, this tendency must be made explicit and resisted. If a university is truly student-ready and designed with equity in mind, the entire university experience would be validating, transformative, and result in educational equity even without programs like Key. Through a lens of critical theory the existing body of literature on HIPs reflects a prioritization of quantification and scaling rather than transformation and equity for those underserved by institutions of higher education (Lange & Stewart, 2019).

The paradigm of a college or university becoming student-ready for structurally underserved students offered a blueprint toward authentic access and equity. According to McNair et al. (2016), a "student-ready college starts with an individual educator and moves on to the collective action of all educators to influence and change the institutional environment to make excellence inclusive by supporting the success of all students" (p. 96). CSU has persistent opportunity gaps in graduation rates for students of color, low-income students, and first-generation college students, which have largely remained unchanged, despite the success in scaling the HIPs discussed here. Striving to be a student-ready university centering educational equity requires unwavering passion and a commitment to (re)designing every function of the university in the mold of our aspirational version of Key that demands authentic access and equity.

CSU, like much of U.S. higher education, is struggling with historical and easily tracked constructs of success as measured quantitatively by retention and graduation rates. As part of this transition, SSI progress is primarily measured quantitatively and with indirect program outcomes presented in this study. These metrics neatly fit into the research questions that administrators have replicated over the years. For example, from this analysis we can conclude that Key's 2nd-year retention rate is 5.5 percentage points higher than for non-Key students. This 5.5 percentage point difference in 2nd-year retention results in an additional 119 students (about 30 per cohort) being retained to the 2nd year. These types of interpretations fit into a neoliberal return on investment mindset that focuses on revenue generation as part of larger free-market ideals, while ignoring other important developmental indicators of success. Reducing equity-focused programs like Key with myopic revenue generation formulas to solely determine success reflect value-absent academic capitalism rather than the values and ethics of creating equitable educational environments that should be prioritized. Although the value of HIP participation should be measured by outcomes/performance/behavior (Kuh & Kinzie, 2018), quantitative metrics and student self-reports fail to help us adequately access perhaps more aspirational outcomes from HIPs, including liberation and agency (Garcia, 2020). In the field of HIPs assessment, we must move toward direct measures of student learning and qualitative inquiries to better understand the quality of experiences from a student-centered perspective (Montenegro & Jankowski, 2017). For example, students in a learning community can be asked to create a blog or vlog reflecting on stated learning outcomes and a reviewer can use a simple rubric to evaluate the demonstration of the objectives.

As universities position themselves to become student-ready campuses, programs like Key have an important place as they provide a unique space for students to learn and thrive in a system that is not designed for them. Until we are at a place where higher education in its entirety provides an experience that honors the identities and learning experiences of Key students, we will continue to offer such programs. Equally important is ensuring those programs do not shoulder a disproportionate amount of the weight of student success. If programs like Key (similar to TRIO programs and cultural centers) become tokenized as the efforts on campus that demonstrate a commitment to diversity and equity continue without institutional systemic changes that are necessary for producing equitable outcomes, then the institution is let off the hook from also shouldering this responsibility. Investment in such programs must also challenge the broader institution to center diversity and equity in order to promote equitable access outside of these special programs. The future success of Key will lean heavily on the broader university making substantial strides toward becoming a student-ready campus focused on student success, with attention to students who have been structurally underserved within higher education.

References

Garcia, G. A. (2020). *Is liberation a viable outcome for students who attend college?* https://www.higheredjobs.com/blog/postDisplay.cfm?post=2256

Garcia, G. A., Núñez, A. M., & Sansone, V. A. (2019). Toward a multidimensional conceptual framework for understanding "servingness" in Hispanic-serving institutions: A synthesis of the research. *Review of Education Research, 89*(5), 745–784. https://doi.org/10.3102/0034654319864591

Harris, J., Barone, R. P., & Patton, L. D. (2015, Winter). Who benefits? A Critical Race analysis of the (d)evolving language of inclusion in higher education. *Thought & Action*, 21–38.

Kuh, G. D., & Kinzie, J. (2018, May 1). What really makes a "high-impact" practice high impact? *Inside Higher Ed.* https://www.insidehighered.com/views/2018/05/01/kuh-and-kinzie-respond-essay-questioning-high-impact-practices-opinion#:~:text=The%20words%20signal%20the%20unusually,historically%20underserved%20populations%20(that%20is%2C

Kuh, G. D., O'Donnell, K., & Reed, S. (2013). *Ensuring quality and taking high-impact practices to scale.* Association of American Colleges & Universities.

Lange, A. C., & Stewart, D.-L. (2019). High-impact practices. In E. S. Abes, S. R. Jones, & D.-L. Stewart (Eds.), *Rethinking college student development theory using critical frameworks* (pp. 221–231). Stylus.

Levitz, R., & Noel, L. (1989). Connecting students to institutions: Keys to retention and success. In L. M. Upcraft & J. N. Gardner (Eds.), *The freshman year experience: Helping students survive and succeed in college* (pp. 65–81). Jossey-Bass.

McNair, T. B., Albertine, S. L., Cooper, M. A., McDonald, N. L., & Major, T. (2016). *Becoming a student-ready college: A new culture of leadership for student success.* Jossey-Bass.

Montenegro, E., & Jankowski, N. A. (2017, January). *Equity and assessment: Moving towards culturally responsive assessment* (Occasional Paper No. 29). University of Illinois and Indiana University, National Institute for Learning Outcomes Assessment (NILOA).

Murnane, R. J., & Willett, J. B. (2011). *Methods matter: Improving causal inference in educational and social science research.* Oxford University Press.

Nosaka, T., & Novak, H. (2014). Against the odds: The impact of the key communities at Colorado State University on retention and graduation for historically underrepresented students. *Learning Communities Research and Practice, 2*(2), 1–20. https://washingtoncenter.evergreen.edu/lcrpjournal/vol2/iss2/3/

Rendón, L. I., Garcia, M., & Person, D. (Eds.). (2004). *Transforming the first-year experience for students of color.* National Resource Center for the First-Year Experience and Students in Transition.

Rosenbaum, P. R., & Rubin, D. B. (1983). *Matched sampling for causal effects.* Cambridge University Press. https://doi.org/10.1017/cbo9780511810725.016

Strayhorn, T. L. (2018). *College students' sense of belonging: A key to educational success for all students* (2nd ed.). Routledge.

Tinto, V. (1993). *Leaving college: Rethinking the causes and cures of student attrition* (2nd ed.). University of Chicago Press.

Witham, K., Malcom-Piquex, L. E., Dowd, A. C., & Bensimon, E. M. (2015). *America's unmet promise: The imperative for equity in higher education*. American Association of Colleges & Universities.

Yosso, T. J. (2005). Whose culture has capital? A critical race theory discussion of community cultural wealth. *Race Ethnicity and Education, 8*(1), 69–91. https://doi.org/10.1080/1361332052000341006

PART TWO

ASSURING FIDELITY

The concept of fidelity is one of the greatest challenges we face in the development and implementation of high-impact practices (HIPs). We see the benefits of promoting fidelity in HIPs design and implementation, resulting in clearly defined and aligned outcomes, activities, and assessments. In turn, these shared expectations will guide professional development for faculty and staff members. Additionally, we need to identify what organizational structures, activities, and evaluation practices best promote the fidelity of HIPs implementation. In these chapters, the authors promote strategies to identify the attributes of HIPs, derived from examining evidence-based practices, supporting the coherence of this work across all formats. The role of professional development and acting upon HIPs assessment results are essential to promoting fidelity across programs, departments, institutions, and entire systems.

Although many institutions offer HIPs, issues of fidelity, equity, and access remain unresolved. A lack of access, as well as lack of consistency in design and implementation, detracts from the promise of HIPs, especially for those students who stand to benefit most from participation. This section of the book is of interest to HIPs stakeholders: program directors, faculty, student affairs directors, and professional development and assessment personnel.

Currently, common understandings and attributes of HIPs are informed by the AAC&U scholarship of Kuh and O'Donnell (2013) regarding foundational HIPs designs, substantiated through National Survey of Student Engagement (NSSE) data and emerging assessment practices. Fundamental characteristics of these experiences include high student effort, collaboration with peers, and interaction with faculty. However, as the field advances, questions arise about the efficacy of HIPs for all students, considerations for faculty development, how to integrate assessment findings into student success strategies, and continuous improvement efforts to ensure fidelity.

In this section, authors describe aspects of fidelity to ensure that HIPs are implemented as originally planned. Common expectations related to fidelity of HIPs represented in this section include designs that are student-centered, equity-minded, and evidence-based, while promoting quality in their implementation. Authors analyze a broad array of HIPs, including capstones, internships, learning communities, service-learning/community-based learning, undergraduate research, and first-year experiences. Chapter 6 explores undergraduate research in a blended general education course, discussing the design approach and theoretical basis for this instance of undergraduate research from three different aspects: course design, distributed mentoring, and scaffolded assignment sequence. Chapter 7 explores the influence of service-learning (SL) and themed learning community (TLC) pedagogies on college students' success and learning. This research explores if there is a differential impact when TLCs and SL are employed concurrently. In chapter 8, the contributors focus on strategies for supporting student work in course-based undergraduate research experiences (CUREs) and for gathering evidence of impact on student learning and success. The contributor of chapter 9 developed and administered the College Internship Study, a concurrent mixed-methods design, where both qualitative and quantitative data are collected and analyzed simultaneously to address research questions about HIPs design, participation, and equity issues. The team in chapter 10 outline five recommendations for structuring high-quality capstone experiences, which include defining goals and pathways, supporting faculty, communicating clearly, tracking participation, and assessing outcomes to provide a road map toward high-quality capstones for all students. And in the final piece of this section, chapter 11, contributors discuss how department culture and design of continuous exposure to HIPs throughout the major positively influence student outcomes.

All of these contributors suggest activities bringing the greatest benefit for students while ensuring high-quality HIPs representing fidelity to commonly derived attributes and expectations. Through research and recommendations about the design, assessment, implementation, and continuous improvement practices of HIPs, these contributors advance the scholarship of HIPs and recommend new considerations for course and program designs that reorient our frameworks for student success by focusing on the fidelity of design and implementation.

Discussion Questions

- How does an institution create a set of shared expectations for quality, fidelity, and equity in HIPs designs?
- How can an institution leverage assessment opportunities to ensure fidelity across HIPs and to improve designs?
- What type of professional development would best help faculty to achieve a shared vision for the design and delivery of quality HIPs?
- How does a department or institution ensure fidelity in the design and implementation of HIPs through multiple delivery models?
- How is the efficacy of HIPs integrated into the design of HIPs across programs, departments, institutions, and systems?

Reference

Kuh, G. D., & O'Donnell, K. (2013). *Ensuring quality and taking high-impact practices to scale*. Association of American Colleges & Universities.

6

A DESIGN APPROACH TO UNDERGRADUATE RESEARCH FOR 1ST-YEAR STUDENTS

William Loker and Thia Wolf

George Kuh's (2008) high-impact practices (HIPs) began as a list. Extracted from an analysis of student responses to classroom practices in the National Survey of Student Engagement (NSSE), HIPs were associated with successful student outcomes. Their purpose was to generate discussion among university faculty and administrators regarding the instantiation of proven pedagogical practices in support of student success. In this, Kuh and collaborators were successful (Finley, 2019). The downside of the list was it ignores certain questions: *Why do HIPs work? Do they work for all students, equally? What are the theories of learning that underlie HIPs, individually and in the aggregate? What are the necessary steps in course design to effectively implement HIPs?*

Our focus in this chapter is undergraduate research, a HIP that aims "to expose and involve students early in . . . systematic inquiry approaches" (Kuh et al., 2017, p. 10). The approach typically includes faculty mentoring (Cuthbert et al., 2012; Leek, 2014; McKillip, 2009) and public presentation of students' work to provide students with an authentic experience of scholarship (McKillip, 2009; Olson-McBride et al., 2016; Wozniak, 2011). Although few faculty members doubt that focused, consequential research projects benefit students, the need for direct mentoring during students' work often limits the number of students reached using this HIP. In a review of the literature, we found that carefully designed undergraduate research projects, with real aims for publication/presentation, most often involved 12 to 20 student researchers at a time. A possible exception to this is projects embedded in multiple sections of a course—for instance, first-year seminars, but even these examples provide roughly every 20 students with direct mentoring by one or more faculty members (Olson-McBride et al., 2016).

In this chapter, we explore undergraduate research in a blended general education course at California State University, Chico. Our campus refers to these blended classes as *U-Courses*, which, in our case, combined introductory English composition and an introduction to cultural anthropology. The course was designed for up to 100 1st-year, mostly first-generation students. We discuss the design approach and theoretical basis for this instance of undergraduate research from three different aspects: course design, distributed mentoring, and scaffolded assignment sequence. We include a discussion of student outcomes and suggestions for future research on HIPs.

Located in far northern California, CSU, Chico historically had a mostly White, largely middle-class student body. For a variety of reasons, including energetic and intentional recruiting, this situation changed rapidly. Table 6.1 shows the ethnic composition of Chico State in 2009 and in the 2016–2019 time period. Note the dramatic increase in the percentage of Hispanic/Latinx students, increasing from 13.5% to 34.2%, and a concomitant decline (in percentage terms) in White enrollment from 64% to 43.6%. At the same time the campus saw a dramatic increase in first-generation and low-income college students; nearly 50% of our students are now either Pell-eligible, first-generation, or both. Despite Chico State's success in recruiting a diverse student body, the university still struggles with a graduation gap: For the 2013 cohort, the 4-year graduation rate for underrepresented minorities was 20%

TABLE 6.1

Ethnic Composition of the Student Body at CSU, Chico, 2009 and 2016–2019

	2009	*2016*	*2017*	*2018*	*2019*
American Indian/Alaskan Native Only	1%	1%	1%	1%	1%
Asian	5%	6%	5%	5%	6%
Black/African American	2%	2%	3%	3%	3%
Hispanic/Latino (any race)	14%	30%	32%	33%	34%
Native Hawaiian/other Pacific Islander	0%	0%	0%	0%	0%
Nonresident alien	3%	4%	4%	3%	3%
Two or more races	2%	5%	5%	5%	5%
Unknown	10%	8%	8%	7%	5%
White	64%	44%	43%	43%	44%

Note. Adapted from California State University, Chico. Institutional Research.

and the 6-year rate was 60%. For traditional students, the corresponding figures are 35% and 71.7%. One of the motivating factors in the design of the U-Courses was (and is) to create an engaging and challenging introduction to college-level learning, with appropriate scaffolding in support of student success. Although the U-Courses are open to all students, a particular effort is made to direct low-income, first-generation, and minoritized students into these classes.

Course Design

In the fall semesters of 2018 and 2019, we offered a combined Anthropology-English course for 97 1st-year students. CSU, Chico's First-Year Experience program (FYE) supported this work by providing a summer design intensive for the faculty team (Wolf and Loker) to develop the course. FYE also trained and provided eight peer mentors who supported enrolled students both academically and socially. The centerpiece of our design was undergraduate research, in this case applied ethnographic research, focused on campus culture. Ethnographic research is the principal method used in cultural anthropology and is widely used in literacy studies as well. This allowed us to teach key concepts from anthropology and English while offering students the identity of researchers contributing to scholarship within the university. The applied dimension encouraged student researchers to focus on aspects of campus life that needed attention from faculty, professional staff, and administrators to improve the student experience. The research project invited students to experience themselves as developing and valued members of the university community, contributing to needed scholarship and providing them with a sense of confidence and belonging.

The Anthropology-English course design used a *communities of practice* framework that refers to the "mutual engagement" of individuals using shared methods/practices in a "joint enterprise" that holds meaning for all members (Wenger, 1998, p. 73–80). Our approach hinged on Wenger's (1998) insight that "[t]here is a profound connection between identity and practice" (p. 149). Indeed, membership in any community of practice, from workplaces to athletic teams, requires a growing sense of one's own value to and competence within the community (Nasir & Cooks, 2009; Wenger, 1998). Every aspect of our course design involved student collaboration, abundant and targeted verbal and written feedback, authentic research tasks (reading, writing, data collection, and analysis), and ample scaffolding—supportive structures to assist students in "pushing the envelope" of their learning through collaboration within and beyond their peer groups.

Distributed Mentoring

One of the chief barriers to wide use of undergraduate research is its perceived labor-intensive nature. To scale up meaningful undergraduate research and extend it to 1st-year students when they are most vulnerable to attrition, our course relied heavily on a distributed mentoring model that involved the creation of purposeful research teams, the provision of peer mentors, and the strategic use of graduate teaching assistants (TAs) and committed faculty. Organization of students into research teams of three to five members enabled progress on significant research questions through a division of labor, drawing on varied strengths of the students involved. With support from faculty (2), TAs (2 for the course), and peer mentors, students created research instruments (interview guides), engaged respondents in interviews, compiled and analyzed information, and wrote up results and recommendations more effectively than solo, novice researchers could have in the same amount of time. Successful research teams formed small communities of practice within the larger classroom community. They helped and critiqued one another, sought help from mentors when needed, and incorporated feedback from faculty. When functioning effectively, and the vast majority did, these teams created a sense of shared purpose as students took on the identity of researchers.

Peer mentors are key members of the teaching team. In our course, eight peer mentors were embedded across approximately 97 enrolled students. This created "pods" of 11–13 students per peer mentor. Peer mentors are *not* subject matter experts; none had taken an introductory anthropology course. As successful undergraduate students, peer mentors modeled effective academic practices such as taking notes on and discussing readings and consulting assignment instructions to help with each stage of work. Faculty met weekly with peer mentors to discuss desired outcomes and activities designed to meet them, enabling peer mentors to "translate" faculty instructions on assignments into language and practices students understood. Perhaps the most important role for mentors is social, fostering cohesive social bonds among students by facilitating community, to support the success of research teams.

Graduate TAs provided backstopping to mentors (e.g., filling in when needed), helped students with more complex problems in addressing course material, and gave assistance with grading weekly assignments associated with the scaffolded sequence of activities. Additionally, they sometimes led short class activities focused on research methods they were using in their graduate studies, thus providing a window for students into trajectories beyond undergraduate study.

Scaffolded Research Assignments

As with overall course design, the outcomes we wanted for students drove the creation and sequencing of assignments. The semester-long ethnographic research project required them to move from their initial status as novice learners to researchers capable of formulating a research question and effectively pursuing answers to that question. As newcomers to the cultural context of the university, focusing their research on the college experience provided a logical and feasible source of research topics. We wanted our students to develop true expertise about their research question(s) while also learning ethnographic research methods, understanding ethical concerns about research, and practicing varied genres of writing (journals, research notes, data presentation and analysis, findings-based recommendations). From the outset, we treated research in our course as more than an assignment: It was a way of being, of participating, and of succeeding at the university.

To successfully provide an authentic, meaningful research project required a scaffolded assignment sequence to support students at every step of the learning process (Vygotsky, 1978). We carefully designed reading-writing assignments, supported by abundant feedback, that assisted students' development as researchers *and* helped students notice their own development and learning along the way. Student research teams engaged in collaborative writing assignments designed to help them construct and demonstrate their understanding of each phase of their research. In addition, students kept individual ethnographer journals, including evaluative writing to help each student monitor their own learning throughout the course—and to help faculty gauge students' development, areas of understanding, and need for support or clarification as work progressed.

The Course in Practice

The practical challenge facing us was how to support and engage this diverse group of students as they navigated difficult reading and writing activities, research design work, data collection, data analysis, and public reporting of their findings. Inviting students to try on a new identity as researchers meant that we addressed them from the 1st day of class as ethnographers-in-the-making. Faculty spoke of "your work as researchers," "your role on campus as an ethnographer," and "the value of your ethnographic research to many members of this campus." We emphasized the *applied* nature of their research and indicated that they would communicate their results to professionals who could learn from their work to improve conditions for students.

To reinforce this message, and heeding Wenger's (1998) idea that an effective learning context "must aim to offer dense connections to communities outside its setting" (p. 275), we invited faculty, administrators, professional staff, and student leaders to discuss research ideas early in the semester. Many of these same individuals returned as part of an interested audience to hear students' research-based recommendations at the end of the semester. We called these individuals *research partners* (following LeCompte & Schensul, 2010) and reminded students frequently throughout the semester of the public audience for their work. These reminders underscored our message that their research mattered to many people in the campus community, allowing students to understand research as a purposeful social activity rather than a school exercise.

Students' research questions/concerns focused on college finances, racial identities, and tensions on campus and in the surrounding community, worries about mental and physical health while adapting to a new environment, interest in campus clubs and majors, and uncertainties about dorm life or living in the Chico community. Our role as faculty was to help students form these concerns into viable research questions. We worked with students to develop strategies for the ethical collection of data (the Human Subjects Research Committee reviewed and approved all research protocols) and to answer their research questions: whom to interview, how to phrase questions, how to record responses, and how to draw meaningful conclusions from their data.

Assisting students to take on the identity of researchers/ethnographers promoted learning, as well as what Wenger (1998) calls "modes of belonging," by inviting students as key contributors into the "processes of negotiat[ing] meaning," "creating images of the world" together through thoughtful reflection on and discussion of their data, and "coordinating our energy and activities . . . [to] contribute to broader enterprises" (pp. 173–174). These modes, according to Wenger, "create relations of belonging" (p. 181) among participants in a community, allowing each person to align their ideas and practices with others while contributing to shared perspectives through proposing meanings and developing ideas/models for collaborative testing and use.

Outcomes

The Anthropology-English U-Course was designed to support novice university students' deep learning and success. This approach used learning theory that applies to all students and that we believed would be particularly useful for students first acclimating to college life and increased rigor in academic studies. Such an approach allowed us to reach and support all students who enrolled, including first-generation students for whom college is sometimes a deeply confusing or even alienating undertaking.

Our experience, the work produced by students, and student commentary on their experience convince us that for the vast majority of students, this was true: They learned, they succeeded, and they learned to succeed. Out of 26 research groups, *all* were able to finish the project on time and present their findings to the public audience at the end of the semester. We observed changes in classroom behavior over the course of the semester that evinced greater commitment in students to the work involved in doing ethnography, improved research and writing practices, clearer understanding of the purposes of a college education, and greater facility in navigating the cultural environment of the university. Practices gained included drawing from published models of writing (in this case, ethnographies) to understand genre features of a writing assignment; focusing on in-class work for increasing amounts of time without deviating from the task at hand; consulting with/asking questions of peers, more advanced peers (mentors and TAs), and faculty in order to gain needed support for accomplishing new tasks; and rereading and revising written products to more clearly articulate research findings.

HIP Quality Indicators

In an important article on the practice of HIPs, Kuh et al. (2013) listed eight quality indicators associated with their effective implementation (see chapter 12). We discuss six of these, drawing on student voices from their written work in the class and an end-of-semester survey to demonstrate the positive gains students experienced through their work as undergraduate researchers.

1. *Significant investment of time and effort by students over an extended period of time.* Students appreciated the chance to implement a semester-long research project. When asked what makes learning interesting in their classes, the most common responses were engaging in hands-on research projects carried out over the course of the semester in research groups (43 comments). Typical responses included the following: "I learned more . . . by doing the semester-long projects" (first-generation, White female student). "The learning in the U-Course was much more critical than my other classes, it definitely took a lot more research. . . . I learned a lot more doing this research project" (first-generation, African American female).

2. *Interactions with faculty and peers about substantive matters.* Students frequently commented on the benefits of working in groups, peer support, and the support of peer mentors. Typical remarks included the following: "It's very different because we do a ton of group work and have mentors to help guide us. I feel like hearing from other students is helpful as I am participating in the class" (first-generation, Hispanic female). "The U-Course is more hands-on and does more group work. I learned more and enjoyed the U-Course more" (first-generation, White female).

3. *Experiences with diversity, wherein students are exposed to and must contend with people and circumstances that differ from those with which students are familiar.* Students both researched diversity and experienced diversity in the classroom: their fellow students, the peer mentors, and the TAs (all of whom were students of color with one international student). Although our end-of-semester survey did not address this directly, a student comment is instructive: "I've learned a lot and have realized a variety of struggles people face in and out of school" (non-1st-generation, White female).

Ethnographic research reports provide in-depth examples of Latinx students grappling with their place on a historically White campus. For example, the ethnography of Research Team 1, *Chico State Diversity: Support Systems for Latinx and Hispanic Students*, concluded:

> Students commonly encountered the same struggles their first year here at Chico State. Most of them felt out of place without the presence of family, friends, familiarity, and culture; the lack of these aspects in their lives caused them to feel disconnected with the university. . . . This can cause some students to feel in disarray when they see the different people around them, especially when you're not involved with a club or program at the school. These organizations are really useful because it can help first years with their transition. The students however that have been able to find a place in a club, program, or organization truly feel like they have found their people at Chico State." (p. 7)

4. *Frequent, timely, and constructive feedback.* Assignment sequencing provided ample time to practice, get feedback, and improve work. Students noticed and commented on this: "It was a great class that supplied enough time to work on projects and get help. Way more feedback than any other class which is great. Instead of learning about something, we learned how to do something" (first-generation, Hispanic male). "[Y]ou could just call for anyone like any teaching aid your age, a mentor at the table or Bill and be like, 'I need help. . . . And you know, they'll just like rush over, they help anyone they can" (1st-generation, Asian American male).

5. and 6. *Opportunities to discover relevance of learning through real-world applications and public demonstration of competence.* We combine these indicators drawn from Kuh et al. (2013) because the applied nature of the ethnographic research was tied tightly to the public audience where students presented the results and recommendations of their research. "I feel I've learned more in the U-Course because it was applied learning" (first-generation, White male). "I find hands-on research projects to be really fun because I get to apply what I am learning. . . . I prefer the style of the U-Course more than other classes because I felt more passionate and interested in what I was learning" (non-first-generation, White female). Regarding the public audience, when asked if having a public audience affected the quality of their work, 61 students mentioned it was motivating or very motivating and only nine indicated it was somewhat motivating or had no effect on motivation. Typical comments included the following: "A public audience was a really big motivator because it made me more aware of my work and pushed me to write better" (first-generation, Hispanic female). "This assignment was great. Having people here that care about what you have to say is just an amazing feeling" (non-first-generation, White male). "Since I had to present and knew my work could make a difference, I worked harder" (1st-generation, White female).

Conclusions

As educators, it is our responsibility to create learning environments that support the success of our students. The HIPs literature emerged in large measure as a systematic attempt to define proven pedagogical practices that foster student success and deep learning (Kuh et al., 2013). One of the criticisms of the HIPs literature is the excessive focus on a list of practices without (a) understanding why and under what circumstances they work, and (b) an uncritical "drop and drag" approach to implementation that neglects important design work necessary to integrate HIPs into course activities and objectives (Finley, 2019).

Our experience implementing undergraduate research in a 1st-year general education course focused on the success of underserved students reinforces the importance of intensive design work to foster a learning environment consistent with the community of practice literature and the need to provide appropriate scaffolding and support to move students toward inclusive excellence. The design features highlighted here emerged dialogically, in conversation between the faculty teaching partners and with the broader teaching team and were informed by a rich literature from the learning sciences. That literature emphasizes that *learning is a process that takes place in community.*

The community of practice approach proved effective when deployed to explicitly support the learning of historically underserved students: low income, first-generation students of color. To these students we owe a particular responsibility given the sacrifices these students, and their families, make to get to and persist in college. For many of us, these historically underserved students form an increasing proportion of our students. To reserve our most effective educational practices, such as undergraduate research, for upper division students in our majors is a disservice to the many underserved students who struggle to succeed on our campuses and in our classes, and who arguably benefit most from a college education.

The pedagogical model described here is not a panacea. It is one attempt to improve learning for our students under the constraints of the contemporary U.S. higher education system. We caution that the creation of learning environments is context-specific—sensitive to institutional cultures, disciplinary norms, and instructor effects. The implementation of undergraduate research in the Anthropology-English course is one example of an approach that builds on the HIPs literature and puts learning theory into practice at a scale that can serve relatively large groups of students. However, undergraduate research, like any HIP, is not replicable in the sense of being uncritically transferable. Thoughtful attention to course and assignment design can bring undergraduate research to more—and more diverse—students, earlier in their academic careers. These are the students who have the most to gain, and lose.

References

Cuthbert, D., Arunachalamm, D., & Licina, D. (2012). "It feels more important than other classes I have done": An "authentic" undergraduate research experience in sociology. *Studies in Higher Education, 17*(2), 129–142. https://doi.org/10.1080/03075079.2010.538473

Finley, A. (2019, November). *A comprehensive approach to assessment of high-impact practices* (Occasional Paper No. 41). University of Illinois and Indiana University, National Institute for Learning Outcomes Assessment (NILOA). https://www.learningoutcomesassessment.org/wp-content/uploads/2019/11/Occasional-Paper-41.pdf

Kuh, G. D. (2008). *High-impact educational practices: What they are, who has access to them, and why they matter.* Association of American Colleges & Universities.

Kuh, G. D., O'Donnell, K., & Reed, S. (2013). *Ensuring quality and taking high-impact practices to scale.* Association of American Colleges & Universities.

Kuh, G. D., O'Donnell, K. O., & Schneider, C. G. (2017). HIPs at ten. *Change: The Magazine of Higher Learning, 49*(5), 8–16. https://doi.org/10.1080/00091383.2017.1366805

LeCompte, M., & Schensul, J. (2010). *Ethnographer's toolkit: Vol. 1. Designing and conducting ethnographic research* (2nd ed.). Rowman Alta Mira.

Leek, D. (2014). Developing U.S. students' skills in communication research through ethnographies of speech in different London settings. *CUR Quarterly, 35*, 14–19. https://link.gale.com/apps/doc/A465436395/AONE?u=nysl_oweb&sid=googleScholar&xid=26b5d588

McKillip, J. (2009). Transformative undergraduate research: Students as the authors of and authorities on their own education. *CUR Quarterly, 30*, 10–15. https://www.cur.org/assets/1/7/winter09mckillip.pdf

Nasir, N., & Cooks, J. (2009). Becoming a hurdler: How learning settings afford identities. *Anthropology & Education Quarterly, 40*, 41–61. https://doi.org/10.1111/j.1548-1492.2009.01027.x

Olson-McBride, L., Hassemer, H., & Hoepner, J. (2016). Broadening participation: Engaging academically at-risk freshmen in undergraduate research. *CUR Quarterly, 37*, 4–10. https://link.gale.com/apps/doc/A465296501/AONE?u=nysl_oweb&sid=googleScholar&xid=8d35687b

Vygotsky, L. S. (1978). *Mind in society*. Harvard University Press.

Wenger, E. (1998). *Communities of practice*. Cambridge University Press.

Wozniak, C. (2011). Freshman fellows: Recruiting and retaining great students through research opportunities. *CUR Quarterly, 32*, 8–15. https://link.gale.com/apps/doc/A274228958/AONE?u=nysl_oweb&sid=googleScholar&xid=6fe7d310

7

THEMED LEARNING COMMUNITIES AND SERVICE-LEARNING LEVERAGED FOR STUDENT SUCCESS

Michele J. Hansen and Thomas W. Hahn

Collegians face an increasingly complex world as they take up adult roles during and after college. Increasing globalization, cultural clashes, and economic challenges are just a few of the major issues that require navigating multiple perspectives to function effectively in a diverse society.

—Baxter Magolda & Boes, 2017, para. 1

As timely as this quote was in 2017, it did not take into account a global pandemic (COVID-19) and protestations against police brutality and racism occurring throughout the country. Clearly, college students today face myriad obstacles to successfully navigating their college years. Promoting retention, academic success, and educating students for both social and personal responsibility will prepare students to become global citizens and navigate the challenges noted in the epigraph. Encouraging the participation of all students in high-impact practices (HIPs) is one strategy to attain this goal.

Campus leaders often desire investigations that allow them to determine which educational practices are the most effective in terms of improving students' levels of academic success and learning outcomes. According to Kuh (2008), creating opportunities for students to participate in at least two HIPs during their undergraduate program, one in the 1st year and one taken later in relation to the major field, is an effective way to enhance students' levels of academic success and engagement. The obvious choices for incoming students are first-year seminars and learning communities.

Kuh also notes that "to engage students at high levels, these practices must be done well" (p. 20). Although research has also shown that being intentional in linking courses and using engaging pedagogies within the context of learning communities can improve academic outcomes (Brownell & Swaner, 2010), there is a gap in the literature on whether this improvement is enhanced when combined with a service-learning course. The present research explored the influence of service-learning (SL) and themed learning community (TLC) pedagogies on college students' success and learning. TLCs with an imbedded first-year seminar and SL are common HIPs available to students at Indiana University–Purdue University Indianapolis (IUPUI). This research explored if there is a differential impact when TLCs and SL are employed concurrently.

Summary of Relevant Literature

SL is a teaching strategy that can generate multiple positive outcomes for students. Research on SL has revealed positive impacts on several facets of students' lives, including cognitive learning outcomes, social responsibility, cultural awareness, and retention. A meta-analysis of 62 studies involving 11,837 students suggested that students participating in SL had significant gains in five outcome areas: attitudes toward self, attitudes toward school and learning, civic engagement, social skills, and academic performance (Celio et al., 2011). Regarding growth in personal development, a meta-analysis by Bowman (2011) found that diversity experiences (a major component of SL done well) are associated with increases in civic attitudes, behavioral intentions, and behaviors. Yorio and Ye's (2012) meta-analysis further supported the hypothesis that SL has a positive effect on understanding of social issues, personal insight, and cognitive development. Lockeman and Pelco's (2013) ex post facto longitudinal study followed a cohort of 3,458 entering undergraduate students for 6 years to explore the differences between students who took SL courses and those who did not. Although SL students and non-SL students had similar precollege academic characteristics, SL students earned more credits, had a higher average college GPA, and graduated at a significantly higher rate than did non-SL students, despite having greater financial need while enrolled. Brown's (2011) experimental study of the impact of SL found that participation in SL led to a decline in social dominance orientation, which is associated with several oppressive attitudes, including sexism and racism.

The intent of TLCs is to facilitate students' transitions to a college or university and promote higher retention rates and levels of academic performance. Research on TLCs has shown that participation in them increases students' engagement levels (e.g., campus involvement), integrative and higher order thinking, and offers a constructive way for students to establish and maintain relationships with peers and faculty (Pike et al., 2011). These levels of engagement can lead to a more successful 1st-year college experience, persistence into the 2nd year, and higher rate of graduation (Andrade, 2008). Qualitative research revealed multiple ways in which the TLC program contributes to student learning. These include receiving college transition assistance, meeting new friends and expanding connections, developing critical thinking skills, being enrolled in linked courses, establishing peer support networks, and becoming more comfortable and confident (Hansen & Rauch, 2017).

Pedagogies and Practices

An interdisciplinary theme shapes each TLC's course design. The integration of course content in each TLC course is intentional, with the course design encouraging integrative thinking in students. The activities that take place out of the classroom are designed to enhance academic content, integrative thinking, and interdisciplinary themes. Active learning strategies are central to each TLC course, and faculty collaboration fosters an integrative approach, exploration of theme, cocurricular experiences, and student development. There are seven essential elements of TLCs provided at IUPUI:

- offered in first fall semester for 1st-year students
- cohort of 25 students
- three or more linked courses
- instructional team (faculty member, advisor, peer mentor)
- all TLCs with an embedded first-year seminar
- interdisciplinary theme and connections
- learning beyond the classroom

TLCs are designed to enhance interdisciplinary knowledge while students grapple with complex issues and explore themes that require higher levels of critical thinking. The following are examples of themes: "Serving Others Through Engineering Design," "Like a Girl—Gender, Language, and Power," "Molecules to Medicines," and "Dangerous Minds, Dangerous Policies." Programs are offered in liberal arts, engineering and technology, science, art, social work, education, business, physical education, public and environmental affairs, University College, and more.

Although there are a variety of definitions of *service-learning*, the IUPUI Center for Service and Learning defines the pedagogy as

> a course or competency-based, credit-bearing educational experience in which students (a) participate in mutually identified service activities that benefit the community and (b) reflect on the service activity in such a way as to gain further understanding of course content, a broader appreciation of the discipline, and an enhanced sense of personal values and civic responsibility. (Bringle & Clayton, 2012, p. 105; adapted from Bringle & Hatcher, 1996)

The Center for Service and Learning offers seminars and ad hoc training to instructors on the following:

- designing an SL course
- best practices for finding and sustaining community partnerships
- navigating logistical issues for an effective service experience
- facilitating critical reflection
- assessing civic outcomes
- visiting scholars throughout the year
- faculty learning communities

Examples of high-quality SL experiences at IUPUI include earth science students conducting soil tests to facilitate lead remediation, sociology students working with the aged, and kinesiology students working with local residents on improving their health outcomes.

Overall Implementation

Fidelity is defined by Webster as "the quality or state of being faithful, the accuracy in details, exactness" (Merriam-Webster, n.d.). Program fidelity assessment offers another level of detail about the program as implemented by examining the degree to which interventions are implemented as theoretically planned. Poor fidelity examples include learning communities implemented with no integrative learning assignments and SL implemented with no structured reflection. It is not possible to test the effectiveness of an intervention if the intervention failed to be implemented as planned (Scott & Sechrest, 1989).

Facilitating and sustaining the quality of HIPs is a priority at IUPUI. The engaged learning taxonomies (formerly Research International Service Learning Experiential [RISE] taxonomies) are a valuable resource for instructors; they have the potential to assist in improving course design and sustaining the quality of HIP experiences offered. Instructors have the opportunity to use these taxonomies to document course revision and enhancement where appropriate (e.g., instructors can see where they are and envision opportunities for growth). For more on the taxonomies for capstones, ePortfolios, first-year seminars, internships, peer mentoring, SL courses, study abroad, summer bridge (an intensive presemester program for incoming students), TLCs, and undergraduate research, see Get Engaged (n.d.).

Evidence of Data-Supported Equity

In Kuh's 2008 seminal research on HIPs he was able to demonstrate that HIPs not only benefited all students who participated but had positive differential effects on historically underrepresented students. HIPs seemed to provide students from historically underrepresented groups the opportunity to engage in deep learning, and these engaging experiences boosted their academic success levels. Given this powerful finding, Kuh advocated that every student should have the opportunity to participate in at least one HIP each year scaffolded through their educational experience. Finley and McNair's (2013) follow-up research also showed that HIPs can have cumulative effects on underserved populations. They advocated that college and university educators adopt equity-minded approaches and take proactive steps toward inclusive excellence. Approaches should be aimed at equitable access, but also equitable achievement of outcomes.

IUPUI campus leaders have implemented a number of initiatives and practices to ensure inclusive excellence and to assess equitable outcomes related to HIPs. The administrative offices for TLCs and the Center for Service and Learning are housed in the Institute for Engaged Learning (IEL). IEL was formed in 2018 to systematically promote and support the equitable progression of undergraduates through pathways of connected and scaffolded curricular and cocurricular HIPs (applied, integrative, and experiential learning opportunities) that prepare students for lives of commitment and success with skills to communicate, innovate, and engage in local and global communities to address 21st-century problems.

IEL partners with other units offering engaged learning experiences in the campus-wide effort to ensure that all undergraduate students participate in at least four scaffolded HIPs by the time they graduate. In an effort to ensure that students have equitable outcomes, IEL also oversees the administration of the Experiential and Applied Learning Record (the Record). The Record is a unique downloadable document for students that provides evidence of experiences they had at IUPUI that are not reflected on their academic transcript. Their Record includes the type of experience, its name, and the learning outcomes associated with it. All experiences included on the Record must be approved and demonstrate learning outcomes, reflection, and assessment. The Record provides evidence that the student participated in and completed these HIPs.

The Office of Institutional Research and Decision Support (IRDS) supports IEL in these efforts through the provision of institutional data and collaboration on assessment and research studies. In an effort to assess campus progress on equity and inclusion goals, IRDS engages in assessment, reporting, and program evaluation activities. IRDS seeks to empower IUPUI leaders, faculty members, and staff at all levels to utilize data, analytics, information, and evidence to make decisions and take actions that benefit students and enhance their learning experiences. Promoting the use of data for decisions that improve equity and success for historically marginalized students is a key element in all IRDS analyses and investigations. Creating culturally responsive institutional research and assessment practices requires moving beyond data disaggregation and moving toward leveraging data to advance more equitable outcomes for all students. Culturally responsive institutional research reminds campus leaders to assess their institutional performance using disaggregated data and to initiate action plans in response to findings. For example, a recent investigation showed that historically underrepresented students (African American, Latinx, two or more races) who participated in TLCs had significantly higher 1-year retention rates (79%) compared to nonparticipants (70%). This finding suggests that the engaging pedagogies occurring in TLCs are having a positive effect on outcomes, and end-of-course questionnaires indicated that the students were having positive learning experiences. If we are to realize the vision of equity-minded practices, we must understand how pedagogical designs and learning contexts affect student circumstances, interests, goals, motivation, self-efficacy, and ability to persist to degree completion.

The Current Study

This study employed a mixed-methods research design to investigate the influences of the independent variables on critical thinking, integrated learning, civic learning, quality interactions with diverse peers, grade point average, and retention at IUPUI—a large, urban public research university in the midwest region of the United States. Multiple sources of data were used to understand the effect of TLC-SLs on student outcomes. Sources of data included institutional data on student demographics, retention, and GPAs; responses from a locally developed end-of-course questionnaire; students' actual work from written reflections; and results from the National Survey of Student Engagement (NSSE).

Participants for this study included 1st-year undergraduate students who participated in TLCs during their first semester. There were 852 total students included, with 352 in a TLC-SL and 500 in a TLC with no SL component. Participants were 4% Asian American, 9% African American, 10% Latinx, 5% two or more races, and 70% White. Sixty-four percent were women, 35% were first-generation college students, 40% were low-income (eligible for a federal Pell Grant), and their average age was 18.23. Participants had an average high school GPA of 3.48 and average SAT score of 1029.

Results

Analysis of covariance and procedures were employed to determine the difference in GPA among TLC participants with and without an SL component. There was a significant effect of TLC-SL on first semester GPA after controlling for high school GPA, SAT score, income level (received a Pell Grant or not), and gender $F(4, 844) = p < .05$. The adjusted mean GPA for TLC-SL was 3.01 compared to 2.89 for TLC without SL.

A series of independent t-test analyses were conducted using data collected from a locally developed end-of-course questionnaire designed to assess civic learning outcomes and integrative learning. Students were asked the extent to which their TLC experience helped them enhance their abilities in various learning areas on a scale that ranged from 0 = "Not at All" to 5 = "Very Much." Students who participated in TLC-SL had significantly higher levels of developing a better understanding of complex real-world social problems ($M = 4.06$ vs. $M = 3.66$), considering problems and issues from multiple perspectives or points of view (ethnic, racial, cultural, religious, etc.; $M = 4.07$ vs. $M = 3.73$), and understanding connections between different disciplines ($M = 3.93$ vs. $M = 3.53$) compared to nonparticipants ($p < .01$). A series of analyses were also conducted to determine if historically marginalized students who participated in TLC-SL had significantly better outcomes compared to nonparticipants. Results indicated that African American students who participated in TLC-SL sections had significantly higher retention rates (85%) compared to nonparticipating African American students (78%). This finding suggested a differential positive effect of TLCs-SLs for African American students, as the overall participant 1-year retention rate was 77%, compared to 74% for all nonparticipants.

Engagement indicator scores based on NSSE results were examined to determine if students who participated in TLCs-SLs had higher levels of engagement. NSSE self-reported results among 1st-year students indicated that students who participated in SL-TLCs had higher engagement indicator scores in the areas of "Higher-Order Learning" (46.36 compared to 40.65 for one HIP, and 38.81 for no HIP) and "Discussions With Diverse Others" (50.45 compared to 40.41 for one HIP, and 38.05 for no HIP).

A content analysis was conducted on student reflection papers that were collected from TLC-SL students. One major theme that emerged from students' written reflections was a deeper understanding of diversity issues. Actual students' comments included the following:

> I've learned a lot about race, especially in aspects I didn't think to focus on or notice, like environmental racism or empowerment. . . . I learned that there is so much more to racism than just police brutality or hate crimes. . . . It stretches so much farther. It really opened my eyes to racism, the fact that it stretches into all areas of life.
>
> As a White female, I have many opportunities and privileges that many people of color do not get. It was interesting to learn and see for myself all of the racial injustice going on around me. It really opened my eyes to see the importance of standing up for racial injustice in the world and made me want to be more helpful.

Another theme that emerged was students' improved sense of selves and awareness of how social issues affect them. One student noted:

> In general, I just started to notice all of the waste everyone around me was producing, myself included. I started to recycle more, I have a lot more reusable cups now, I produce less food waste, etc. Now I'm just trying to have my family follow suit. For me, the experience where I developed a deeper understanding for sustainability and others was the day we did our service project.

Conclusion

Results suggest that pedagogical strategies that facilitate a sense of community, integrative learning, and positive peer interactions may be the most effective strategies for enhancing students' overall academic success and learning experiences. It is evident that TLCs coupled with SL create positive learning experiences and allow students to develop the global learning skills necessary for future success. TLCs and SL create a synergistic effect in which their TLC cohort experiences help students feel a sense of belonging, engage in meaningful interactions with diverse peers, explore complex issues through an interdisciplinary lens, participate in critical reflection, and analyze and solve real-world complex social problems.

This current study suggested that students who participated in TLCs with SL experiences had significantly higher levels of critical thinking, integrated and civic learning, quality interactions with diverse peers, as well as higher GPA and retention rates compared to students who participated in TLCs with no SL. The evidence suggests that the TLC-SL instructional teams on campus have developed pedagogical strategies that facilitate positive connections and interactions, equip students with skills necessary to effectively adjust to college, and help students make connections between courses. Furthermore, this research enhances understanding regarding the effectiveness of integrative learning experiences as components of HIPs.

This study also provides insights to help researchers and assessment specialists develop methods and techniques to investigate how TLC-SL experiences affect academic success and learning outcomes. As a result of this research, the institution offers faculty development and incentives for TLC teams to create SL experiences integrated across multiple TLC courses. This work is guided by the campus taxonomies for TLC and SL, for project planning and institutional assessment. Future investigations will use actual student work as authentic evidence of integrative learning in order to determine meaningful impacts on student learning outcomes.

References

Andrade, M. S. (2008). Learning communities: Examining positive outcomes. *Journal of College Student Retention*, *9*(1), 1–20. https://doi.org/10.2190/E132-5X73-681Q-K188

Baxter Magolda, M. B., & Boes, L. M. (2017). Educational theory and student civic outcomes. In J. A. Hatcher, R. G. Bringle, & T .W. Hahn (Eds.), *Research on student civic outcomes in service learning: Conceptual frameworks and methods* (pp. 115–133). Stylus.

Bowman, N. A. (2011). Promoting participation in a diverse democracy: A meta-analysis of college diversity experiences and civic engagement. *Review of Education Research*, *81*(1), 29–68. https://doi.org/10.3102/0034654310383047

Bringle, R. G., & Clayton, P. H. (2012). Civic education through service learning: What, how and why? In L. McIlrath, A. Lyons, & R. Munck (Eds.), *Higher education and civic engagement: Comparative perspectives* (pp. 101–124). Palgrave.

Bringle, R. G., & Hatcher, J. A. (1996). Implementing service learning in higher education. *Journal of Higher Education*, *67*, 221–239. https://doi.org/10.1080/00221546.1996.11780257

Brown, A. (2011). Learning from service: The effect of helping on helper's social dominance orientation. *Journal of Applied Social Psychology, 41*(4), 850–871. https://doi.org/10.1111/j.1559-1816.2011.00738.x

Brownell, J. E., & Swaner, L. E. (2010). *Five high-impact practices: Research on learning outcomes, completion, and quality.* Association of American Colleges & Universities.

Celio, C. I., Durlak, J., & Dymnicki, A. (2011). A meta-analysis of the impact of service-learning on students. *Journal of Experiential Education, 34*(2), 164–181. https://doi.org/10.1177/105382591103400205

Finley, A., & McNair, T. (2013). *Assessing underserved students' engagement in high-impact practices.* Association of American Colleges & Universities.

Get Engaged. (n.d.). *Engaged learning taxonomies.* Indiana University–Purdue University Indianapolis. https://getengaged.iupui.edu/faculty-and-staff/taxonomies/index.html

Hansen, M. J., & Rauch, J. (2017). *Themed learning communities (TLCs) qualitative report.* Office of Institutional Research and Decision Support.

Kuh, G. (2008). *High-impact educational practices: What they are, who has access to them, and why they matter.* Association of American Colleges & Universities.

Lockeman, K. S., & Pelco, L. E. (2013). The relationship between service-learning and degree completion. *Michigan Journal of Community Service Learning, 20*(1), 18–30. http://hdl.handle.net/2027/spo.3239521.0020.102

Merriam-Webster. (n.d.). Fidelity. In *Merriam-Webster.com dictionary.* Retrieved August 18, 2021, from https://merriam-webster.com

Pike, G. R., Kuh, G. D., & McCormick, A. C. (2011). An investigation of the contingent relationships between learning community participation and student engagement. *Research in Higher Education, 52*(3), 300–322. https://doi.org/10.1007/s11162-010-9192-1

Scott, A. G., & Sechrest, L. (1989). Strength of theory and theory of strength. *Evaluation and Program Planning, 12*(4), 329–336. https://doi.org/10.1016/0149-7189(89)90049-9

Yorio, P. L., & Ye, F. (2012). A meta-analysis on the effects of service-learning on the social, personal, and cognitive outcomes of learning. *Academy of Management Learning & Education, 11*(1), 9–27. https://doi.org/10.5465/amle.2010.0072

8

DATA COLLECTION IN COURSE-BASED UNDERGRADUATE RESEARCH EXPERIENCES

Best Practices and Lessons Learned

Sara Z. Evans and Jocelyn Evans

Undergraduate research (UGR) allows students to leave the traditional lecture-based classroom and apply knowledge in a new and novel way. High-impact practices (HIPs) such as UGR also provide an exponential positive impact for first-generation and underrepresented minority (URM) students (Kuh et al., 2017). UGR can take many forms, but this chapter specifically focuses on course-based undergraduate research experiences (CUREs), where an entire class of students engages in undergraduate research project(s) that include the essential elements of a HIP defined by Kuh et al. (2013). CUREs increase access to research experiences for URM students because they are embedded courses within the curriculum (Bangera & Brownell, 2014). This chapter focuses on strategies for supporting student work in CUREs and for gathering evidence of impact on student learning and success.

Strategies for the Design of Student-Centered CUREs

UGR is most importantly about student personal and professional development. Much like internships or directed studies, a student-centered approach benefits and enhances the student experience. To be student-centered is to fully consider student preparation to confront theoretical and methodological material. Mentoring students within a major is, in some ways, easier than guiding 1st-year students in general education courses. Advanced students have taken research methods courses and have basic statistical knowledge. UGR rewards with seniors might be more straightforward, including successful admission to graduate school or easier pathways to employment. However, mentoring 1st-year students can reveal a range of disciplinary perspectives, natural skills, and academic backgrounds. UGR projects with 1st-year students can transform their understanding of science, whether or not they pursue a STEM major or career (Brownell et al., 2015; Kortz & van der Hoeven Kraft, 2016). The UGR experience is a tremendous recruitment tool for majors and minors and an opportunity to find young collaborators to work on projects spanning multiple years.

Given differences in student expectations and preparation, it is critical to scaffold assignments appropriately within CUREs. The instructor should include activities and assignments yielding the greatest benefit to students and ensuring the highest quality experience for them. Keep students on track with a large project such as a paper or presentation by requiring small formative assignments with low stakes that focus on detailed constructive feedback rather than punitive grading to help students build confidence early. Individual assignments, such as "Research Topic," "Research Question," "Paper Proposal," "Annotated Bibliography," and rough drafts scaffold the development of the final product. Instructor feedback provides students with encouragement early in the semester, with plenty of time to correct mistakes before the final product is due. To maintain a student-centered perspective, we conceive of assignments as a workbook and develop scaffolded assignments for each student level (see also Evans & Evans, 2021).

Give students agency in managing data collection. Data collection tools can empower students to "grow" datasets and see the fruits of their labor, even while protecting data integrity and human subjects. If students need certification and institutional review board (IRB) approval, one could make this task an assignment in the course to increase both buy-in and accountability. Other faculty view favorably students with experience such as this early in their academic careers, and these students often are given future research opportunities because of their advanced preparation to handle research tasks. For this reason, it is essential to emphasize that IRB certification is of value to their entire academic career and professional development.

Students benefit from feeling ownership of data collection and analysis. They are empowered by managing data collection. They see the data as "theirs" and value contributing to the scholarly enterprise and the broader community (Ahlm, 1997). Data management can involve frustration and unanticipated obstacles, but the end result illuminates course material in ways no traditional class lecture can. Through data analysis and theoretically driven modeling, research comes alive for students.

Instructors play an important role in facilitating and guiding the data collection process, and several strategies can be implemented to mitigate potential problems. If students will be asked, for example, to collect observational data using Qualtrics or Google Forms, to code for content analysis, or to transcribe historical records, consider a practice session in which they collect data from the same source or location. Each individual collecting data should have a unique identifier. Comb through results to look for discrepancies, discuss them with the group, and repeat the process until you are confident that all coders are interpreting observations similarly. Graduate students can be "mock participants" for students prior to fieldwork, acting as specific archetypes of human subjects (i.e., "the questioner," "the combative respondent," "the easy respondent"), while instructors offer real-time feedback. Provide a "Frequently Asked Questions" document for students in the field, with business cards for all instructors. We support students with answers to common questions, such as "Why are you doing this research?" and "Who is in charge of this project?" as well as some that were specific to our own research context such as "Are you doing this because you think there is a lot of crime here?" Lastly, distribute a "script" for students to follow when approaching participants to ease their anxiety about asking for participation. These strategies ensure quality data, give students confidence, and reduce anxiety in the field. In a lab environment, students can complete practice experiments prior to ensure procedural accuracy and identify questions; during these practice sessions faculty can interpret results in real time and check for accuracy in lab reports prior to completing tasks with data the instructor hopes to use.

Despite the diversity of data informing faculty research agendas, there are several common issues that may arise. Consider that "analysis" of data can take many forms, and often does not need to include all students having access to primary data (with human subjects research, this may also introduce unnecessary risk for participants). For some student populations, analysis might include interpreting results produced by faculty or graduate student(s). For upper level students, perhaps allow estimation of results using primary data and statistical analyses. In other situations, such as lab work, students can conduct experiments generating primary data. There are ways to ensure data integrity and protection of human subjects in all of these examples, but taking time to consider what analysis and retention of data will include prior to the project's launch pays dividends later (see Dehn, 2010, for resources on ethics in UGR). Researchers must also be able to access all raw, original data in case they must recreate a file later. Once data has been entered completely, we provide separate "working files" for students to use when recoding/analyzing data.

Regardless of methods for data collection, management, and analysis, all researchers should consider several aspects regarding data integrity. Prior to beginning, develop expectations for timely collection of data and procedures for periodic checks for accuracy. How will you ensure that data is being collected on time? This is easier to accomplish by creating graded course assignments associated with data collection in a CURE. Multiple deadlines prior to the semester's end allow time for improvement from early mistakes. Formative assignments contribute to timely completion of final projects, and essential training prior to data collection improves results. In one course project, we neglected this to our detriment with errors that could have been avoided using earlier check-ins with 1st-year students.

Finally, it is important to provide opportunities for students to present the research experience and results to appropriate stakeholders. At the outset identify where results will be disseminated, such as a class presentation in which the faculty member invites fellow colleagues and other students, the institution's annual research symposium, or a professional conference. Conference presentations allow students to connect the experiences of class discussion with actual research communication and articulate these connections in a meaningful way to a scholarly audience (see Millspaugh & Millenbah, 2004). Through presentations, especially at national and regional disciplinary conferences, students undergo powerful transformation from passive learners to active scholars.

Measuring the Outcomes of CUREs

The most powerful way we can continue to demonstrate UGR's substantial impact is to gather high-quality supporting evidence. Assessment data provides valuable information about student learning gains as evidence for scholarship on teaching and learning and can bring about change at departmental, college, and university levels. When considering UGR's effectiveness, there are multiple dimensions for evaluating efficacy and impact. In the following, we describe examples from our own CURE research over the last 5 years. Although these projects were implemented with diverse student populations, we deliberately designed rubrics and assignments that aligned so we could compare results (see also Evans & Evans, 2021). Additionally, we recommend building an assessment plan that allows your units to gather evidence of student learning aligned with the institution's accrediting bodies and continuous quality improvement plans.

First, collect evidence aligned with course learning outcomes. This ensures assessment of course effectiveness overall, even when including a nontraditional component such as UGR. The best choice of assessment mechanism depends on course content and level, but many instructors choose an end-of-course project, paper, and/or presentation. Group projects accommodate larger classes, but consider group dynamics and functionality when designing a course to involve group work. For example, one of our CUREs enrolled 75 honors 1st-year students, with each student completing their own paper using the same dataset (observational data collected by the class earlier in the semester). The dataset itself was not incredibly large (60 cases; 150 variables), but students explored a variety of topics.

Second, assess the student experience. The benefits of UGR go beyond traditional classroom learning, which is what makes the experiences so powerful. Often, these benefits include improvements in self-efficacy, confidence, public speaking skills, and a deeper understanding of content (Crews, 2013; Linn et al., 2015; Lopatto, 2010). Furthermore, although outcomes are similar for students in CUREs compared to those in a traditional apprenticeship UGR experience, those in a CURE report higher gains in learning the scientific process (Kinner & Lord, 2018). Gains will not be captured by examining course learning outcomes alone. There are two main ways to assess these gains, and we recommend both. Structured, critical reflection provides valuable information regarding student experiences, challenges, gains in personal traits and learning, and synthesis of content. Critical reflection is an essential HIP element (Kuh et al., 2013) and opportunities should be both summative and formative. Reflection throughout the semester can identify both challenges and successes in real time and provide opportunities to change course before the semester and project are over. Additionally, these formative reflections contribute to summative reflection for students. In the past, we have utilized formative reflection on data collection days in particular. At the end of each day of data collection, students write (by hand) a short narrative account of the experience, describe any problems, discuss any apprehensions, and identify information learned in class that was helpful in the field. On the following days, they repeat the process and compare with prior data collection experiences.

Ash and Clayton (2009) designed one procedure for critical reflection based on the "DEAL" model (describe–examine–articulate learning). This approach depends upon well-designed learning objectives aligned with assessment products. It requires significant presemester planning but results in richer and more meaningful feedback. Several of our UGR projects included a similar model; one is outlined by Abderhalden et al. (2016). Students in this course indicated it was a powerful experience allowing them to apply classroom content in a hands-on way.

Most of our students complete a quantitative questionnaire modified from one developed by Gordon et al. (2009). This evaluation contains 22 Likert-scale questions asking students to indicate agreement/disagreement with statements such as "I learned through direct experience in this class," "Working with my peers was a good way to facilitate learning," and "This experience taught me more than books or lectures." Results suggest overwhelmingly positive evaluations of the course and delivery method. Students also answered several open-ended questions regarding course attributes and offered suggestions for improvement (see Table 8.1).

Five major themes emerged from closed- and open-ended student feedback. Table 8.1 displays answers to the closed-ended questions, and

TABLE 8.1
Quantitative Feedback From Spring 2018 (N = 63)

	Strongly Disagree	*Disagree*	*Agree*	*Strongly Agree*
I had little interaction with my classmates during this semester.	46%	35%	13%	6%
I had little interaction with my instructor.	30%	41%	14%	14%
This course allowed me to engage in activities, problems, and tasks.	0%	10%	43%	48%
I learned through direct experience in this class.	6%	11%	43%	40%
I had to synthesize information from divergent sources and viewpoints and draw reasonable conclusions.	0%	10%	48%	43%
I had to exhibit disciplined work habits as an individual.	2%	11%	38%	49%
I had to conceive, plan, and execute a group service project.	2%	5%	30%	64%
Working with my peers was a good way to facilitate learning.	5%	11%	33%	51%
My sense of community was enhanced.	6%	16%	29%	49%
I worked with students outside the classroom to enhance my learning.	5%	10%	37%	49%

(*Continues*)

TABLE 8.1 (*Continued*)

	Strongly Disagree	*Disagree*	*Agree*	*Strongly Agree*
I learned more in this class doing field research than in a traditional classroom.	13%	24%	37%	27%
This experience taught me more than books or lectures.	10%	22%	30%	38%
Through the hands-on experience I learned more about myself.	14%	25%	29%	32%
I would take another class like this one with hands-on learning.	6%	18%	38%	38%

we refer periodically to responses from the open-ended responses throughout this discussion. All assessment results speak to essential elements of HIPs. First, students valued the learning experience provided by fieldwork and thought "this experience taught [them] more than books or lectures" (68%). It gave them a sense of agency—leaving the comfort zone of campus and traveling to a field site (in this case a community park) to collect observational and survey data. They had to "exhibit disciplined work habits as an individual" (87%) and learn to adapt in the face of unexpected developments. Challenges led to greater resiliency, with 61% of students suggesting that through the hands-on experience they learned more about themselves. They saw a long-term benefit in learning about survey methodology and the value of information good surveys can provide. Taken together, the experience involved appropriately high performance expectations, a significant investment of time and effort, and multiple experiences with diversity (Kuh et al., 2013).

Second, applied research required students to draw from the course content and extend it locally. They engaged in solving problems and accomplishing tasks (91%). For many, it made scientific inquiry relevant. Students saw research as beneficial for society; they felt they helped the community and were "doing something bigger than just the class." Some also reported learning more about the community, the contours of the local public, and the face of citizenship in everyday life (see Miller et al., 2013, for substantiation of these benefits in a natural science setting). The experience involved opportunities for integrating coursework and discovering its relevance through real-world application (Kuh et al., 2013).

Third, they reported increased participation in the course, engagement with the content and project, and value in interactivity. It gave them opportunities to know their peers better, to bond as a community, and to establish and grow friendships. They appreciated the support they received from their classmates through the process. In turn, they found that their "sense of community was enhanced" (78%). The experience provided frequent interactions with faculty and fellow students about matters of substance. Fourth, students valued a culminating opportunity to share research findings with community stakeholders. It clearly made a strong impression on them. This was an opportunity to dress professionally, participate in an oral presentation, and field questions and answers from community representatives to defend the rigor of their work and address the implications of their findings. The experience required students to demonstrate competence in a public forum (Kuh et al., 2013).

Finally, the course provided an invaluable experience for critical thinking about contemporary issues in a synthesizing way. The research combined quantitative and qualitative measures and uncovered findings that built upon student understanding of key concepts. Research became something real that involved posing questions and searching for answers, rather than something abstract and boring. In fact, 91% reported they "had to synthesize information from divergent sources and viewpoints and draw reasonable conclusions." In this way, students benefited from regular opportunities for reflection, integration, and synthesis (Kuh et al., 2013). We present results from only one course here but have found similar responses across both honors courses and upper level criminal justice courses (see Evans & Evans, 2021).

Instructors also can assess UGR effectiveness as a HIP. Despite growing evidence regarding impacts on learning outcomes and other student gains such as those described previously, little work considers the assessment of each experience and to what degree it meets the definition and criteria of a HIP. A few taxonomies exist, but it is still a relatively new exercise. Fischer et al. (2021) had a taxonomy for assessing UGR experiences. This taxonomy identified elements of "research breadth" and "research depth" and presented milestones of student involvement and engagement. Other taxonomies have been developed by Indiana University–Purdue University Indianapolis (n.d.) and the Tennessee Board of Regents (n.d.). Additionally, Kinzie et al. (2021) are in the process of collecting data investigating how well HIPs achieve the outcomes aligned with Kuh's (2008) definitions and essential elements (Kuh et al., 2013; Winkler, 2018). Shortlidge and Brownell (2016) have provided a comprehensive and useful instructor guide to develop a CURE assessment plan. Faculty engaged in UGR report benefits including increased job satisfaction, quality pilot data for external funding applications, and improved student learning outcomes (Shortlidge et al., 2017). In our experience, UGR leads to increased faculty collaboration, scholarly publications, and quality pilot data to support external research grant activity. Additionally, faculty leadership in this area impacts institution-wide strategic planning, budget allocation, and assessment for accreditation around HIPs.

This chapter identified strategies for engaging in data collection within the CURE context. There is no "one size fits all" approach to UGR, given vast differences across disciplines and institutional types. One major advantage of implementing a CURE rather than working with individual students is the opportunities CUREs provide for students who might not have the ability to participate in research otherwise. Many individual, mentored UGR projects require time and resources outside of class. Students from underrepresented minority backgrounds in STEM, arts, and humanities might not have access to either. Additionally, underrepresented students might not know of the existence or benefits of UGR or might feel uncomfortable approaching faculty members to discuss opportunities (Bangera & Brownell, 2014). Evidence from a longitudinal sample of underrepresented students indicates that participants in at least two semesters of URE were more likely to graduate with a science degree (Hernandez et al., 2018). Faculty should consider overall institutional diversity when aiming for specific targets of underrepresented participation in research. With planning and forethought, CUREs can increase access to UGR, benefit faculty research agendas, and provide high-quality experiences for undergraduate students.

Acknowledgments

The authors would like to thank Jamie Snyder and John D. Morgan for their contributions in the course and survey development in the early stages of this work. We would also like to thank Frances Abderhalden for her tireless work as an undergraduate and graduate student on this project.

References

Abderhalden, F. P., Snyder, J. A., & Evans, S. Z. (2016, February). Crime, camping, and fear: Developing high impact practices in criminal justice. *Journal of Criminal Justice Education, 1253*, 1–22. http://doi.org/10.1080/10511253.2016.1144990

Ahlm, K. (1997). A researcher's guide to key assessment principles and techniques. *CUR Quarterly, 18*, 70–72.

Ash, S. L., & Clayton, P. H. (2009). Generating, deepening, and documenting learning: The power of critical reflection in applied learning. *Journal of Applied Learning in Higher Education, 1*(1), 25–48. https://scholarworks.iupui.edu/handle/1805/4579

Bangera, G., & Brownell, S. E. (2014). Course-based undergraduate research experiences can make scientific research more inclusive. *CBE—Life Sciences Education, 13*, 602–606. https://doi.org/10.1187/cbe.14-06-0099

Brownell, S. E., Hekmat-Scafe, D. S., Singla, V., Seawell, P. C., Imam, J. F. C, Eddy, S. L, Stearns, T., & Cyert, M. S. (2015). A high-enrollment course-based undergraduate research experience improves student conceptions of scientific thinking and ability to interpret data. *CBE—Life Sciences Education, 14*, 1–14. https://doi.org/10.1187/cbe.14-05-0092

Crews, A. (2013). A partnership for the future: Undergraduate research's mutual benefits for students and administrators. *CUR Quarterly, 33*(3), 3–6.

Dehn, P. F. (2010). Responsible conduct of research: Administrative issues concerning research integrity and compliance. *CUR Quarterly, 30*(2), 27–34. https://link.gale.com/apps/doc/A228908816/AONE?u=nysl_oweb&sid=googleScholar&xid=ca27b984

Evans, S. Z., & Evans, J. (2021). Undergraduate research embedded across the curriculum through scaffolded projects. *Journal of the Scholarship of Teaching and Learning, 21*(1). https://doi.org/10.14434/josotl.v21i1.30552

Fischer, A. E., Immel, K. R., Wilkum, K., & Lee, L. R. (2021). A taxonomy for developing undergraduate research experiences as high-impact practices. *Journal of the Scholarship of Teaching and Learning, 21*(1). https://doi.org/10.14434/josotl.v21i1.30564

Gordon, J. A., Barnes, C. M., & Martin, K. J. (2009). Undergraduate research methods: Does size matter? A look at the attitudes and outcomes of students in a hybrid class format versus a traditional class format. *Journal of Criminal Justice Education, 20*(3), 238–239. https://doi.org/10.1080/10511250903200493

Hernandez, P. R., Woodcock, A., Estrada, M., & Shultz, P. W. (2018). Undergraduate research experiences broaden diversity in the scientific workforce. *BioScience, 68*(3), 204–211. https://doi.org/10.1093/biosci/bix163

Indiana University–Purdue University Indianapolis. (n.d.). *Engaged learning taxonomies.* Institute for Engaged Learning. https://getengaged.iupui.edu/faculty-and-staff/taxonomies/index.html

Kinner, D., & Lord, M. (2018). Student-perceived gains in collaborative, course-based undergraduate research experiences in the geosciences. *Journal of College Student Teaching, 48*(2), 48–58. https://www.jstor.org/stable/26616270

Kinzie, J., McCormick, A. C., Gonyea, R. M., Dugan, B., & Silberstein, S. (2021, March 3). *Getting beyond the label: Three takes on quality in high-impact practices.* https://www.aacu.org/blog/getting-beyond-label-three-takes-quality-high-impact-practices

Kortz, K. M., & van der Hoeven Kraft, K. J. (2016). Geoscience education research project: Student benefits and effective design of a course-based undergraduate research experience. *Journal of Geoscience Education, 64*, 24–36. https://doi.org/10.5408/15-11.1

Kuh, G. D. (2008). *High-impact educational practices: What they are, who has access to them, and why they matter*. Association of American Colleges & Universities.

Kuh, G. D., O'Donnell, K., & Reed, S. (2013). *Ensuring quality and taking high-impact practices to scale.* Association of American Colleges & Universities.

Kuh, G. D., O'Donnell, K. O., & Schneider, C. G. (2017). HIPs at ten. *Change: The Magazine of Higher Learning, 49*(5), 8–16. https://doi.org/10.1080/00091383.2017.1366805

Linn, M. C., Palmer, E., Baranger, A., Gerard, E., & Stone, E. (2015). Undergraduate research experiences: Impacts and opportunities. *Science, 347*(6222), 627. https://doi.org/10.1126/science.1261757

Lopatto, D. (2010). Undergraduate research as a high-impact student experience. *AAC&U Peer Review, 12*, 27–30. http://proxy.binghamton.edu/login?url=https://www.proquest.com/scholarly-journals/undergraduate-research-as-high-impact-student/docview/734767118/se-2?accountid=14168

Miller, C., Hamel, J., Holmes, K. D., Helmey-Hartman, W. L., & Lopatto, D. (2013). Extending your research team: Learning benefits when a laboratory partners with a classroom. *BioScience, 63*(9), 754–762. https://doi.org/10.1525/bio.2013.63.9.11

Millspaugh, J. J., & Millenbah, K. F. (2004). Value and structure of research experiences for undergraduate wildlife students. *Wildlife Society Bulletin (1973–2006), 32*(4), 1185–1194. https://doi.org/10.2193/0091-7648(2004)032[1185:VASORE]2.0.CO;2

Shortlidge, E. E., Bangera, G., & Brownell, S. E. (2017). Each to their own CURE: Faculty who teach course-based undergraduate research experiences report why you too should teach a CURE. *Journal of Microbiology & Biology Education, 18*(2), Article 18.2.29. https://doi.org/10.1128/jmbe.v18i2.1260

Shortlidge, E. E., & Brownell, S. E. (2016). How to assess your CURE: A practical guide for instructors of course-based undergraduate research experiences. *Journal of Microbiology & Biology Education, 17*(3), 399–408. https://doi.org/10.1128/jmbe.v17i3.1103

Tennessee Board of Regents. (n.d.). *Undergraduate research taxonomy—Revised 2019.* https://www.tbr.edu/student-success/hip-taxonomy-undergraduate-research-creative-activities

Winkler, C. (2018). *IU research Center to study reach and quality of high-impact practices.* https://education.indiana.edu/news-events/_news/2018/jul-dec/2018-11-16-high-impact-practices.html

9

INTERNSHIPS FOR ALL?

How Inequitable Access to Internships Hinders the Promise and Potential of High-Impact Practices and Work-Based Learning

Matthew T. Hora

Finding and completing an internship was always going to be a problem for Javier, a senior at a college where internships had recently become required for graduation. As he explained to our research team, "I just don't have the resources to do an internship," because he worked two jobs—one as a bank teller to pay for college and the other in a restaurant to help support his elderly parents. As we traveled across the country collecting data for the College Internship Study, a national mixed-methods study conducted through the Center for Research on College-Workforce Transitions (CCWT) at the University of Wisconsin-Madison, we, unfortunately, discovered that Javier's experience was not an isolated case.

Javier's predicament should raise red flags for those of us in higher education because internships are an increasingly important signal to employers that students are ready to enter the workforce (National Association of Colleges and Employers [NACE], 2018). A growing body of research is also showing that internship participation leads to higher rates of employment after graduation, higher wages and job satisfaction, and even better grades for student interns than those who don't take an internship (Binder et al., 2015; Jung & Lee, 2017; Silva et al., 2018). Simply put, internships can be a transformative experience for a college student, one that can "open the doors to opportunity" (Saniter & Siedler, 2014, p. 22), which is one reason they are considered as a high-impact practice (HIP) in which college students should participate before they graduate (Kuh, 2008).

But internships are not a universally possible or positive experience for all students. Besides long-standing concerns with inadequate mentoring, menial tasks, workplace harassment, and even illegal exploitation of unpaid student labor, for too many students these issues are irrelevant because an internship experience is simply out of reach (Chan et al., 2015; Perlin, 2012). This may especially be the case for low-income, first-generation students who may lack financial resources and social connections that help students locate and successfully pursue internships (Curiale, 2009; Finley & McNair, 2013). Consequently, some fear that internships may represent yet another vehicle for reproducing privilege for well-connected and wealthy students, raising questions about being required for graduation or promoted as a HIP without additional support systems put in place to ensure that all students can pursue and complete these experiences (Perlin, 2012).

Research on Internships and Access-Related Issues

Although the empirical research literature on HIPs is growing in scope and sophistication, limitations to the evidentiary base on HIPs include findings that students' precollege and background characteristics influence the impact of HIPs, and the acknowledgment that the implementation quality and efficacy of a HIP can vary substantially from campus to campus (Kuh & Kinzie, 2018; O'Neill, 2010; Seifert et al., 2014). The literature on internships is also hindered by the fact that some surveys ask students to report participation in a wide range of distinct types of programs (e.g., co-ops, apprenticeships, internships), instead of solely focusing on internships alone. Complicating matters, however, is that even if an instrument focused on internships, there is no single type or format of an internship, as they come in all shapes and sizes, varying along a variety of dimensions that include differences in program modality (e.g., online or in person), disciplinary or professional affiliation, duration, location, activities, and supervision (Bayerlein & Jeske, 2018; Hora et al., 2017). In practice, internships encompass an immense range of programs and student experiences. Further complicating advocacy for internships in higher education is the fact that equal access to these potentially transformative experiences does not yet exist. Research documenting the obstacles to internships focus on three distinct types of barriers: financial, sociocultural, and institutional.

Research and debate about the financial barriers to internship participation has a long history, with much of the discussion focused on issues related to unpaid labor, including its legality or the ethics of unpaid internships (e.g., Morris, 2018; Svacina, 2012). However, although many scholars have examined the role of compensation in shaping internship outcomes, surprisingly little empirical research exists on the nature and impacts of financial barriers to internship participation (e.g., Crain, 2016; McHugh, 2017). In a study on internships in the creative industry, Shade and Jacobson (2015) interviewed women who were unpaid interns in Toronto and New York City and found that the students would have been unable to participate in an unpaid internship without parental financial support in the form of helping to pay for room, board, and travel expenses.

Another set of barriers to internships includes sociocultural factors such as social and professional networks. For example, Milburn (2009) documented how internships "operate as part of an informal economy in which securing an internship all too often depends on who you know and not on what you know" (p. 99). The influential role of social and professional contacts to obtain an internship is common in creative industries such as advertising and in professions such as finance and law that have historically relied on informal networks as well as elite alumni networks for recruitment (Boulton, 2015; Frenette, 2013; Shade & Jacobson, 2015). However, some students may not have immediate access to these networks and resources (e.g., Parks-Yancy, 2012).

Finally, some research focuses on instructional and/or structural barriers to internship participation reflected by institutional provision (or lack thereof) of career-related advising and services. For example, Allen et al. (2013) found that elite institutions in the United Kingdom provide extensive coaching on how to access internships, including interview coaching and résumé audits, whereas universities that serve working-class students tend to lack such services. For institutions with fewer programs and services related to internships, students may struggle to find and successfully pursue internships (Finley & McNair, 2013). Given these varied obstacles that may keep some college students from pursuing and successfully completing an internship, it is imperative that postsecondary institutions identify solutions that level the playing field for all students, regardless of income, social connections, institutional affiliation, and geography.

Findings From the College Internship Study

The College Internship Study uses a concurrent mixed-methods design, where both qualitative and quantitative data are collected and analyzed simultaneously to address the research questions. The dataset used in this analysis includes a survey and focus groups with students at nine postsecondary institutions that include three historically Black colleges and universities

(HBCUs), two Hispanic-serving institutions (HSI), three public 4-year universities, and one technical college. The sampling frame for the study included students in their second half of their degree programs in order to increase the prospects that a student had completed an internship. Based on constraints of financial resources and time, the size of the study sample was capped at each institution at 1,250 students. The survey was completed by a total of 2,495 students across the nine institutions, with an average response rate of 26%. After completing the survey, students were asked if they were willing to participate in a focus group, and 171 students self-selected into the qualitative portion of the study.

Results

For the students who answered no to having participated in an internship in the past 12 months, 67% (n = 1,175) stated that they had hoped to obtain an internship but could not for a variety of reasons. This finding alone indicates a substantive number of college students want to pursue internships but cannot, thereby underscoring the fact that access to internships themselves is a considerable problem. Some demographic characteristics of the study sample include their academic enrollment (79% full time, 21% part time), race and ethnicity (37% White, 28% Black, 23% Hispanic, and 7% Asian or Asian American), first-generation status (53% continuing generation, 47% first generation), and employment status (55% part-time employed, 26% no employment, 19% full-time employed). Among the six barriers to internships included in the survey, the most common reason that prevented students from taking an internship was the need to work at their current paid job (63%), followed by a heavy course load (60%), a lack of internships in their discipline or field (49%), insufficient pay (37%), lack of transportation (26%), and lack of childcare (16%).

Next, due to the prospect that some students may experience more than one of these barriers at a time, we report how individuals reported combinations of these barriers. The most common combination was the need to work at their current paid job and a heavy course load, followed by those who had a heavy course load, needed to work, and had few opportunities, and those who reported the three barriers but also the obstacle of finding internships with sufficient pay. At the same time, some students did report only a single obstacle, such as the need to work or a heavy course load. What is notable in these data is not only the fact that multiple obstacles overlap or co-occur in the lives of individual students, but also that the need to work and a heavy course load are present in the four most frequently reported sets of barriers to internship participation.

Focus Group Data

Next, we turn to the focus group data, and thematic analysis of the text revealed that students described various obstacles, struggles, and concerns related to internship participation.

Internship Compensation

The most commonly discussed barrier to internship participation pertained to compensation—specifically, unpaid or inadequately paid internships. Some students had avoided pursuing internships because they believed them to be mostly unpaid, or because they could not find any that paid enough for them to consider leaving other employment. As one working student explained of the low-paying internships he found online, "They were paid, but I mean, it's not like my salary, so that's just not feasible." For many students who have bills, phone, rent, and even one-time expenses like a wedding, they sometimes organize their thinking into such lists of financial responsibilities, to which they viewed the addition of an unpaid or inadequately paid internship to be impossible.

Internship Scheduling

Another barrier to pursuing an internship was the competing demands of students' paid work, academic obligations, and family-related responsibilities, which left little time for an internship. As one student said, "I pretty much do not have enough time to give to an internship even if it's just part-time. . . . I just don't think there's enough time in the day." Some students who worked full-time shared that adding an internship to their schedule could put their main jobs at risk. For example, one student was a manager of a restaurant felt that she could not risk losing a stable job by taking on a second job, which could anger her supervisor and/or lead to exhaustion. These findings indicate that internships may not only be an inconvenience for students with existing work obligations but that they may in fact threaten their job security and/or career development.

Internship Availability

Participants in our focus groups also expressed concerns about the limited availability of internships in their disciplines or chosen profession. One student in a physics and applied math program explained that he had not taken an internship simply because "There aren't any here offered for me in my field." In addition, some students observed that although their career services offices and/or departments had staff to help locate an internship, there simply was a lack of internships in their field. As one student said, "We have an internship coordinator in our department, but there's not a ton of opportunities." In addition, the potentially irrelevant nature of internship work (e.g., repetitive data entry, pouring coffee) was a major concern for students, especially those who had not yet had an internship.

Internship Location

Finally, a major obstacle to accessing an internship involved the expenses related to travel, relocation, and living expenses for internships located in large metropolitan areas, where many internships are located. Although some students who had taken an internship had family who subsidized their living expenses, especially those who had to work in cities like New York or San Francisco. Consequently, some students only applied to internships that were close to home where these expenses would not be an issue. For example, one student at a Wisconsin university declined a highly desirable summer internship in the mining industry because it would lead them to incur substantial relocation and living expenses, while also providing no pay for a substantial amount of work. Consequently, this student took an on-campus undergraduate research position, and had to forgo his "dream internship."

Implications

One of the primary conclusions that we can draw from the data is that there are large numbers of college students who are effectively "screened out" or unable to pursue one of the most widely promoted HIPs in higher education—that of the college internship—largely due to their need to work consistently for pay, take a full slate of courses, or a simple lack of opportunities in their fields and/or geographic areas. The data also highlights how these obstacles to internships accumulate in the lives of individual students, not unlike the ways in which structural inequalities in our labor market, education, and criminal justice systems intersect with one another to effectively limit the opportunity for marginalized populations (Bourdieu, 1986; Crenshaw, 1991). Of course, these barriers are unfortunate for all students, but may be especially problematic for low-income, first-generation, and/or minoritized students for whom an internship may be an especially valuable professional experience. This is due to the fact that students in these groups are at a higher risk for dropping out of college (Museus & Quaye, 2009), often have less robust social networks (Parks-Yancy, 2012), and are at a disadvantage with respect to the elite and White-dominated cultural capital implicated in employers' hiring practices (Hora, 2020; Rivera, 2012).

Simply put, the long-standing concerns that internships may be reproducing patterns of privilege and inequality (e.g., Curiale, 2009) are borne out in our data, as 67% of the students in our study who had wanted to take an internship could not. This state of affairs raises questions about the degree to which colleges and universities should promote these experiential learning programs and what they can do to increase access to all students regardless of race, socioeconomic status, institutional and disciplinary affiliation, and physical location. Consequently, one of the most pressing issues facing higher education and the notion of HIPs is to determine ways to dismantle persistent structures of inequality and inaccessibility to an experience that is likely to "open the doors" of opportunity for college students (Saniter & Siedler, 2014). Although addressing these obstacles will be complex work, here I offer three concrete ways that higher education professionals can begin to democratize access to internships for *all* college students.

1. *Develop alternative forms of experiential education, especially work-integrated learning.* There are many ways for college students to be exposed to real-world problems and to be introduced to workplace norms, expectations, and situations. Although work-based learning programs like internships are valuable immersive experiences, work-integrated learning experiences where workplace problems are incorporated into academic courses and projects via problem-based learning, guest lectures, and consultations with outside experts can be equally valuable (Hmelo-Silver, 2004).

Furthermore, given the access issues outlined previously and the challenges of ensuring quality control in off-campus internships, work-integrated learning offers the advantage of being available to all enrolled students while also remaining under the auspices and oversight of faculty and other postsecondary professionals (Jackson, 2018). As a result, the category of HIPs that includes internships and other forms of work-based learning should be expanded to include campus-based work-integrated learning experiences. Doing so will be especially important for the large number of college students who are working part- or full-time jobs (Perna, 2010), which represent the single most prevalent barrier to internship participation documented in our study.

2. *Expand online or remote internships.* Even before the COVID-19 pandemic, online and remote internships were growing in popularity, given the growth in remote work more generally and also because of the potential to bring internships to new populations of college students. Although the potential for online internships to ameliorate problems with equitable access has not yet been empirically demonstrated, the very nature of the modality

means that students who cannot afford to relocate to expensive metropolitan areas, who lack personal transportation, and who may have existing work, family, or academic obligations may now be able to pursue an internship experience (Hora et al., 2020).

Online internships, however, should not be viewed as a panacea to accessibility problems, as they are not yet available at scale in formats that reflect best practices in internship design (e.g., appropriate tasks, effective mentorship, etc; Jeske & Axtell, 2016). Furthermore, one of the most common forms of online internships—the "micro-internship"—is an extremely brief (i.e., 4 to 40 hours) experience that does not meet the criterion of what constitutes a "legitimate" internship (NACE, 2018). For the promise and potential of online internships to be realized, colleges and universities will need to invest considerable resources in academic and career advisors who can partner with employers to design high-quality experiences. But the potential for online internships to address—if not eliminate—many of the problems with equitable access outlined in this chapter makes such investments worthwhile.

3. *Work with employers to increase accessible, paid opportunities across the disciplines.* Finally, if all college students are to have the opportunity to pursue an internship, it is clear that more placements will be required, especially in rural areas and in disciplines that do not have a long tradition of paid work-based learning (e.g., arts and humanities). Although online internships may help to address this issue of scale and despite the fact there is no reliable count of the total number of internships in the United States with which to estimate the true nature of supply and demand in the internship market, it is evident that more positions will need to be created if all college students are to have the opportunity to pursue this HIP.

Ultimately, addressing the challenges to internship access will require more collaboration among the various stakeholders of the internship process to provide creative ways to engage all college students in these valuable opportunities. It will also be essential to maintain a critical and evidence-based stance that maintains a commitment to equity, fairness, and social justice so that internships cease to act as yet another vehicle for reproducing inequality.

References

Allen, K., Quinn, J., Hollingworth, S., & Rose, A. (2013). Becoming employable students and "ideal" creative workers: Exclusion and inequality in higher education work placements. *British Journal of Sociology of Education, 34*(3), 431–452. https://doi.org/10.1080/01425692.2012.714249

Bayerlein, L., & Jeske, D. (2018). Student learning opportunities in traditional and computer-mediated internships. *Education + Training, 60*(1), 27–38. https://doi.org/10.1108/ET-10-2016-0157

Binder, J. F., Baguley, T., Crook, C., & Miller, F. (2015). The academic value of internships: Benefits across disciplines and student backgrounds. *Contemporary Educational Psychology, 41*, 73–82. https://doi.org/10.1016/j.cedpsych.2014.12.001

Boulton, C. (2015). Under the cloak of whiteness: A circuit of culture analysis of opportunity hoarding and colour-blind racism inside US advertising internship programs. *tripleC: Communication, Capitalism & Critique, 13*(2), 390–403. https://doi.org/10.31269/triplec.v13i2.592

Bourdieu, P. (1986). The forms of capital. In J. Richardson (Ed.), *Handbook of theory and research for the sociology of education* (pp. 241–258). Greenwood.

Chan, J., Pun, N., & Selden, M. (2015). Interns or workers? China's student labor regime. *Asian Studies, 1*(1), 69–98. https://doi.org/10.6551/AS.0101.04

Crain, A. (2016). *Understanding the impact of unpaid internships on college student career development and employment outcomes.* NACE Foundation. https://www.naceweb.org/uploadedfiles/files/2016/guide/the-impact-of-unpaid-internships-on-career-development.pdf

Crenshaw, K. (1991). Mapping the margins: Identity politics, intersectionality, and violence against women. *Stanford Law Review, 43*(6), 1241–1299. https://doi.org/10.2307/1229039

Curiale, J. L. (2009). America's new glass ceiling: Unpaid internships, the Fair Labor Standards Act, and the urgent need for change. *Hastings Law Journal, 61*, 1531–1560. https://heinonline.org/HOL/P?h=hein.journals/hastlj61&i=1541

Finley, A., & McNair, T. (2013). *Assessing underserved students' engagement in high-impact practices.* Association of American Colleges & Universities.

Frenette, A. (2013). Making the intern economy: Role and career challenges of the music industry intern. *Work and Occupations, 40*(4), 364–397. https://doi.org/10.1177/0730888413504098

Hmelo-Silver, C. E. (2004). Problem-based learning: What and how do students learn? *Educational Psychology Review, 16*(3), 235–266. https://doi.org/10.1023/B:EDPR.0000034022.16470.f3

Hora, M. T. (2020). Hiring as cultural gatekeeping into occupational communities: Implications for higher education and student employability. *Higher Education, 79*(2), 307–324. https://doi.org/10.1007/s10734-019-00411-6

Hora, M. T., Vivona, B., Chen, Z., Zhang, J., Thompson, M., & Brown, R. (2020). *What do we know about online internships? A review of the academic and practitioner literatures* (Research Brief No. 10). Center for Research on College-Workforce Transitions, University of Wisconsin-Madison.

Hora, M. T., Wolfgram, M., & Thompson, S. (2017). *What do we know about the impact of internships on student outcomes? Results from a preliminary review of the scholarly and practitioner literatures.* Center for Research on College-Workforce Transitions, University of Wisconsin-Madison.

Jackson, D. (2018). Developing graduate career readiness in Australia: Shifting from extra-curricular internships to work-integrated learning. *International Journal of Work-Integrated Learning, 19*(1), 23–35. https://files.eric.ed.gov/fulltext/EJ1179832.pdf

Jeske, D., & Axtell, C. M. (2016). How to run successful e-internships: A case for organizational learning. *Development and Learning in Organizations, 30*(2), 18–21. https://doi.org/10.1108/DLO-09-2015-0073

Jung, J., & Lee, S. J. (2017). Impact of internship on job performance among university graduates in South Korea. *International Journal of Chinese Education, 5*(2), 250–284. https://doi.org/10.1163/22125868-12340070

Kuh, G. D. (2008). *High-impact educational practices: What they are, who has access to them, and why they matter.* Association of American Colleges & Universities.

Kuh, G., & Kinzie, J. (2018, May 1). What really makes a high-impact practice high impact? *Inside Higher Ed.* https://www.insidehighered.com/views/2018/05/01/kuh-and-kinzie-respond-essay-questioning-high-impact-practices-opinion

McHugh, P. (2017). The impact of compensation, supervision and work design on internship efficacy: Implications for educators, employers and prospective interns. *Journal of Education and Work, 30*(4), 367–382. https://doi.org/10.1080/13639080.2016.1181729

Milburn, A. (2009). *Unleashing aspiration: The final report.* Panel on Fair Access to the Professions, Cabinet Office.

Morris, D. Z. (2018, July 8). Are unpaid internships exploitation or opportunity? Twitter has some opinions. *Fortune.* https://fortune.com/2018/07/08/unpaid-internships-twitter-debate/

Museus, S. D., & Quaye, S. J. (2009). Toward an intercultural perspective of racial and ethnic minority college student persistence. *The Review of Higher Education, 33*(1), 67–94. https://doi.org/10.1353/rhe.0.0107

National Association of Colleges and Employers. (2018, August). *Position statement: U.S. internships.* http://www.naceweb.org/about-us/advocacy/position-statements/position-statement-us-internships

O'Neill, N. (2010). Internships as a high-impact practice: Some reflections on quality. *Peer Review, 12*(4), 4–8. https://www.proquest.com/scholarly-journals/internships-as-high-impact-practice-some/docview/822747510/se-2?accountid=14168

Parks-Yancy, R. (2012). Interactions into opportunities: Career management for low-income, first-generation African American college students. *Journal of College Student Development, 53*(4), 510–523. https://doi.org/10.1353/csd.2012.0052

Perlin, R. (2012). *Intern nation.* Verso.

Perna, L. (2010). *Understanding the working college student: New research and its implications for policy and practice.* Stylus.

Rivera, L. A. (2012). Hiring as cultural matching: The case of elite professional service firms. *American Sociological Review, 77*(6), 999–1022. https://doi.org/10.1177/0003122412463213

Saniter, N., & Siedler, T. (2014). *Door opener or waste of time? The effects of student internships on labor market outcomes* (IZA Discussion Paper No. 8141). The Institute for the Study of Labor (IZA).

Seifert, T. A., Gillig, B., Hanson, J. M., Pascarella, E. T., & Blaich, C. F. (2014). The conditional nature of high impact/good practices on student learning outcomes. *Journal of Higher Education, 85*(4), 531–564. https://doi.org/10.1080/00221546.2014.11777339

Shade, L. R., & Jacobson, J. (2015). Hungry for the job: Gender, unpaid internships, and the creative industries. *The Sociological Review, 63,* 188–205. https://doi.org/10.1111/1467-954X.12249

Silva, P., Lopes, B., Costa, M., Melo, A. I., Dias, G. P., Brito, E., & Seabra, D. (2018). The million-dollar question: Can internships boost employment? *Studies in Higher Education, 43*(1), 2–21. https://doi.org/10.1080/03075079.2016.1144181

Svacina, L. S. (2012). A review of research on unpaid internship legal issues: Implications for career services professionals. *Journal of Cooperative Education and Internships, 46*(1), 77–87. https://www.researchgate.net/profile/Norah-Mcrae/publication/268926074_Co-operative_Education_and_Student_Recruitment_Engagement_and_Success_Early_Findings_for_a_Multi-institutional_Study_in_British_Columbia/links/557dd0ad08aec87640dc61ab/Co-operative-Edu

10

LIVING UP TO THE CAPSTONE PROMISE

Improving Quality, Equity, and Outcomes in Culminating Experiences

Caroline J. Ketcham, Anthony G. Weaver, Jessie L. Moore, and Peter Felten

Capstone and culminating experiences have existed in some form at many colleges and universities for decades (Gardner & Van der Veer, 1998; Levine, 1978). A senior thesis is perhaps the most traditional capstone, but other varieties have flourished, ranging from internships and integrative portfolios to a required course in the major or core curriculum. Although in theory an undergraduate capstone is nothing new, this category of high-impact practices (HIPs) lacks coherence because it spans so many experiences, goals, and curricular contexts. Indeed, in the foundational HIPs text, Kuh (2008) defined *capstone courses and experiences* quite loosely:

> Whether they're called "senior capstones" or some other name, these culminating experiences require students nearing the end of their college years to create a project of some sort that integrates and applies what they've learned. The project might be a research paper, a performance, a portfolio of "best work," or an exhibit of artwork. Capstones are offered both in departmental programs and, increasingly, in general education as well. (p. 34)

Research reveals significant variation in student outcomes depending on the type of experience within the capstone category; for instance, a large national survey found that field experiences correlate with the most self-reported student gains among capstone types and a required course in the major with the fewest (NSSE, 2007). Simply labeling an experience a capstone does not make it high impact (Finley, 2019).

Recognizing these challenges with defining the capstone, scholars increasingly have concentrated on the *qualities* that make such experiences HIPs (Kuh et al., 2013, 2017). Scholars associated with the Association for American Colleges & Universities have coined the term *signature work* to identify three essential quality components: (a) integrating multiple aspects of a student's education, (b) providing the student with some agency in shaping their capstone, and (c) prompting the student to "apply their learning to real-world issues that matter to society and to the student" (Peden, 2015, p. 22). Put another way, the three necessary parts of any high-quality capstone are integration, agency, and application. Taken together, these attributes transform a generic "capstone" into the "keystone" of a student's education, locking together the diverse aspects of their undergraduate studies and providing the foundation for successful life after graduation (Ketcham & Weaver, 2017). High-quality culminating experiences not only benefit individual students but also answer the critique that college is nothing more than a jumble of disconnected experiences that too many students drift through aimlessly (Kinzie, 2013).

High-quality capstones cannot achieve their promise if all students do not have equitable access to and experiences in this HIP. Data documenting disparities in capstone participation suggest significant inequities exist (NSSE, 2014; Padgett & Kilgo, 2012; Young et al., 2017). Drawing on National Survey of Student Engagement (NSSE) data, Kinzie (2018) concluded that "white students participate in capstones more than students in all other racial/ethnic groups, and first-generation students have lower levels of participation than their non-first-generation peers" (p. 30). This is particularly disturbing because Finley and McNair (2013) demonstrated that capstones have a "compensatory effect" for first-generation and other students who historically have been marginalized in higher education, helping to close equity gaps in graduation rates and to produce many other positive outcomes. To live up to the quality and equity promise of capstones for all students, faculty and administrators should adopt five recommendations (Figure 10.1 summarizes concrete action steps related to each).

Recommendation 1: Articulate Shared Goals and Pathways

To achieve the promise of capstones, institutions must articulate clear, consistent goals for and pathways into capstone experiences for all students. An institution's approach to capstones should build on its own students' strengths and interests as well as align with that institution's mission. This does *not* mean capstones must become a homogenous practice within an institution; rather, variations across programs can be constructive if students,

Figure 10.1. Recommendations to support sustained and evidence-informed practices for mission-driven high-quality capstone experiences.

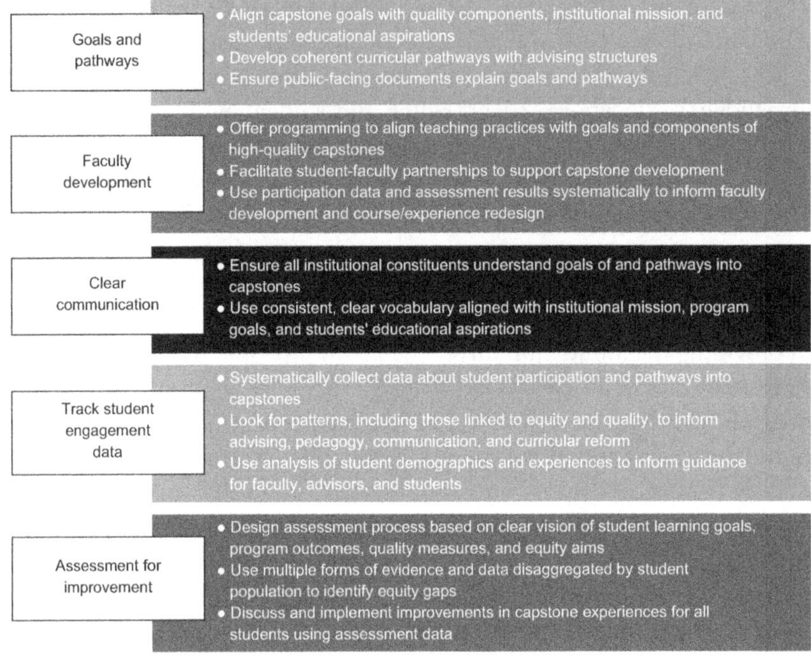

faculty, and staff have a shared vision for the goals of their capstones, and students understand how their education is building toward a culminating experience to integrate and apply their learning.

Unfortunately, research suggests that students either are not experiencing capstones or they do not know that they are. In one survey, only 45% of U.S. seniors indicated that they had participated in a capstone (NSSE, 2019). To try to determine why that percentage is far lower than what is reported in surveys of campus administrators (e.g., Young et al., 2017, found 99% of U.S. 4-year institutions offer capstones), Bean et al. (2019) analyzed the descriptions of capstones in institutional public-facing documents (e.g., catalogs, program descriptions, general education requirements) at 499 institutions, including all higher education institutions in Australia and the United Kingdom and a systematic sample of more than 300 4-year institutions in the United States. Overall, only 11% of the universities in this study publicly stated that a capstone experience was required (5% in Australia, 4% in the United Kingdom, 15% in the United States). This suggests that institutions are doing a poor job of articulating pathways into capstones, either because capstones are required but students are not told that they are (or even what they are) or because faculty and institutions assume availability means universal access to capstones. Simply put, if a program or institution believes that a high-quality capstone is essential for undergraduates, it should require all students to complete one—and explain how and why to do so.

A similar inconsistency exists in the stated purposes for capstones. In a thematic analysis of the capstone descriptions at institutions that do require a capstone experience, Bean et al. (2019) found integration to be the most commonly identified goal (in 63% of descriptions) and agency/self-directed learning (28%) and application (30%) to be much less frequently mentioned. In short, even at institutions that require capstones, most do not explain that the markers of high-quality culminating experiences are the explicit goals for their capstones. Gresham et al.'s (2020) survey research of U.S. faculty further suggests that faculty identify a wide range of different purposes and practices for capstones in their programs, with significant variation not only across institutions but also within the same institution. Given these findings, to develop high-quality and equitable capstone experiences, faculty and program leaders should ensure that capstones have clearly articulated goals—shared in public-facing documents—that align with the components of quality (integration, agency, application), their institution's mission, and their students' educational aspirations.

Recommendation 2: Provide Faculty Development for Capstone Instructors

Once capstone goals and curricular pathways are clear, the next step is to support faculty in designing and teaching high-quality culminating experiences. The University of North Carolina at Pembroke (UNCP, n.d.) offers one example of a focused faculty development initiative to support effective capstone teaching that includes both the flexibility of major-specific capstones and university-wide goals for these courses. UNCP's faculty first identified four shared learning outcomes for capstones across the university's 36 undergraduate degree programs. UNCP next created a series of stipend-supported faculty development offerings to foster the design or redesign of capstone experiences that align with those four outcomes, including workshops on best practices in teaching and assessing integrative thinking and reflective writing. This institution-wide commitment not only helps faculty who are teaching these capstones but also increases the likelihood of equitable experiences for all students across the university. As Pearl et al. (2020)

demonstrated, once institutions like UNCP have focused on this alignment in goals and teaching, faculty and staff should partner with students to research specific outcomes of and experiences with capstones—and to use what is learned to continue to enhance faculty development. Pedagogical partnerships are effective for pedagogical improvement and course design and they also can be used for broader program-wide and curricular reform efforts (Cook-Sather et al., 2019).

Beyond tailored faculty development and partnership programs, institutions must provide the resources necessary to demonstrate the importance and value of faculty involvement with culminating experiences. In a survey of faculty at five diverse U.S. institutions, Laye et al. (2020) uncovered significant enthusiasm for teaching capstones, but also considerable faculty concern about whether this work would be rewarded in the long term during promotion/tenure decisions and in the shorter term with financial support and release time for course development. To cultivate high-quality and equitable capstone experiences, faculty and program leaders should ensure development programs support faculty to align their teaching with the goals for and components of capstones, facilitate student–faculty partnerships in capstone development, and connect quality capstone teaching to faculty promotion and review processes.

Recommendation 3: Communicate Clearly About Capstones

A clearly defined and well-taught capstone will not meet its full promise if students (and others at the institution) do not understand the purposes of this culminating experience. Pearl et al. (2020) examined institutional messaging around capstones, diversity, inclusion, and equity in Australia, Canada, and the United States, collaborating with student researchers at Deakin University (Australia) and the University of Calgary (Canada). The researchers found that students consistently interpreted institutional messaging quite differently than faculty do, reinforcing the value in partnering with students (Cook-Sather et al., 2014) to communicate capstone experience goals in student-centered language. This finding aligns with advice from Budwig and Low (2018) to use common, consistent vocabulary to establish a shared understanding of goals and pathways related to capstone experiences. Budwig and Low (2018) also emphasized communicating regularly with all stakeholders, including faculty and academic advisors, to be sure they can use their day-to-day interactions with students to reinforce the value and purposes of capstones. Finally, Budwig and Low (2018) stressed the importance of communicating about capstones with students at all points in the curriculum; waiting until undergraduates reach their final year might be too late to allow all students to understand the merits of capstones. To clearly and consistently communicate about capstones, program leaders should ensure all institutional constituents, including students, understand the goals of and pathways into capstones.

Recommendation 4: Track and Analyze Data About Student Engagement

Tracking and disaggregating student engagement with capstones is essential for understanding students' experiences, for advising and teaching effectively, and for refining policies and practices. Of course, data alone does not lead to positive change, but having valid and useful information about student participation in capstones is a necessary step in any effort to enhance learning and equity (Hutchings et al., 2015). Collecting this kind of data presupposes answers to some of the questions raised earlier in this chapter about the definition and qualities of capstones in your context.

The questions asked of this data should be shaped by those in position to use and act on this analysis. For instance, academic advisors could use capstone participation data and enrollment mapping analysis to inform the advice they offer students about the best ways to prepare for and benefit from capstones—and to tailor guidance to specific student groups, such as first-generation or Latinx students. When should a student enroll in a capstone? What courses should they take before they enroll? Are there experiences, such as internships or undergraduate research, that are particularly effective stepping-stones to a capstone?

Faculty also can use participation and enrollment data to improve capstone course design. For instance, at Elon University, the registrar creates tailored reports for faculty teaching capstone courses. Because Elon's core curriculum requires all undergraduates to enroll in an interdisciplinary capstone, these seminars often include seniors from a variety of majors. The diversity of knowledge, experiences, and interests these students bring to the capstone could be an asset in the classroom, but historically faculty could not learn much about their students before the first day of class. Drawing on existing institutional data, the registrar worked with capstone faculty to identify the kinds of information about students that would be helpful (and ethical) to have before the semester begins—including not only majors and minors but also data about students' participation in experiential learning activities, including where and when students have completed internships, conducted undergraduate research, and studied abroad. Capstone faculty now receive a report with that data weeks before the term begins, giving them the chance to plan their courses to build on the learning and experiences students bring to class. One humanities faculty member "was stunned that nearly every student in my [capstone] had taken economics during the completion of their core requirements," so they worked with a colleague in economics to modify readings and assignments to draw on the expertise and interests their students brought to the classroom that semester (Parks, 2019). To track participation in capstones, faculty and program leaders should systematically collect data about student participation with and pathways into capstones and analyze it to look for patterns, including those linked to equity and quality, that should inform advising, pedagogy, communication, and curricular or programmatic reform.

Recommendation 5: Assess to Improve

Finley (2019) suggested that HIP assessment should begin by articulating a clear vision of student learning goals, program outcomes, quality measures, and equity aims. Those should guide an assessment process that draws on a variety of data sources and research methodologies, and that disaggregates data across student populations to assess equity gaps. This complex, iterative approach should not seek scientific perfection, but rather "good (enough) evidence" to "target improvement of practices and promote conversations among stakeholders focused on evidence-based decision-making" (Finley, 2019, pp. 9–10; see also Mansilla & Dusaising, 2007).

For instance, an assessment project at Boston College has aimed to understand what students and faculty perceive to be the attitudes, skills, and values developed through the capstone experience. The director of the Capstone Senior Seminars Program partnered with colleagues from two additional North American institutions to survey capstone students and faculty about their perceptions of outcomes, providing a list of possible attitudes, skills, and values (Vale et al., 2020). This multi-institutional research allowed collaborators to examine school-specific data and to make comparisons across institution types. The survey produced a rich set of data about Boston College capstones that suggested both congruence in some areas (e.g., both students and faculty report self-awareness is the most common attitude outcome) and significant disjuncture in others (e.g., 52% of faculty perceive the capstone to develop the value "intercultural sensitivity" but only 23% of students do). Perhaps the most valuable outcome of the survey is *not* the specific findings but rather the evidence-informed conversations among various stakeholders about the possible meanings and implications of these results for the ways that capstones are designed, described, taught, and assessed.

Because high-quality capstones focus on integration, agency, and application, high-quality assessment of capstones should include some direct evidence related to these. Documenting student agency and real-world application of knowledge can be vexing because curricular structures tend to put undergraduates in "high cue" environments that explicitly signal to students about what to do (e.g., "I am in a physics class so this exam problem surely is asking me to use a formula I've learned in physics"). The world outside of school, however, tends to be "low cue" because professional, civic, or personal activities typically require people to determine how to act without the scaffolding provided in the classroom. When capstone experiences immerse students in dynamic environments—in or beyond the classroom—then the "low cue" writing and other academic work students do reveals their capacity to integrate and apply what they have learned (Felten, 2017).

Perhaps the ultimate evidence of capstone outcomes would come from alumni. How did their capstone, and college in general, prepare them with the knowledge, attitudes, skills, and values required for them to flourish professionally and personally? Many institutions survey alumni, but that data typically is *not* collected to assess curriculum design or program outcomes. Perhaps the future of capstone assessment will weave together evidence from current students and alumni to better understand the short- and longer term impacts of culminating experiences in college. To assess capstones, faculty and program leaders should start with a clear vision of student learning goals, program outcomes, quality measures, and equity aims; use multiple forms of evidence; and disaggregate data by student population to look for equity gaps.

Living Up to the Capstone Promise

As institutions struggle to meet the dynamic challenges of higher education in the 21st century, capstones offer a unique opportunity to bring together integration, agency, and application to contribute to a transformational undergraduate experience for every student. Fulfilling that promise, however, is not easy. High-quality and equitable capstones demand alignment of goals, pedagogy, curriculum, faculty development, institutional resources, communication, tracking, and assessment. Creating and sustaining that alignment is immensely difficult and requires persistent and flexible effort toward evidence-informed improvement, even when the data does not provide perfect clarity about how to proceed (Finley, 2019). Despite the challenges and uncertainties, the results of this labor are valuable for individuals, institutions, and communities. When done with integrity and fidelity, this work will support faculty, staff, programs, and institutions to develop clear and coherent capstone experiences that build on their students' strengths and that prepare their graduates to thrive in work and life.

References

Bean, J., Beaudoin, C., Lewis, D. I., Van Zile-Tamsen, C., & Von Der Heidt, T. (2019, October 12). *Committing to capstones: What motivates institutions, faculty, and students* [Conference session]. International Society for the Scholarship of Teaching and Learning, Atlanta, GA, United States.

Budwig, N., & Low, K. (2018). Institutional readiness for signature work. *Peer Review, 20*(2), 20–23. https://link.gale.com/apps/doc/A547869400/AONE?u=nysl_oweb&sid=googleScholar&xid=f34567c4

Cook-Sather, A., Bahti, M., & Ntem, A. (2019). *Pedagogical partnerships: A how-to guide for faculty, students, and academic developers in higher education*. Center for Engaged Learning.

Cook-Sather, A., Bovill, C., & Felten, P. (2014). *Engaging students as partners in learning and teaching: A guide for faculty.* Jossey-Bass.

Felten, P. (2017). Writing high-impact practices: Developing proactive knowledge in complex contexts. In J. L. Moore & R. Bass (Eds.), *Understanding writing transfer: Implications for transformative student learning in higher education* (pp. 49–58). Stylus.

Finley, A. (2019, November). *A comprehensive approach to assessment of high-impact practices* (Occasional Paper No. 41). National Institute for Learning Outcomes Assessment.

Finley, A. P., & McNair, T. (2013). *Assessing underserved students' engagement in high-impact practices.* Association of American Colleges & Universities.

Gardner, J., & Van der Veer, G. (1998). *The senior year experience: Facilitating integration, reflection, closure and transition.* Jossey-Bass.

Gresham, M., Laye, M., Boswell, C., Smith-Sherwood, D., & Anderson, O. S. (2020, January 24). *Changing landscape of inclusive capstone experiences: Influences, impacts, and design* [Conference session]. Association of American Colleges & Universities, Washington DC, United States.

Hutchings, P., Kinzie, J., & Kuh, G. (2015). Evidence of student learning. In G. Kuh, S. Ikenberry, N. Jankowski, T. Cain, P. Ewell, P. Hutchings, & J. Kinzie (Eds.), *Using evidence of student learning to improve higher education* (pp. 27–50). Jossey-Bass.

Ketcham, C., & Weaver, T. (2017, August 7). *"Capstone" experience in higher education: Defining, characterizing, and assessing as a high impact practice in a multi-institutional research context.* Center for Engaged Learning. https://www.centerforengagedlearning.org/capstone-experience-in-higher-education/

Kinzie, J. (2013). Taking stock of capstones and integrated learning. *Peer Review, 15*(4), 27–30. https://www.proquest.com/scholarly-journals/taking-stock-capstones-integrative-learning/docview/1506113339/se-2?accountid=14168

Kinzie, J. (2018). Assessing quality and equity: Observations about the state of signature work. *Peer Review, 20*(2), 29–31. https://www.proquest.com/scholarly-journals/assessing-quality-equity-observations-about-state/docview/2077518950/se-2?accountid=14168

Kuh, G. D. (2008). *High-impact educational practices: What they are, who has access to them, and why they matter.* Association of American Colleges & Universities.

Kuh, G. D., O'Donnell, K., & Reed, S. (2013). *Ensuring quality and taking high-impact practices to scale.* Association of American Colleges & Universities.

Kuh, G. D., O'Donnell, K. O., & Schneider, C. G. (2017). HIPs at ten. *Change: The Magazine of Higher Learning, 49*(5), 8–16. https://doi.org/10.1080/00091383.2017.1366805

Laye, M., Boswell, C., Gresham, M., Smith-Sherwood, D., & Anderson, O. S. (2020). Multi-institutional survey of faculty experiences teaching capstones. *College Teaching, 68*(4), 201–213. https://doi.org/10.1080/87567555.2020.1786663

Levine, A. (1978). *Handbook of undergraduate curriculum.* Jossey-Bass.

Mansilla, V., & Dusaising, V. (2007). Targeted assessment of students' interdisciplinary work: An empirically grounded framework proposed. *Journal of Higher Education, 78*(2), 215–223. https://doi.org/10.1080/00221546.2007.11780874

National Survey of Student Engagement. (2007). *Experiences that matter: Enhancing student learning and success.* https://scholarworks.iu.edu/dspace/handle/2022/23412

National Survey of Student Engagement. (2014). *Bringing the institutions into focus: Annual Results 2014.* https://scholarworks.iu.edu/dspace/handle/2022/23405

National Survey of Student Engagement. (2019). *Engagement insights: Survey findings on the quality of undergraduate education.* https://scholarworks.iu.edu/dspace/handle/2022/23392

Padgett, R. D., & Kilgo, C. A. (2012). *2011 national survey of senior capstone experiences: Institutional-level data on the culminating experience.* National Resource Center for the First-Year Experience and Students in Transition, University of South Carolina.

Parks, R. (2019, June 6). Comprehensive learner profiles: Helping faculty improve pedagogy in the classroom. *Educause Review.* https://er.educause.edu/blogs/2019/6/comprehensive-learner-profiles-helping-faculty-improve-pedagogy-in-the-classroom

Pearl, D., Dyer, S., McGrath, M., de St. Jorre, T., & Rankin, J. (2020, January 24). *Changing landscape of inclusive capstone experiences: Influences, impacts, and design* [Conference session]. Association of American Colleges & Universities.

Peden, W. (2015). Signature work: A survey of current practices. *Liberal Education, 101*(1/2), 22–29. https://www.aacu.org/liberaleducation/2015/winter-spring/peden

University of North Carolina Pembroke. (n.d.). *QEP executive summary.* https://www.uncp.edu/academics/academic-resources/quality-enhancement-plan/qep-executive-summary

Vale, J., Kirkscey, R., & Weiss, J. (2020, June). *Faculty and student perceptions of personal development capstone experiences at Boston College* [Conference session]. Center for Engaged Learning Research Seminar, Elon, NC, United States.

Young, D. G., Chung, J. K., Hoffman, D. E., & Bronkema, R. (2017). *2016 national survey of senior capstone experiences: Expanding our understanding of culminating experiences.* National Resource Center for The First-Year Experience & Students in Transition, University of South Carolina.

11

IDENTITY AND COMMUNITY AMONG FIRST-GENERATION STUDENTS

High-Impact Practices and Communicating Belonging Throughout Department Design

Adrienne Viramontes and Theresa Castor

The purpose of this project was to analyze the role of high-impact practices (HIPs) in one academic department by focusing on first-generation student (FGS) perspectives of community-based learning (CBL). Our department commitment to student success is centered around intentionally designed HIPs across our curriculum. We believe this approach benefits FGSs by reframing the classroom power dynamic and empowering FGSs by valuing them for their *assets* rather than *deficits*. HIPs provide educational and professional benefits within a classroom context where students feel respected and experience a sense of belonging through reflection and integration of their learning (Kuh, 2008). This is developed through a framework of HIPs that students experience in a departmental culture that prioritizes social justice, critical pedagogy, and a student-centered, experiential learning–based curriculum. Having such a department culture enables us to seamlessly integrate best practices with respect to implementing HIPS (see Kuh et al., 2013). Whatever a department's starting point, the implementation of a HIP practice should integrate quality best practices to help create a positive learning experience for students. In this chapter, we provide background information and a brief review of scholarship on FGS identity. We discuss our department's teaching philosophy as it contributes to equity and accessibility within a curricular design that integrates CBL throughout the academic program. Our department uses HIPs to foster students' sense of belonging. We conclude by recommending a department-level curricular design that addresses the achievement gap for FGSs and students of color.

First-Generation Students

Our literature review focuses on FGS experience and the performance of identity to inform about the cultural contexts and experiences of FGSs and students of color and what they bring with them to our classrooms. These concepts underwrite our department's mission to design our curriculum with a continuous set of HIPs that promote student success in ways that address the challenges that first-generation students face. This body of knowledge contributes to our department's pedagogical practices and curricular decision-making as well as aligns with our own research specializations. Much of the qualitative research that exists about FGSs and FGSs of color discuss how they understand themselves and perform within the context of higher education given their racial, cultural, and economic backgrounds. For example, Roksa and Whitley (2017) discussed how some African American students do not benefit from academic motivation in the same way other students do and that interactions with faculty who are concerned about student learning matter significantly. Guiffrida (2005) explored how some FGSs of color decided which faculty could be trusted and with whom they felt they could communicate safely. Saunders and Serna (2004) studied a small group of Latina/o students and highlighted a common component of FGSs of color, which is the perception by friends and family that enrolling in college is a rejection of culture—an act of cultural treason.

Orbe (2004) uncovered that for some FGSs and FGSs of color, their identities were prominent in certain contexts, yet not so for others—it depended on the circumstances of the student, his or her race, class, gender, and type of college institution. He examined how they negotiated their identities as FGSs across interactions and concluded that identity is an ongoing performance dependent upon interactional contexts of multiple frames of reference. In general, FGSs are different in terms of race, class, gender, sexuality, family structure, and age. It is unrealistic to understand these students as a homogenous category because each student has a unique life situation. Although these studies are informative, they offer only a broad understanding of the experiential scope of FGSs.

The students at the University of Wisconsin-Parkside are predominantly working class, FGSs, and students of color from a variety of social, economic, racial, and cultural backgrounds. Most if not all our students need to work part-time (sometimes two or three) or full-time jobs. Many have children and families to care for while enrolled as full-time students. They are diverse students with a multitude of complicated, complex needs. The intentional design of our curriculum dates to the early 1990s (Rakow, 1993). Although the program has undergone revisions, it is guided by a critical perspective that values integration across the curriculum and is inclusive and visionary. As a department, we feel that the most pedagogically appropriate ways to fulfill these principles is through the integration of a variety of HIPs and specifically scaffolding CBL at the upper level of our program. Our students have access to multiple HIPs experiences and, as a department, we can act on the importance of equitable access (McNair, 2012). Department students and faculty invest significant amounts of time and effort over extended periods throughout our HIPs program.

Our Department

UW-Parkside is a public, 4-year comprehensive university with over 50% FGSs and is the most racially/ethnically diverse campus within the University of Wisconsin System. The Communication Department reflects and amplifies this diversity in attracting, retaining, and graduating students from diverse backgrounds, including FGSs, those from underrepresented racial and ethnic groups, and/or nontraditional students. Another distinction is that a majority of faculty members are former FGSs, female, and from various minority and class groups and are all committed to social justice in what we teach and how we facilitate knowledge.

As FGSs who are now faculty members, we share similar frames of reference with the FGSs that were discussed in the literature review. Our unique experiences as FGSs invite current students to discuss with us their FGS identities, experiences, struggles, and achievements without fear, creating community and an inherent support system. In addition, we magnify our first-generation relational group identity with the added intense learning environment created by implementing CBL, often achieving transformative educational experiences that Freire would describe as *liberatory* due to their dependence upon dialogue and shared values.

Scaffolding HIPs

As a department, we have implemented HIPs throughout the major. Our department has placed HIPs within lower and upper-level core courses and in upper-level electives so that students move progressively through the major, developing a greater understanding of content, which leads to greater independence in the learning process (see Table 11.1). Each course identified in Table 11.1 is linked to one or more department learning outcomes and this relates to the choice of most appropriate HIP to use for each course. This process is what ensures fidelity for the use and integration of HIPs throughout the curriculum. For example, some courses at UWP are designated as DV (diversity) based on the University of Wisconsin system-wide definition of *diversity*, which means it must contain content about underrepresented minority groups (Latina/o, Asian American, African American, and/or Native American).

CBL Designs

Our program requires the completion of 15 elective credits in communication; 10 courses have integrated a CBL project or structured the entire course as a CBL project. Table 11.1 is a sample of courses that integrate HIPs. The

TABLE 11.1
Scaffolding of HIPs

Course Requirement	*Type of HIP*	*Curricular Location*
COMM 107: Communication and the Human Condition	Diversity	Lower-Level Core; General Education
COMM 205: Oral Interpretation	Embodied Performance of Text[a]	Lower-Level Core; General Education
COMM 207 and 208: Introduction to the Communication Discipline, Parts 1 and 2	Undergraduate Research; Diversity	Lower-Level Core
COMM 295: Sophomore Seminar	E-Portfolios; Collaborative Learning	Lower-Level Core
300–400 Level Communication Electives (includes internships and independent study)	Collaborative Learning; CBL; Undergraduate Research; and/or Diversity	Upper-Level Requirement
COMM 495: Senior Seminar	E-Portfolio; Autoethnographic Writing; and/or CBL	Upper-Level Requirement

[a]"Embodied performance of text" is not listed in the taxonomy of HIPs; however, it is a form of experiential learning that we consider to be a high-impact teaching practice.

program is dedicated to the practice of CBL, especially in our upper division courses, in part because of CBL's power to transfer classroom experiences, as in the following two examples:

1. *Digital Legacy Stories Project.* Working in partnership with Hospice Alliance of Kenosha, COMM 340: Health Communication students interviewed patients to create oral histories, showing students how communication and respect matter in the face of life and death.
2. *Homeless Assistance Leadership Organization Project.* COMM 485: Interventions in Conflict Management students interacted with homeless citizens and engaged in weekly dialogues, inviting students to a nuanced understanding of the conditions in people's lives that make becoming homeless a reality.

Community-based projects bring faculty and students to a location where the usual classroom power dynamic is altered. The "authority" that the faculty member possesses in the classroom shifts to a consulting role. Given the seriousness of the context, the students experience learning with greater intensity and weight: Decisions matter. The environment transforms the locus of power to create a collaborative learning space among faculty *and* students and is the impetus that drives students to "develop skills in collecting, evaluating, and synthesizing resources as they first define and then propose a solution to a multi-faceted problem" (Major & Palmer, 2001, para. 2). Of equal importance, CBL facilitates interaction between faculty and students, which can foster meaningful relationships leading to exceedingly positive outcomes for some FGSs (McKay & Estrella, 2008). CBL has become a part of our curricular tapestry of HIPs, and our department remains committed to reflecting our critically pedagogic teaching philosophy.

Methods

To gather data on FGS perspectives about their college experiences with our department active learning practices, we distributed an online survey to communication majors consisting of 16 open, closed, and demographic questions. Although 56 students responded, only 18 met our criteria of being FGSs. Among these, 16 identified as female and two as male, reflecting the trend within our program of mostly female students. In terms of sexuality, 16 identified as straight, one as lesbian, and one as asexual. For racial/ethnic self-identification, seven indicated they were White/European/American, six were Latina/o, three were African American/Black, and two were Asian

American. Students ranged in age from 20 to 58, with an average age of 30. Half of our respondents were 25 years or older, an age that has typically been used to delineate traditional-aged college students.

Positive Results

The following thematic analysis was performed on the responses to open-ended questions. Respondents were asked to describe one or more teaching practices that positively affected them. Most of the responses described instructional communication behaviors.

Theme 1: Encouragement

Three of the 15 responses described how an instructor's positive, constructive feedback communicated confidence in the student. That simple act in the context of a classroom assignment or activity had a tremendous impact on the student. As one Latina/o student explained:

> I have never experienced such positive feedback from a professor, or professors rather, until I became a Comm major. It reinforced my skill not only as a student, but as an equipped human being. Critical examination is always key, coupled with critique, it's a recipe for improvement. But nothing boosts morale and makes you succeed more than a professional letting you know you're doing something right, and maybe you should pursue said skill or talent. Everything is now so competitive; it'd be nice if in some instances it's about where you excel most yourself.

Of note in this student's comments is the connection they make between encouragement, confidence, *and* their identity ("not only as a student *but as an equipped human being*" [emphasis added]).

Another student connected a CBL experience as important for learning about course material *and* enhancing the student's sense of empowerment: "[Integrated Marketing] taught me how marketing has a big impact in our society and that through marketing I can make a change." Additionally, CBL coursework provides an organizational and college socialization experience for students:

> It made me become more engaged within the community and learn more about it. It really made me understand the materials taught in class, it helped me [to] stay on track, knowing that I had to work with a business/org in the community.

CBL courses allow students to develop and demonstrate their skills in a tangible way to see for themselves what they are capable of doing. For FGSs who may not have the benefit of parent or older sibling perspectives on college and professional socialization, the CBL experience provides a structured way for such socialization. One student summarized this dual function perfectly: "I think CBL is great for a résumé and it makes you feel like you are making some sort of difference."

Theme 2: Open Discussion

Three respondents reported that open discussions in class helped them to express their opinions. The discussion format was framed by the professor as having no absolute right or wrong responses. This allowed the student to express what they really thought, prompting a genuine learning opportunity. According to an Asian American respondent, "[Communication] professors encouraged students [to trust that in group discussions] that there are no wrong answers. There is always a discussion [about] every question and answer, which leads to an understanding of both."

For some college professors/instructors, telling students that there is no absolute right or wrong answer contrasts with their disciplinary ways of thinking. However, this kind of discussion is what Sawyer (2004) called "creative teaching or improvisational performance" (p. 11–12). Sawyer (2004) explained:

> Conceiving of teaching as improvisation emphasizes the interactional and responsive creativity of a teacher working with a unique group of students. In particular, effective classroom discussion is improvisational because the flow of the class emerges from the actions of all participants, both teachers and students. (p. 12)

This highlights the ways in which teaching is a performance with ever-changing classroom dynamics.

Other Themes: Classroom Ambiance, Instructor Attitude

A few students mentioned the positive effect that an open-minded instructor brings to a classroom. When the instructor explicitly recognized that they are not the only one in the room who is *right*, it invites students to feel less threatened and establishes inclusivity. When the instructor demonstrates an openness to other ideas, it allows students to be more vulnerable in class and allows for meeting students where they are in terms of their knowledge and experiences. This is in direct opposition to the banking model of education, which positions knowledge as "a gift bestowed by those who consider themselves knowledgeable upon those whom they consider to know nothing" (Freire & Shor, 1987, p. 72).

Negative Results

The following themes describe some of the negative experiences reported by students.

Theme 1: Lost, Confused

When asked how they felt in a classroom upon starting college, seven students wrote that they felt lost and/or confused about the expectations of professors/instructors. They were also unsure of what kinds of academic support (e.g., tutoring, advising) were available. These students did not know what to expect and were unsure of what to do in class.

Theme 2: Discouraged, Belittled, Feeling Like I Don't Belong

Four students expressed some variation of being "discouraged, belittled or feeling excluded." These FGSs felt discouraged by professors/instructors' communication, which was rooted in their attitude about certain students. For example, a Latina respondent described how the instructor perceived students who needed remedial coursework by stating, "[Y]ou people wouldn't even be here if it wasn't for this class. [Y]ou all obviously have learning issues with English and literature."

Another response from a nontraditional White male described how an instructor made him feel ignored and excluded because of his advanced age. Because of how the instructor interacted with what he called "traditional students," he felt discouraged, excluded, and not motivated to engage the coursework.

The positive survey responses highlight for us what is working effectively and what could be modified in our curriculum to better address student needs and the benefits of HIPs. We identified the following responses:

1. *Response to the theme of lost and/or confused.* Our department could benefit from a 1st-year student seminar to introduce students to the culture of higher education and to improve the student's relationship with the university community. As a more budget-friendly alternative, issues related to introducing students to the culture of higher education could be incorporated more directly into current 100- and 200-level required program courses.
2. *Response to the theme of discouraged, belittled, and excluded.* When a student feels belittled or ostracized, this kind of situation may be created by a failure to effectively perform the "college student role" (Collier & Morgan, 2008, p. 427). Accordingly, "roles serve as *resources,* which individuals use to pursue their goals through interactions with others"

(p. 427). However, Collier and Morgan (2008) placed the responsibility of a successful relationship solely on the student's performance and did not discuss the degree to which teaching and learning is dyadic, which suggests that the instructor may have failed to successfully perform the role/profession of "effective instructor." The HIPs design provides students and faculty with multiple opportunities to interact over sustained periods of time. Our findings support the need for a student-centered curriculum focused on equity and accessibility.

Implications for Practice

HIPs have been implemented into our curriculum from beginning to end *because* of our philosophy and dedication to the needs of our diverse student body. As mentioned previously, our students are predominantly FGSs, of the working class, and are diverse in terms of age, race, ethnicity, and gender. To provide an engaging, equitable, and accessible curriculum, we structure our courses and program with HIPs. Our faculty follow a critical pedagogy philosophy and are keenly aware of classroom power relations and the ways in which classroom dynamics can reflect systemic racism, classism, ageism, and sexism in higher education. Our scholarly study of culture strongly influenced our design of the curriculum and learning experiences to include the integration of HIPs. Our department is student-centered because if we do not put students at the center of what we do, we run the risk of perpetuating the status quo of inequities. Our department supports HIPs, *because* our faculty believe that knowledge is not a competition. We do not know *more* than our students. We know *differently.* Teaching through HIPs supports our students by providing multiple opportunities to respond to the social, political, and economic matrix within which their lives are situated. HIPs make possible moments for reflecting on who we are and how we know. This is how a HIPs-infused curriculum helps students discover their strengths, address their weaknesses, and cultivate their voices. We use HIPs to teach in ways that honor the humanity in our students.

Our research has demonstrated how the integration of HIPs throughout our department curriculum has contributed to students' sense of self and belonging. Our department design makes it possible for communication students to complete at least six HIPs by graduation. By offering a coherent and contiguous set of HIPS at the department level, FGSs greatly benefit from the opportunity to experience learning as praxis. Our HIPs-infused department curriculum has been 30 years in the making and, though still evolving, at this point we can reflect on recommendations that could be utilized by other programs that seek to increase the number of HIPs and the qualitative nature of those HIPs for students. The Communication Department's commitment to implementing HIPs throughout our curriculum has been a long, ongoing process that required discussion, consensus, vulnerability, risk, and trust in ourselves and each other. The recommendations we offer in the following are a reflection of a collection of lessons learned. These recommendations are grouped in terms of department curriculum, departmental culture and personnel, and the university context.

Department Curriculum

- Scaffolding HIPs through lower level core *and* upper level courses can allow departments to build a progressive, coherent programmatic learning experience for students. This allows HIPs to be a part of the department–student culture *and* fosters the formation of a department–student culture.
- Implementing a sophomore seminar class that explicitly introduces students to the department and higher education culture and to HIPs can help students in understanding educational and professional norms and expectations.
- Implementing CBL projects in upper division courses can enhance student experience, student learning, and faculty–student relationships (which enhance retention and graduation rates).

Departmental Culture and Personnel

- Developing new faculty position descriptions that *explicitly* call for new colleagues who are able to teach in ways that integrate CBL and diversity can support the maintenance of a student-centered and HIPS-focused department culture.
- For merit and personnel evaluation purposes, faculty teaching, research, and/or service that advances HIPs should be positively evaluated. For instance, in our program, integration of a CBL project into a course counts positively toward merit scores.
- Mapping course offerings with department learning outcomes sheds light on how each course contributes to or connects with learning outcomes. Courses that don't align with goals can be changed or eliminated.
- Embracing assessment as an evaluative tool for curricular decisions creates a department culture that is *responsive* to ever-changing student needs.

University Context

- The department curriculum should also meet the overarching goals within the university's academic plan.
- Faculty should be encouraged in taking advantage of professional development opportunities related to HIPs. For instance, at our university we have a CBL fellows' program that several of our colleagues have participated in.

In this chapter, we discussed how HIPs and specifically CBL benefit FGSs. Structuring classes using HIPs allows students equal access to course material and invites them to engage coursework using skills they already possess as they also discover and develop new capabilities. Based on our intentional departmental design and faculty culture, we believe that multiple HIPs have influenced student success. As Paulo Freire wrote, "What the educator does in teaching is to make it possible for the students to become themselves" (Horton & Freire, 1990, p. 302). We have experienced firsthand how HIPs make this transformation possible.

References

Collier, P. J., & Morgan, D. L. (2008). "Is that paper really due today?": Differences in first-generation and traditional college students' understandings of faculty expectations. *Higher Education*, *55*(4), 425–446. https://doi.org/10.1007/s10734-007-9065-5

Freire, P., & Shor, I. (1987). *A pedagogy for liberation: Dialogues on transforming education*. Bergin and Garvey.

Guiffrida, D. (2005). Othermothering as a framework for understanding African American students' definitions of student-centered faculty. *Journal of Higher Education*, *76*(6), 701–723. https://doi.org/10.1080/00221546.2005.11772305

Horton, M., & Freire, P. (1990). *We make the road by walking: Conversations on education and social change* (B. Bell, J. Gaventa, & J. Peters, Eds.). Temple University Press.

Kuh, G. D. (2008). *High-impact educational practices: What they are, who has access to them, and why they matter*. Association of American Colleges & Universities.

Kuh, G. D., O'Donnell, K., & Reed, S. D. (2013). *Ensuring quality and taking high-impact practices to scale*. Association of American Colleges & Universities.

Major, C. H., & Palmer, B. (2001). Assessing the effectiveness of problem-based learning in higher education: Lessons from the literature. *Academic Exchange Quarterly*, *5*(1). http://www.rapidintellect.com/AEQweb/mop4spr01.htm

McKay, V. C., & Estrella, J. (2008). First-generation student success: The role of faculty interaction in service learning courses. *Communication Education*, *57*(3), 356–372. https://doi.org/10.1080/03634520801966123

McNair, T. (2012). Seeking high-impact learning: The imperative of faculty development and curricular intentionality. *Peer Review, 14*(3), 4. https://link.gale.com/apps/doc/A311500174/AONE?u=nysl_oweb&sid=googleScholar&xid=f4cd3968

Orbe, M. P. (2004). Negotiating multiple identities within multiple frames: An analysis of first-generation college students. *Communication Education, 53*(2), 131–149. https://doi.org/10.1080/0363452041000l682401

Rakow, L. F. (1993). The curriculum is the future. *Journal of Communication, 43*(4), 154–162. https://doi.org/10.1080/03057640050005825

Roksa, J., & Whitley, S. E. (2017). Fostering academic success of first-year students: Exploring the roles of motivation, race, and faculty. *Journal of College Student Development, 58*(3), 333–348. https://doi.org/10.1353/csd.2017.0026

Saunders, M., & Serna, I. (2004). Making college happen: The college experiences of first-generation Latino students. *Journal of Hispanic Higher Education, 3*(2), 146–163. https://doi.org/10.1177/1538192703262515

Sawyer, R. K. (2004). Creative teaching: Collaborative discussion as disciplined improvisation. *Educational Researcher, 33*(2), 11–20. https://doi.org/10.3102/0013189X033002012

PART THREE

ACHIEVING SCALE

Educational innovations deemed effective are expected to be scaled up so more students benefit. However, "achieving scale" is a formidable goal for the growth and sustainability of innovations, and high-impact practices (HIPs) are no exception. To make HIPs more widespread and available to students, colleges and universities have been expanding opportunities. More service-learning courses have been created, course-based undergraduate research is popular, and at some institutions, capstone courses are now required. Taking HIPs to scale demands more offerings and intentionality in design. It may also mean making them required or inescapable by embedding them in the curriculum to ensure student participation. Scaling HIPs also demands systematic tracking and monitoring to maintain attention to participation rates, while ensuring consistent quality of experiences, as described in the previous section.

We know that higher education is a difficult context for scaling instructional programs or proven practices. Many aspects of the college and university setting influence the expansion of beneficial interventions, including the importance faculty place on the initiative, student interest, institutional promotion and support, and financial constraints. Higher education leaders interested in achieving scale should be aware of the interrelated dimensions of scale that Coburn (2003) defined: flexible adaptation by taking account of situational variations and needs, sustainability over time, system-wide spread, institutional and curricularly embedded efforts, and innovations that achieve internal understanding and support.

The seven chapters in this section explore a variety of strategies to scale HIPs. The contributors of chapter 12 discuss the ways in which research on HIPs informed a decision at Community College of Baltimore County to buttress a guided pathways model with the infusion of HIPs in high-enrollment general education courses to make it possible for all students to participate in high-impact experiences. The University of South Carolina's systematic documentation of student participation in HIPs and corresponding assessment of quality (chapter 13) made it possible to identify participants and involve nonparticipants and ensure HIPs are designed with quality. Two institutions, Bradley University (chapter 14) and Slippery Rock University (chapter 16) built HIPs into the curriculum through required experiences and assure fidelity in design through systematic curricular review and professional development. Chapter 15 describes Florida State University's experiential learning graduation requirement and their emphasis on two work-based experiences, student employment and internships, as vehicles for more widespread HIP engagement. Finally, monitoring, tracking, and assessing HIPs are critical to tailoring and sustaining desired practices. Chapters 17 and 18 document how institution-level assessment and tracking across a university and community college system, respectively, expanded HIP opportunities and achieved greater scale.

Discussion Questions

- What are the prospects for making HIPs required experiences? Where is there space in the curriculum to design HIPs for all?
- Scaling HIPs requires buy-in across the institution. Who needs to be involved to move HIPs from individual opportunities to widespread experiences?
- Maintaining quality during scaling and beyond can be challenging. What aspects of the HIP experience should be assessed and monitored in the scaling process?

- What student information campaigns and professional development supports are needed to achieve and sustain HIPs at scale?
- What tracking, evaluation, and records are needed to document and sustain HIPs at scale?

Reference

Coburn, C. E. (2003). Rethinking scale: Moving beyond numbers to deep and lasting change. *Educational Researcher*, *32*(6), 3–12. https://doi.org/10.3102/0013189X032006003

12

HIGH-IMPACT PRACTICES AND EQUITY

Pathways to Student Success in General Education Courses at a Large Urban Community College

Dallas M. Dolan, Jennifer Kilbourne, Monica Walker, and Glenda Breaux

The Community College of Baltimore County (CCBC) is an Achieving the Dream Leader College well known for developmental education reform and a strong equity agenda focused on fostering a college climate of equity, civility, and inclusion. CCBC is a large urban community college in Baltimore County, Maryland, serving about 30,000 credit students a year and an additional 25,000 noncredit students. CCBC's student population is quite diverse, with over 50% of our students coming from minoritized groups, the largest population being African American students (41%), a large number of first-generation college students, and with much of the student body attending part time (89%) and working 20 or more hours a week (49%). CCBC's President Sandra Kurtinitis (2020), along with senior leadership and the Diversity, Equity and Inclusion Advisory Council, have recently recommitted the college to a series of "actions that matter" to include measures to decrease equity gaps and increase retention and success rates. In addition, CCBC has undertaken a thorough review of academic policies that may perpetuate structural barriers to these success efforts. "The work of the President's Diversity, Equity and Inclusion Advisory Council will guide our college to stay true to three simple premises: quality in the classroom, dignity for every individual, and equal access and opportunity for everyone" (para. 4).

At CCBC we have been aware of significant achievement gaps between White and African American students for some time. Although achievement gaps have closed somewhat over the past 10 years, we continued to see larger gaps than we hoped. As a result, as we actively sought interventions to reduce these gaps, we likewise consciously avoided the deficit narrative often associated with the discourse on achievement gaps that can be proxy for institutional racism, in full recognition that socioeconomic factors are not necessarily the determinants of those gaps.

In 2015, CCBC adopted a pathways model that has led to changes in the way the student experience is organized and supported. We also wished to work through our general education core courses to provide additional ways to keep students engaged with the college and making progress toward a degree, certificate, or other credentials. High-impact practices (HIPs) seemed a good fit for reaching our goals. According to Finley and McNair (2013), HIPs are impactful because they lead to deeper student learning and engagement. This is especially significant in traditionally underserved populations where students are less likely to have been exposed to deep learning and engagement strategies. Considering the demography at CCBC, this consideration was particularly important.

As we worked at CCBC to expand the use of HIPs in student coursework, we targeted general education courses for infusion projects in order to maximize equitable student access. CCBC's general education outcomes include written and/or oral communication, local/global diversity, critical analysis and reasoning, technological competency, information literacy, personal and professional ethics, and scientific, quantitative, or logical reasoning, and lend themselves to incorporation of HIPs. We envisioned CCBC's general education course curricula with the intentional infusion of HIPs would enable students to acquire the knowledge and skills to participate effectively in our ever-evolving multicultural context and address the challenges in building an equitable society (CCBC, 2019).

Starting in 2015, CCBC's Office of Instruction identified the most highly enrolled general education courses, because these courses cut across academic pathways at CCBC, as general education courses are taken by students in all credit majors. Our rationale was that once fully scaled, most (if not all) CCBC credit students would be exposed to one HIP in the required Academic Development course (first-year experience) and at least one HIP in a general education course. The list of the most highly enrolled general education courses included the following: College Composition I, Technology and Information Systems, Introduction to Psychology, Introduction to Sociology, Fundamentals of Communication, Health and Wellness, Biology 1: Molecules and Cells, and a variety of mathematics courses.

Initial funding for this work was provided by Achieving the Dream's (ATD) Engaging Adjunct Faculty in the Student Success Movement grant (Achieving the Dream, 2016), along with institutional support from the

CCBC President's Office. An application process was developed, and the faculty of the highly enrolled general education courses were encouraged to work collaboratively, within their disciplines, to assemble a working team. The teams were composed of a team leader and several full-time and adjunct faculty members, and were charged with selecting the HIP to adopt for that course. Groups of interested faculty were led through a process of proposing their HIP and exploring how that HIP would be designed to meet the criteria for a high-quality HIP. Proposals were evaluated using Kuh et al.'s (2013) list of eight dimensions of high-quality HIPs:

1. Performance expectations set at appropriately high levels
2. A significant investment of time and effort by students over an extended period of time
3. Interactions with faculty and peers about substantive matters
4. Experiences with diversity wherein students are exposed to and must contend with people and circumstances that differ from those with which students are familiar
5. Frequent, timely, and constructive feedback
6. Periodic, structured opportunities to reflect and integrate learning
7. Opportunities to discover the relevance of learning through real-world applications
8. Public demonstration of competence

Intentionality in designing and assessing HIPs is critical to HIPs fulfilling their promise as deep learning experiences. "As is the case with every campus initiative, HIPs need to be implemented intentionally to assure quality and to promote the equitable participation of diverse students" (National Association of System Heads, n.d., para. 2). It is important to regularly assess the equitable involvement and the impact of HIPs. According to Finley (2019) of the Association for American Colleges & Universities,

> A good assessment plan for HIPs starts with acknowledging three things. One, the name alone does not make them high-impact. Two, evidence of effect requires assessing more than outcomes, alone. And three, an assessment must be, at every stage, attentive to equity. (p. 4)

Finley went on to point out that "the biggest impediment to assessing high-impact practices may very well be the name itself. The term 'high-impact' almost assumes efficacy" (p. 4). Focusing intentionally on assessing outcomes at the project level, teams of full-time and adjunct faculty identified the types of assessment (focus groups, student and faculty reflections, surveys, etc.)

that would best meet their need to know if the HIP was leading to the kinds of outcomes hoped for—student engagement and success. At the college-wide level, we also collected data on student success within HIPs-infused courses and the persistence of those students who were exposed to HIPs to the next semester (semester-to-semester retention).

During the 2016–2017 academic year, the HIPs Infusion Steering Committee was formed. The HIPs Steering Committee was charged with oversight of the committees working to infuse HIPs, guiding professional development efforts to increase faculty knowledge of HIPs, expanding the infusion of HIPs to new disciplines, and reviewing data related to the projects to assess the efficacy of the interventions. The committee was intentionally cross-functional and multidisciplinary, composed of full-time and adjunct faculty members, administrators from Academic Advising; Enrollment and Student Services; Planning, Research and Evaluation; and the Office of Instruction, as well as coordinators and faculty members in the disciplines that were building, implementing, assessing, or scaling HIP infusion projects.

In the fall of 2016, the first two HIP infusion projects were initiated in College Composition and Technology and Information Systems. The HIPs Steering Committee subsequently revised the application process before seeking new HIP infusion projects for the next cycle, and ultimately accepted five more disciplines to begin building their HIP infusion projects. With the inclusion of projects in Introduction to Psychology, Biology 1: Molecules and Cells, Fundamentals of Communication, Health and Wellness, and Introduction to Sociology, CCBC now has HIP projects infused in seven of its eight most highly enrolled general education courses. Table 12.1 shows the seven disciplines/courses, their chosen HIP, and their methods of infusing that HIP.

TABLE 12.1
Seven High-Impact Infusion Projects at CCBC

Course	*HIP*	*Pedagogy*
College Composition	Diversity/Global Learning	Intentionally and transparently include diverse voices in writing and explore diversity-related issues in discussion.
Technology and Information Systems	Collaborative Assignments	Students collaborate in small groups with activities related to career development.

Course	*HIP*	*Pedagogy*
Biology 1: Molecules and Cells	Collaborative Assignments/Common Intellectual Experience	Student groups collaborate to create a group poster presentation to be presented at an end-of-semester symposium.
Introduction to Psychology	Common Intellectual Experience	Students complete a faculty-assigned project in their psychology class, then create a poster presentation and participate in a conference with other psychology students.
Health and Wellness	Common Intellectual Experience	Students complete one of several faculty-identified projects focused on resilience. All sections of the course complete a common preevaluation and reflection papers.
Fundamentals of Communication	Diversity/Global Learning	Intentional infusion of cultural activities, assignments, and projects throughout the course. A common end-of-course assignment is completed.
Introduction to Sociology	Service-Learning	Students participate and reflect on a service-learning project throughout the semester.

Fidelity in Implementation

In the absence of fidelity to agreed-upon standards, HIPs lack the requisite detail or structure in order to render them impactful for student success and intended outcomes. As such, we were ever-mindful of conditions that support student engagement in HIPs (Kuh et al., 2013) when designing this project, recognizing that our HIPs infusion projects had to be done well, but also with fidelity (Kuh, 2008). Yet challenges associated with fidelity in HIPs implementation did arise in terms of how to balance the academic creativity of our faculty with the consistency of the HIPs infusion and measuring outcomes with precision. In HIPs Steering Committee meetings, members contemplated how to (a) determine the proper "dosage" of HIP a faculty member needs to infuse as a threshold to yield results and (b) balance fidelity with concerns about academic freedom and creativity. For example, within the College Composition project the faculty sought to answer clarifying questions to both address and ensure fidelity. During the piloting phase, the College Composition HIP faculty leader was instrumental in guiding conversations with participating faculty about what level of implementation of HIP constituted participation in the diversity/global learning HIP.

Research Questions

In developing our research questions, we considered the role of general education courses in the overall student experience as well as the outcomes for all students and particularly historically underserved student populations. Here are the questions CCBC considered when implementing HIPs infusion projects:

1. Is infusing HIPs into general education courses an effective strategy for increasing the number of students exposed to HIPs, as well as the number of HIPs to which students are exposed?
2. Will students in general education course sections infused with HIPs be retained (semester to semester) at higher levels than students in non-HIPS sections?
3. Will students in minoritized groups in general education course sections infused with HIPs have higher retention (semester to semester) and success rates (earned A, B, or C grades in the course) than similar students in non-HIPs sections?
4. Will traditionally underserved populations of students show a compensatory effect when they experience HIPs (as in the literature)?

Data Collection and Analysis

To answer these important questions relative to the infusion of HIPs into general education courses, we collected data at the course and institutional levels. Each of the seven HIPs infusion projects at CCBC collected data to include student and faculty reflections, focus groups, and surveys. At the institutional level, we examined success in the course (disaggregated by race, age, and gender), persistence within the term, and retention to the next term (student enrolled at the 3rd week of the subsequent semester) for students in the HIPs course sections and students in the non-HIPs sections for the same course. Two of the HIPs projects (Technology and Information Systems and Health and Wellness) scaled to all sections of the course in one semester. These two projects scaled up so quickly that there was no comparison group available. For each research question, our analysis method is as follows.

Exposure to HIPs

We determined exposure rate by calculating the percentage of total enrollment in each term between fall 2016 and fall 2019 in all seven highly enrolled courses by HIPs status, which was based on whether a course section infused a HIP. We calculated the number of HIPs to which a student was exposed by counting the number of times each student enrolled in a section of the seven highly enrolled courses that infused HIPs and in the Academic Development course between fall 2016 and fall 2019.

Retention and Success Rates

In each course, we calculated the retention rate (to the next semester) and success rate (earned A, B, or C grades in the course) for students in HIPs and non-HIPs sections. We compared the rates for each term between fall 2016 and fall 2019 for relevant courses and calculated the number of comparisons favoring each group. We also noted the number of comparisons showing statistical significance. We used a two-sample z-test of proportions to test the statistical significance ($p \leq 0.05$) of differences between rates.

Achievement Gaps

As a majority-minority institution, with the largest minority group being African American, we analyzed the gap between White students' performance and African American students' performance with respect to course success in fall 2018 and the retention of fall 2018 students (in spring 2019). We compared the size of the gap between racial groups for HIPs and for non-HIPs students to determine whether the gap is smaller for HIPs students. We used a two-sample z-test of proportions to test the statistical significance ($p \leq 0.05$) of differences between gap magnitudes.

Results

In the following we present our findings related to exposure to HIPs, retention, success rates, and achievement gaps. Each topic is in a separate section that contains an introductory narrative that summarizes the findings, followed by a table that illustrates the results.

Exposure to HIPs

Infusing HIPs into highly enrolled general education courses led to a significant increase in the percentage of students exposed to at least one HIP between fall 2016 and fall 2019. In fall 2016, HIPs were infused in two courses (Technology and Information Systems and College Composition). As a result, only 4% of students who enrolled in a highly enrolled course were exposed to HIPs. By fall 2019, HIPs had been infused into seven highly enrolled courses and 63% of enrolled students in the seven courses experienced at least one HIP. As shown in Table 12.2, the rate of HIPs exposure increased each term. In some cases, every section of the course infused a HIP by fall 2019 (e.g., Fundamentals of Communication, Technology and Information Systems, Health and Wellness).

In addition to increasing overall exposure, infusing HIPs into highly enrolled general education courses increased the number of HIPs to which students were exposed over the course of their time at CCBC. Table 12.3 shows that students participated in as many as eight HIPs experiences (including the HIP associated with Academic Development, a first-year experience course, which 40% of students took). The largest share of students (58%)

TABLE 12.2
HIPs Exposure Rate in Highly Enrolled Courses

	HIPs	*Non-HIPs*
Fall 2016	4%	96%
Spring 2017	14%	86%
Fall 2017	15%	85%
Spring 2018	32%	68%
Fall 2018	44%	56%
Spring 2019	52%	48%
Fall 2019	63%	37%

TABLE 12.3
Number of HIPs Experiences for Students

Number of HIPs	*8*	*7*	*6*	*5*	*4*	*3*	*2*	*1*	*Total*
Count	1	23	78	354	1,167	2,596	5,487	6,933	16,639
Percentage	0.01%	0.1%	0.5%	2%	7%	16%	33%	42%	100%

was exposed to two or more HIPs in their general education classes, with 42% being exposed to one HIP-infused general education course.

Retention Rates

Students enrolled in HIPs sections had higher retention rates than students in non-HIPs sections. Across the seven courses and six semesters, we ran a total of 22 comparisons between these groups. Of these 22 comparisons, 20 (91%) showed higher retention rates among HIPs students. Of these 20, almost half (9) were statistically significant (see Table 12.4). Among significant results, the 95% confidence intervals showed an advantage to HIPs students that ranged from a low of 2 percentage points to a high of 53 percentage points. The result was not statistically significant in either case where the retention rate was higher for non-HIPs students.

When we looked within each racial group, students in HIPs sections had a retention advantage over students in non-HIPs sections in both White and African American groups (see Table 12.5). There was a total of 20 terms between fall 2016 and fall 2019 where HIPS and non-HIPs data could be compared. Out of 20 comparisons for each racial group, 16 (80%) favored White HIPs students versus White non-HIPs students and 16 (80%) favored African American HIPs students versus African American non-HIPs students. Out of 40 total comparisons, 32 (80%) favored HIPs students over non-HIPs students and 13 (33%) were statistically significant. Twelve of the statistically significant results were in favor of HIPs students and seven involved African American HIPs students being retained at higher rates than African American non-HIPs students.

TABLE 12.4
Retention Rate Comparisons Between HIPs and Non-HIPs Course Sections

	Fall 2016	*Spring 2017*	*Fall 2017*	*Spring 2018*	*Fall 2018*	*Spring 2019*	*Total*	*Statistically Significant*
Higher retention in HIPS sections	2	1	4	4	4	5	20	9
Higher retention in non-HIPS sections	0	0	1	1	0	0	2	0

TABLE 12.5

Retention Rate Comparisons Between HIPs and Non-HIPs Course Sections by Race

	Fall 2016	*Spring 2017*	*Fall 2017*	*Spring 2018*	*Fall 2018*	*Spring 2019*	*Fall 2019*	*Total*	*Statistically Significant*
Higher retention among White HIPs students	1	1	2	3	4	4	1	16	5
Higher retention among White non-HIPs students	0	0	2	1	0	0	0	3	1
Higher retention among African American HIPs students	1	1	2	3	4	4	1	16	7
Higher retention among African American non-HIPs students	0	0	1	2	0	1	0	4	0

Note. There was one tie between White HIPs and non-HIPs students in spring 2019.

Success Rates

Results for success rate were less promising, with a small advantage to non-HIPs students overall. Out of 18 comparisons for each racial group, seven (39%) were in favor of White HIPs students versus White non-HIPs students and nine (50%) were in favor of African American HIPs students versus African American non-HIPs students. Out of 36 total comparisons, 16 (48%) were in favor of HIPs students over non-HIPs students and eight (24%) were statistically significant (see Table 12.6).

TABLE 12.6
Success Rate for HIPs and Non-HIPs Students by Race

	Fall 2016	*Spring 2017*	*Fall 2017*	*Spring 2018*	*Fall 2018*	*Spring 2019*	*Fall 2019*	*Total*	*Statistically Significant*
Higher success among White HIPs students	0	0	0	3	0	3	1	7	1
Higher success among White non-HIPs students	1	1	4	1	3	1	0	11	1
Higher success among African American HIPs students	0	0	1	2	3	2	1	9	3
Higher success among African American non-HIPs students	1	1	3	2	0	2	0	9	3

Achievement Gaps

As Table 12.7 shows, results were highly variable for retention rates, with only one instance of gap reduction among HIPs students out of five comparisons. Results were more promising for success rates. For non-HIPs students, success rate gaps ranged from 8 to 28 percentage points across courses. For HIPs students, the gaps ranged from 1 to 23 percentage points. Although the achievement gap remained, there was progress toward closing it when HIPs were introduced into courses. When we examined each course, we found that the gap between White and African American HIPs students closed significantly in three of the four courses. The size of the gap decreased by as much as 20 percentage points in one course (Biology 1: Molecules and Cells).

TABLE 12.7
Retention and Success Rate Gap Comparisons for White and African American Students by HIP Status

Course	*Retention Gap (Spring 2019)*	*Success Gap (Fall 2018)*
Biology 1: Molecules and Cells	Closed significantly for HIPs (–24)	Closed significantly for HIPs (–20)
Fundamentals of Communication	No significant difference (+4 vs. +6)	Closed significantly for HIPs (–7)
College Composition	Widened significantly for HIPs (+21)	Widened significantly for HIPs (+8)
Introduction to Psychology	No significant difference (+6 vs +6)	Closed significantly for HIPs (–11)
Introduction to Sociology	Widened significantly for HIPs (+10)	N/A[a]

[a]Introduction to Sociology began its HIP infusion project in spring 2019.

Discussion

CCBC has had notable success with infusing HIPs in general education courses. Beginning in fall 2016 through fall 2019, over 23,000 students have experienced a HIP in their general education coursework. Infusing HIPs in general education courses addresses CCBC's equity agenda by ensuring that all students, including historically minoritized populations, have access to these practices and experience comparable levels of success. As demonstrated previously, CCBC is seeing a compensatory effect for minoritized groups that is reflected in diminished achievement gaps in some HIPs-infused courses. Expansion of HIPs across the curriculum in both general education and in a student's major is an important next step to better serve our students and to further the important equity agenda work at CCBC. Having ongoing and deep discussions of fidelity in the implementation of HIPs in general education courses is important to attend to early in the planning process, and to return regularly to be sure the HIP is, and remains, impactful. In the future, departmental committees should consider the minimal level of infusion (i.e., activity specifics, class time) prior to HIPs infusion program implementation.

With promising results in our efforts to infuse HIPs in highly enrolled general education courses, our next steps in our continued implementation and scaling of HIPs infusion at CCBC include mapping current and future HIPs projects to the eight quality measures proposed by Kuh et al. (2013) and continuing efforts to get disaggregated HIPs data into the hands of faculty members teaching those courses so that actionable strategies can be designed to continue to close achievement gaps. Our CCBC HIPs have become a signature initiative that has bolstered the college's efforts to build capacity and to inform solutions narrowing both opportunity gaps and achievement gaps. HIPs infusion is now a preferred strategy for advancing our equity agenda and larger scale student success agenda at CCBC.

References

Achieving the Dream. (2016, July 28). *New initiative at six Achieving the Dream colleges harnesses faculty expertise to improve student success.* https://www.achievingthedream.org/press_release/16087/new-initiative-at-six-achieving-the-dream-colleges-harnesses-faculty-expertise-to-improve-student-success

Community College of Baltimore County. (2019). *Cultural diversity report.* http://dlslibrary.state.md.us/publications/Exec/MHEC/ED11-406(d)(2)_2019.pdf

Finley, A. (2019). *A comprehensive approach to assessment of high-impact practices.* National Institute for Learning Outcomes Assessment. https://eric.ed.gov/?id=ed604467

Finley, A., & McNair, T. (2013). *Assessing underserved students' engagement in high-impact practices.* Association of American Colleges & Universities. https://eric.ed.gov/?id=ed582014

Kuh, G. D. (2008). *High-impact educational practices: What they are, who has access to them, and why they matter.* Association of American Colleges & Universities.

Kuh, G. D., O'Donnell, K., & Reed, S. (2013). *Ensuring quality and taking high-impact practices to scale.* Association of American Colleges & Universities.

Kurtinitis, S. (2020). *Charge to the Diversity, Equity, and Inclusion Advisory Council.* https://libraryguides.ccbcmd.edu/c.php?g=346661&p=8097436

National Association of System Heads. (n.d.). *High-impact practices: An educator's guide.* http://www.hips.nashonline.org

13

DOCUMENTING HIGH-IMPACT PRACTICES IN INSTITUTIONAL DATA

Pam Bowers and Lara Ducate

To improve, organizations need to be able to see the system that is producing the current results (Bryk et al., 2015). Missing or poor quality of data on college learning experiences influences universities' ability to examine the educational environment and its impact on students (Astin & Antonio, 2012). Pascarella (2006) discussed the importance and challenges surrounding the availability of good data for identifying connections among college experiences and student learning and development and described good data as those that provide insights to inform decision-making and educational practice.

Universities are under increasing pressure to advance success for all students and to provide evidence of effectiveness in producing student learning, but often have limited ability to use institutional data to achieve these objectives. Results of a national landscape study on data analytics in higher education (Parnell et al., 2018) found that the information collected in student information systems, such as data on admissions, financial aid, and academic courses, are "the only student data systematically collected, integrated, and used to any meaningful extent" (p. 10). Practices for collecting and managing important institutional data have not kept pace with the growing interest in using analytics tools to advance student success, in general, and the quality and equity of high-impact practices (HIPs) and the cocurriculum, in particular. The quality of student learning data collected in traditional education records is also insufficient for reporting individual student learning achievement. Traditional transcripts focus on the instruction received by a student, providing information about courses completed and grades earned but excluding specific information about learning outcomes or the learning activities students experience in college (Laitinen, 2012). This information about student learning achievement is not included in traditional student education records and, therefore, not available for reporting on student transcripts.

Understanding how an institution engages students in educationally purposeful activities and the results achieved is essential to inform improvement and advance student learning and development. What students do in college, how they engage in both curricular and cocurricular activities, affects the educational impact on the student (Astin, 1984; Pascarella & Terenzini, 2005), but these educationally purposeful activities are not traditionally recorded in institutional data. Astin and Antonio (2012) described the difficulties in regard to obtaining data on students' educational experiences: "The methodological challenge for the researcher is to identify such experiences and to devise an appropriate means for measuring them and for determining whether each student encountered such an experience while enrolled" (p. 99).

Over the last decade, research on HIPs has illuminated a path to improving data on student engagement and learning by identifying the characteristics of these practices that are essential for producing a high educational impact (Kuh et al., 2013, 2017). Identification of these key elements provides a means for universities to proactively improve HIPs by documenting the design of educational practices to ensure the inclusion of essential components, rather than focusing solely on outcome measures to determine the extent to which a program achieved high impact.

Beyond the Classroom Matters: A Data Strategy

The University of South Carolina (UofSC) implemented an initiative to improve institutional data on student engagement and learning, initially focusing on noncredit-bearing HIPs and the cocurriculum provided by student affairs. UofSC created a supplemental student information system, Beyond the Classroom Matters (BTCM), that enables documentation of the educational purpose and design of HIPs and other cocurricular programs, events, and activities (called Engagements); systematically records student involvement in documented Engagements; and links these records with each student's academic records to create a more comprehensive education record for each student. Engagement records are recognized as official student education records in university policy (University of South Carolina, 2020b).

The primary objectives initially were to improve visibility of the educational purpose of student affairs programs, improve evidence of the impact of the cocurriculum on student learning and development, and increase student engagement in these important educational experiences. To achieve these objectives, the university implemented a strategy to integrate these new education records into institutional data. Historically, student affairs data have not been included in education records because student engagement in noncredit programs, although educationally purposeful, is not required for graduation and does not produce grades or credit hours. Education records and the information systems used to collect and manage the records were designed to monitor student progress to graduation, so student participation in the cocurriculum has traditionally been neither systematically defined nor recorded.

Design

The UofSC model includes the following components: documenting program design using a framework based in part on the characteristics of HIPs; within that design, defining learning activities, learning outcomes, and other characteristics using standard definitions and naming conventions; and defining methods for verifying and recording students' satisfactory completion of documented programs. The framework for the model parallels academic information to the extent possible, including defining Engagements within academic terms (semesters), so that student records of Engagement can be linked to academic records to provide a more comprehensive record of student engagement and learning during each term.

The BTCM project expanded beyond student affairs in support of a new academic affairs initiative to increase student engagement in credit-bearing HIPs, as existing institutional data had limitations for supporting the effort. Neither data on content and design of credit-bearing HIPs nor data on student participation in these programs were readily available. HIPs are offered by many departments—curricular and cocurricular—in multiple formats and with variations in definitions and naming conventions, making it difficult to identify characteristics of existing educational programs across the institution. In order to ensure that all students had the opportunity to participate and achieve equitable educational benefits, more comprehensive data about student engagement in these educational programs were required.

Credit-bearing HIP programs share some relevant characteristics, from a data-improvement perspective, with the noncredit student affairs programs that were the initial focus of BTCM. HIPs are often encouraged, but usually not required, for graduation and are often defined at the program or department level. Across an institution, colleges and academic departments have different naming practices and variations in criteria that define experiences such as internships or service-learning courses. BTCM staff had worked through similar issues in systematically documenting cocurricular programs across the Division of Student Affairs, moving from previous department- or unit-level practices.

Implementation Workflow

The UofSC model requires educators to propose a course, program, event, or activity (called an Engagement) for cataloging in the BTCM system. An Engagement must have a stated educational purpose, intentional and coherent design, defined successful completion, and a means to monitor student completion, as defined. Engagements are categorized into three levels, based on the nature and depth of the student experience. Those that demonstrate essential elements of HIPs such as engaging with students on substantive matters over an extended period of time, providing feedback on their performance and development, and offering structured activities for their reflection on learning are categorized at the highest level.

With the launch of the provost's initiative to engage all students in experiential learning, credit-bearing Engagements and noncredit-bearing Engagements that demonstrate HIPs characteristics are designated as Experiential Learning Opportunities. To receive this designation, educators must provide supporting documentation in a syllabus or rubric that demonstrates an experiential component as well as alignment of the program's design with the essential elements of HIPs.

In an online proposal form, educators provide a brief description of the nature and format of the program in which they describe it from the perspective of the student (item 1 in the following list). Educators answer additional questions aligned with the essential elements (such as those listed in the following) by choosing from a dropdown menu of response options.

1. What does the student do? What are the required tasks or actions of student participants?
   For example, a service-learning course has this response: *Students work directly with a local immigrant service provider to gain an in-depth, direct understanding of refugee-resettlement processes taking place in the Midlands region. Students contribute to the operations of a refugee social service agency and fulfill tasks and duties as specified by the agency.*
2. What is the time-on-task for students who engage in this program, as designed?
3. With whom does the student interact?

4. How does the student experience diversity in this course/program?
5. How does the student receive feedback?
6. How is the student engaged in structured opportunities to reflect and integrate learning?
7. What knowledge and skills do students apply and practice as they engage?

In the proposal process, educators reflect on the purpose and design of their programs through the lens of HIPs characteristics. Systematically documenting purpose and design in this way encourages the educator's reflection on the intentionality and coherence of the design of their program, increasing opportunity for recognition of design gaps, modifications to close the gaps, and improvement of the quality of the program. These measures of alignment with the essential characteristics provide leverage points for implementing practices that are likely to have high impact. For example, when an educator is asked to provide information about how they engage students in structured reflection on their learning, they may recognize an opportunity for improvement and identify a modification to add or strengthen the reflection component of their program.

Educator responses to the online proposal provide the basis for reviewers to evaluate the extent to which an Engagement embodies the essential elements of HIPs; those designed with HIPs characteristics are designated in the data. Responses are collected in the BTCM system to improve the institution's ability to understand the range and depth of HIPs available on the campus, report individual student engagement and learning (in an extended transcript), and improve analysis of inclusion and equity of the educational impact of participation. By collecting these descriptive data elements, analysis of educational impact can go beyond examining the impact of participation in a HIP to exploring, more specifically, how essential elements of HIPs, regardless of the kind of program, may have a conditional impact on student populations.

Table 13.1 illustrates how documentation of program content and design creates data for analysis of the impact of methods of structured reflection on learning. Connecting this information to student demographic records enables analysis of the conditional impact of a reflection method on student populations.

In some HIPs, such as internships, the experience has unique characteristics for individual students. The essential elements of the experience are the same from a program design perspective, but individual students may engage in different settings and perhaps on different topics. The UofSC model captures these student-specific data elements. For example, students

TABLE 13.1
Frequency of Documented Reflection Methods in HIPs and Counts of Students Who Participated in Engagements

Primary Structured Reflection Activity	*Engagement Count*	*Student Count*
1–1 session with faculty	16	776
1–1 session with professional staff	22	454
Students produce written reflection	23	940
Group/class session with faculty	10	1,362
Group/class session with professional staff	12	261
With external supervisor/partner	4	483
Total	87	4,276

Source: J. Poon, personal communication, September 26, 2020.

in a credit-bearing internship interact with the faculty member in the same way (e.g., required tasks, feedback, and reflection on learning), but their employment experiences are with different employers. Engagement data collected for internship Engagements include each student's job title, employer name, and location. This provides institutional data on employers who engage UofSC students as interns and provides specific, validated learning experiences that a student can report on in an official extended transcript provided by the university. Similarly, undergraduate research data include the type of research program (e.g., grant, independent, paid), each student's research topic, and research mentor name and department. BTCM staff work with educators to collect this information using electronic transfer of records where possible. The university considers these data to be important assets for achieving institutional objectives for student learning and success, and it is an ongoing priority to improve the quality and availability of the data.

Strategies for assuring quality currently vary based on credit-bearing status. BTCM staff assist student affairs educators with using tools in the university's learning management system (Blackboard) to monitor fidelity of implementation of HIP Engagements as each Engagement is underway. Students who participate in student affairs HIP Engagements receive a survey at the end of the term with questions designed to indicate the extent to which programs they completed were delivered with fidelity to their visible, intentional design. Students in credit-bearing Engagements currently receive a traditional course evaluation survey; closer alignment of survey tools for credit- and noncredit-bearing Engagements is an area identified for future development to improve the initiative. For both types of surveys, results are reported to educators to inform improvement of their programs. If an Engagement designated as a HIP is not implemented with fidelity to its stated design, the faculty/staff governance group may remove the special designation and correct the documentation of the program's design in institutional data.

Using Data to Achieve Institutional Objectives

Each student and their advisor can access the student's Engagement records for use in holistic education and career planning, and reflection on learning from completed Engagements. Comprehensive advising conversations are informed by review of each student's records and may include a broad range of educationally purposeful activities such as new student orientation programs, career development activities, student organization membership, student leadership roles, HIPs, and more. Knowledge and skills developed in documented Engagements are visible in student records. Student records can be reported (at the student's request) in an official, extended transcript that supplements the academic transcript to provide a more comprehensive record of a student's learning experiences at the university.

Data visualization tools and reports are available to educators. The data displayed in this chapter were prepared by professional staff in the UofSC Office of Institutional Research, Assessment, Analytics. In interactive dashboard reports, student participant data can be disaggregated on characteristics such as first-generation status, Pell eligibility, race/ethnicity, and other data elements. Data files can be extracted from the institution's data warehouse for further analysis. Table 13.2 illustrates disaggregation of HIPs data by participants' status as "first-generation" or "not first-generation" college students as defined in the university admissions application, and comparison to the population in their enrollment cohort group. Because HIPs data are linked with the university's academic and demographic student-level records, data can be disaggregated on many data elements and examined in a variety of ways, including analysis of the conditional effects of participation in HIPs on historically underserved student populations.

Data Analysis

Examining students' involvement in educationally purposeful Engagements, including HIPs and the cocurriculum, illustrates how student learning and institutional objectives are being achieved and informs efforts for

TABLE 13.2
Percentage of HIPs Participants in a Specified Term Who Identify as First-Generation College Students and Their Percentage in the Cohort Population for Fall 2019

	First-Gen		*Non First-Gen*	
	Engagement Proportion	*Population Proportion*	*Engagement Proportion*	*Population Proportion*
Civic Engagement and Service-Learning Programs	25%	14%	75%	86%
Education Abroad Programs and Services	11%	14%	89%	86%
Internship Programs	18%	14%	82%	86%
Student Leadership Programs	17%	14%	83%	86%
Undergraduate Research Programs	14%	14%	86%	86%

Source: J. Poon, personal communication, September 26, 2020.

improvement. One measure includes investigating how participation in recorded Engagements contributes to student success, as defined by student retention and completion. These analyses of student engagement play a key role in the recently adopted UofSC strategic plan and also in the 2021 Quality Enhancement Plan submitted as a component of the Southern Association of Colleges and Schools Commission on Colleges (SACSCOC) reaffirmation of institutional accreditation.

Engagements are categorized into three tiers, based on the educational depth and structure of the learning activities. Preliminary analysis of the records of student engagement in the three tiers (see Table 13.3) indicates that in fall 2018, there were 6,195 students classified as 1st-year students and 6,448 sophomores, where 2,598 (42%) of 1st-year students participated in at least one Tier 1 and at least one Tier 2 Engagement. Of those 2,598 1st-year students, 91% of them returned for fall 2019. Among the 1,380 (22%) students classified as 1st-year students who participated in at least one Tier 2 Engagement, 84% returned. It is encouraging to note that overall, 78% of the freshman class was able to participate in at least one recorded Engagement during their 1st year at the University. This high percentage of participation serves to alleviate initial faculty concerns that these types of activities might not be available to all students or that students do not have the time or interest to participate.

When examining the data in Figure 13.1 (see note on p. 260) on juniors and seniors from fall 2018 to fall 2019 who engaged in Tier 1, 2, and 3 Engagements, and juniors and seniors who did not engage, it is evident that the majority of students who engaged were slightly more successful in terms of graduation or retention than students who did not participate.

TABLE 13.3
Engagement and Persistence of UofSC 1st-Year Students and Sophomores 2018–2019

BTCM Engagement Combination in Fall 2018			*Rate of Return in Fall 2019*		*Head Count Fall 2018*	
Tier 1	*Tier 2*	*Tier 3*	*Freshman*	*Sophomore*	*Freshman*	*Sophomore*
+	+	+	97%	94%	35	119
+	+		91%	94%	2,598	1,542
+			73%	94%	765	1,881
+		+	90%	98%	10	53
	+		84%	85%	1,380	983
	+	+	86%	93%	14	57
		+	50%	95%	2	21
			66%	86%	1,391	1,792

Source: J. Poon, personal communication, September 26, 2020.

Figure 13.1. Engagement and success outcomes of UofSC juniors and seniors.

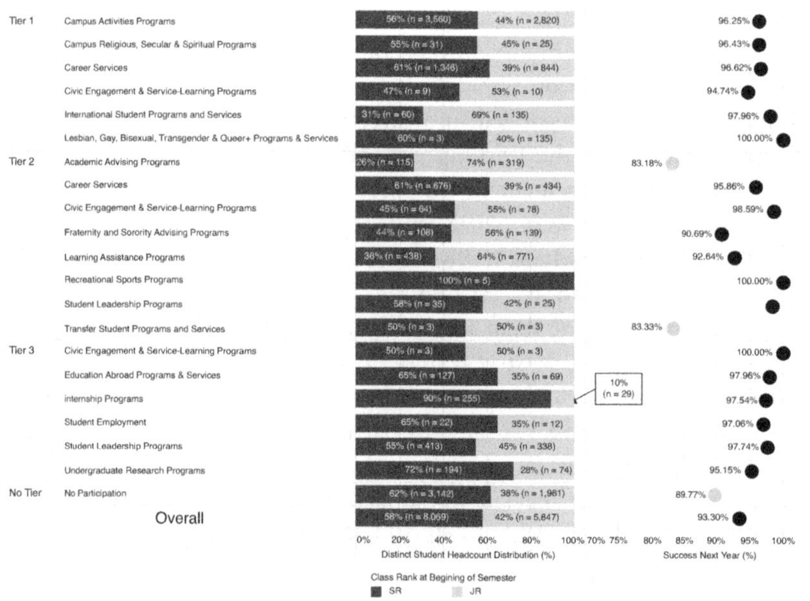

Future Directions

These analyses are likely to proceed in multiple directions. In a study underway, the data already described are disaggregated and analysts are examining the success of various student populations, including first-generation students, underrepresented minorities, and Pell-eligible students. As there is currently limited research that demonstrates the exact effects of HIPs on students (Kuh et al., 2017), the specificity of this data will also allow an examination of the influence of specific types of HIPs and Engagements on different types of student involvement and success. Plans for additional inquiry include assessing the extent to which participation in recorded Engagements led to a higher likelihood of returning in fall 2020, especially considering the influence of COVID-19 on students' decisions.

These analyses of student engagement and learning in HIPs and the cocurriculum help quantify how the university is able to meet its strategic goals. The university identifies plans to "increase experiential learning opportunities for students to engage in real-world community research and service experiences" (University of South Carolina, 2020a, p. 22) as the university becomes more engaged in community partnerships. This expanded university engagement aims to include a 10% increase in students participating in documented experiential and cocurricular learning, a 5% increase in community engagement, and a 5% increase in study abroad each year through 2025. Another university goal is to "cultivate a more diverse, equitable, and inclusive campus culture where every individual, regardless of background, has the full opportunity to flourish and thrive" (p. 29). To achieve this goal, the university seeks to "increase participation among undergraduate students from underrepresented, low-income, and other marginalized groups in HIPs by enhancing the availability of access to and support for internships, study abroad (grant-funded) research and other experiential learning opportunities" (p. 29). A quantitative metric of this goal is to double participation in HIPs among students from underrepresented, low-income, and other marginalized groups by 2025. Systematically documenting student Engagements in HIPs and the cocurriculum makes it possible to identify which students are engaging and which are not and consider ways to involve the nonparticipants.

A primary goal of the UofSC initiative described in this chapter is to improve the quality of institutional data on student engagement and learning in HIPs and the cocurriculum in order to help the organization achieve its objectives to advance student learning and success for all students, while demonstrating effectiveness and efficiency. An organization needs information about how it operates to produce current results, in order to improve future results. To deliver on the promise of HIPs, an institution needs to be able to see, in its data, the current state of those practices. Improving institutional data in the ways described in this chapter requires educator reflection on the deliberate design of educational programs at the micro level—within a HIP or cocurricular activity—and enables institutional reflection on design at the macro level—of the whole student experience. The resulting comprehensive student education records enable institutional reflection on the current design of the broader student learning experience and facilitate taking deliberate action to design a holistic college experience that leverages all student learning opportunities, within and beyond the classroom.

References

Astin, A. W. (1984). Student involvement: A developmental theory for higher education. *Journal of College Student Personnel, 25*, 297–308. https://eric.ed.gov/?id=EJ309521

Astin, A. W., & Antonio, A. L. (2012). *Assessment for excellence: The philosophy and practice of assessment and evaluation in higher education* (2nd ed.). Rowman & Littlefield.

Bryk, A. S., Gomez, L. M., Grunow, A., & LeMahieu, P. G. (2015). *Learning to improve: How America's schools can get better at getting better*. Harvard University Press.

Kuh, G. D., O'Donnell, K., & Reed, S. (2013). *Ensuring quality and taking high-impact practices to scale*. Association of American Colleges & Universities.

Kuh, G. D., O'Donnell, K., & Schneider, C. G. (2017). HIPs at ten. *Change: The Magazine of Higher Learning, 49*(5), 8–16. https://doi.org/10.1080/00091383.2017.1366805

Laitinen, A. (2012). *Cracking the credit hour.* https://www.newamerica.org/education-policy/policy-papers/cracking-the-credit-hour/

Parnell, A., Jones, D., Wesaw, A., & Brooks, D. C. (2018). *Institutions' use of data and analytics for student success: Results from a national landscape analysis*. NASPA–Student Affairs Administrators in Higher Education; the Association for Institutional Research; EDUCAUSE. https://library.educause.edu/resources/2018/4/institutions-use-of-data-and-analytics-for-student-success

Pascarella, E. T. (2006). How college affects students: Ten directions for future research. *Journal of College Student Development, 47*(5), 508–520. https://doi.org/10.1353/csd.2006.0060

Pascarella, E. T., & Terenzini, P. T. (2005). *How college affects students: A third decade of research* (Vol. 2). Jossey-Bass.

University of South Carolina. (2020a, August). *For South Carolina: A path to excellence.* https://sc.edu/about/our_leadership/president/strategic_plan/index.php

University of South Carolina. (2020b, May 28). *Undergraduate student records of experiential and cocurricular learning* (Academic Affairs Policy 2.14). http://www.sc.edu/policies/ppm/acaf214.pdf

14

REQUIRED EXPERIENTIAL LEARNING

Cultural Change and Commitment to Student Success

Jon C. Neidy, Kelly McConnaughay, and Jennifer Gruening Burge

Fundamental shifts are needed for campuses to productively alter their culture for learning and realize their full promise for a transformative undergraduate education. "These shifts should engage us all and support all our efforts as laborers in the messy process of initiating and sustaining steps—large or small steps and nudges" (Harward, 2012, p. 25). This chapter examines how Bradley University used large steps, small steps, and nudges to engage in campus-wide cultural change to implement a requirement for all students to complete two experiential learning activities prior to graduation. This effort provided the opportunity for campus administrators, faculty, and student affairs staff to investigate and debate the value of such experiences for all students, especially those who are traditionally considered underserved.

In 2015, the university developed and approved a revised general education program, known as the Bradley Core Curriculum. The curriculum included many unique aspects, including the addition of core practices and high-impact practices (HIPs) inspired by the Association of American Colleges & Universities (Kuh, 2008). The campus community approved writing-intensive courses to be included in the Bradley Core Curriculum as the first core practice. Following approval of the Bradley Core Curriculum, the community was engaged in a strategic planning process, which refined the mission and vision statements, affirming the university's commitment to student success and student engagement. At the same time, the university began working on a Quality Initiative for accreditation. These processes served to reinforce the university's commitment to experiential learning (EL).

The Bradley University construct of EL emerged from an analysis of the eleven HIPs championed by Association of American Colleges & Universities (AAC&U) and campus practices considered student success predictors (Kuh, 2008). Specifically, we reviewed campus practices, such as engagement with experiential activities like internships, study abroad, undergraduate research, service-learning, and capstones, with the career outcomes of students and then aligned them with detailed descriptions of the HIPs on a matrix. The HIPs identified through this analysis include capstone courses and projects, diversity/global learning, internships, service-/community-based learning, and undergraduate research. Although enriching experiences like these permeate learning at Bradley University and were reinforced in the development of the Bradley Core Curriculum, the selection of EL as the Quality Initiative project for accreditation helped campus stakeholders understand that EL should be required for all students who graduate with a baccalaureate degree. Empirical data supported this internal analysis and principles from the National Society for Experiential Education's Principles of Best Practice in Experiential Education grounded the campus-wide cultural change for EL.

Evidence of Data-Supported Equity

The promotion of equity and access for traditionally underserved student populations is deeply embedded in the premise of requiring EL for all baccalaureate graduates. Analysis of Bradley's centralized career center data indicates that traditionally underserved student populations were not participating in "registered practical experiences" or EL as often as their peers. Embedding and integrating the construct of EL within the cocurriculum, the Bradley Core Curriculum, and already existing major and minor curricula makes EL more accessible for traditionally underserved students (racially minoritized populations) and, with curricular integration, has the potential for deeper, more transformative learning outcomes. The Bradley University Undergraduate Learning Experience provides a visual model for this commitment (Figure 14.1).

EL as a requirement for all students began with the incoming class in the fall of 2019. Analyses of initial outputs indicate that students who are traditionally underserved are participating in EL at more consistent rates but are not yet engaging in EL in parallel to the existing student population (see Table 14.1). However, as traditionally underserved students matriculate, they should become more equally represented within the undergraduate student population engaged with EL.

Figure 14.1. Visual model of the commitment.

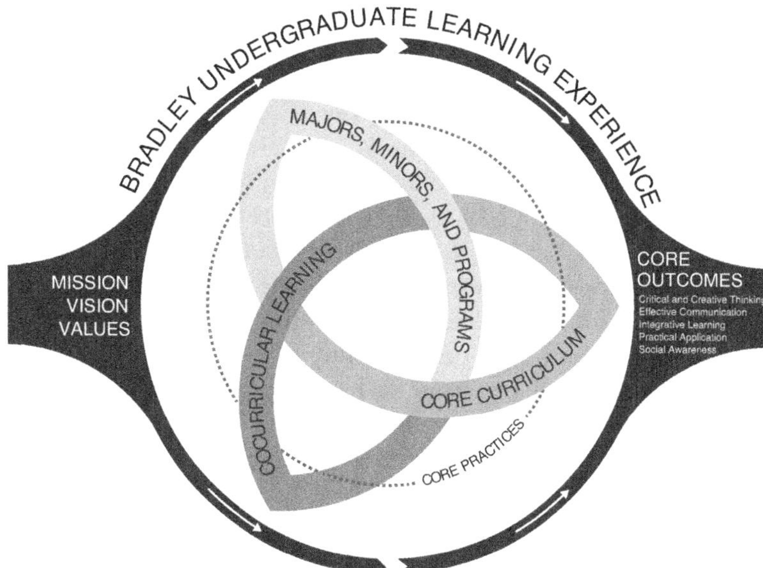

TABLE 14.1
Comparison of Total Undergraduate Populations to EL Engaged: Academic Year 2019–2020

Population	*Asian*	*Black*	*Caucasian*	*Hispanic*	*Native American/ Alaskan*	*Multirace*	*Nonresidents*	*Unknown*
Total Undergraduates	3.9%	7.0%	71.3%	11.2%	—	3.1%	1.9%	1.3%
EL Engaged Undergraduates	3.8%	5.4%	77.7%	8.1%	—	2.4%	1.0%	1.3%

In addition, a data-gathering effort will allow for an analysis of EL activities by category as compared to student participation. This will allow the campus community to identify, review, and address which types of EL are being completed by traditionally underserved populations. A preliminary analysis of the 2019–2020 academic year data indicates that 77% of those completed were capstone courses, 16% were internships or practica,

5% were undergraduate research or creative production, and 2% were other. The ultimate goal is to reduce inequities in participation in HIPs and to ensure underserved students are getting exposure to EL opportunities vital to their success.

The emphasis on serving the underserved through EL has also generated related new initiatives on campus. For example, motivated by the connection between EL and positive career outcomes, the centralized career center established a goal for the 2020–2021 academic year focused on examining 5 years' worth of data related to underserved students and postgraduation success as it relates to EL. As the first class of required EL students advances toward graduation in the spring of 2023, student engagement and EL participation is being monitored and assessed to ensure the cultural and curricular changes and EL requirement are having the desired impact. The primary goal of this effort was to embed significant cultural change within the context of the university community and thereby reduce inequities of participation in HIPs.

Relevant Literature

Increasing students' attainment of educational objectives, such as postgraduation employment or matriculation into graduate school, are the primary motivators for Bradley University to engage in this substantive curricular and EL work. Kuh's (2008) belief that an institution should make it "possible for every student to participate in at least two HIPs during his or her undergraduate program, one in the first year, and one taken later in relation to the major field" (p. 21), in addition to his assertion that "some groups of historically underserved students are less likely to participate in HIPs—those first in their family to attend college and African American students in particular" (p. 27), amplify the importance of this effort.

The demonstrated relationship between student success and EL also animates Bradley's efforts. For purposes of this chapter "student success is defined as academic achievement; engagement in educationally purposeful activities; satisfaction; acquisition of desired knowledge, skills, and competencies; persistence; and attainment of educational objectives" (Association for the Study of Higher Education, 2007, p. 9). With Kuh's (2008) research as a foundation, many other studies have demonstrated the influence of HIPs on student success, including Anderson et al. (2019), Brownell and Swaner (2009), Coker et al. (2017), Hart Research Associates (2016), Kilgo et al. (2015), Neill (2010), and Trolian and Jach (2020), who have provided additional confirmation of the value of requiring such experiences. As a cautionary consideration it is important to note that Finley and McNair (2013) asserted that

> it is imperative, therefore, for campus practitioners to examine their own equity effects by disaggregating their data and comparing their findings. Such analyses can provide the information needed for evidence-based decisions about how to improve programs that strive toward, advance, and support equitable outcomes for students across all groups, particularly underserved students. (p. 19)

With this in mind, Bradley is committed to disaggregating EL data for underserved student populations and acting to ensure representational equity in HIPs participation.

Implementing Cultural Change

"Creativity and innovation are particularly important in organizations not wedded to the status quo. In the 21st century, postsecondary institutions need to change if they are to succeed" (Tierney, 2008, p. 10). Success for students and the institution serve as the foundation for the implementation of the significant cultural changes necessary to require EL for all students at Bradley University. In his inspiring work, *The Impact of Culture on Organizational Decision-Making: Theory and Practice in Higher Education,* Tierney (2008) asserted, "An understanding of culture has become essential for those who to seek to understand how to foment change in the organization" (p. 9). Explication of the cultural steps and shifts to achieve Bradley's EL requirement is essential to the story of institutional change.

The Bradley University construct of EL stands on a strong historical foundation as the university was founded in 1897 as a polytechnic institute, with the "first object of this Institution to furnish its students with the means of living an independent, industrious and useful life by the aid of a practical knowledge of the useful arts and sciences" (Bradley University, n.d., para. 3). One hundred and fifteen years later, beginning in 2012, a nexus of "large steps, small steps, and nudges" would occur that would allow EL to emerge as a graduation requirement for all baccalaureate students by embedding the requirement within the newly revised general education program (Harward, 2012, p. 25).

Nexus of Events Leading to Required EL

A few large steps, including a commitment on the part of the University Senate to review and revise the general education program, the emergence of

EL as an initiative for accreditation, and the approval of EL as a requirement for graduation, were essential to the changes at Bradley. Examples of small steps included the identification of curricular elements, alignment with the university strategic plan, and piloting proposals through an approval process. A few nudges included participation in an AAC&U conference on HIPs by a group of key influencers, the commitment by various campus-wide committees to the EL construct, listening tours throughout campus, and the presentation of available data at university-wide conferences.

The first goal, curricular change, was achieved by operationalizing the idea and requiring students to complete two courses or activities that meet the requirements of the EL core practice in the Bradley Core Curriculum. Curricular change was supported by providing campus-wide professional development to ensure a deep understanding of course modification approaches, new course creation, and the identification of cocurricular EL activities. As an institution, success of the second goal, campus engagement, was ensured by utilizing a university-wide committee composed of faculty, staff, students, and administration to ensure that the diverse courses and activities gathered together under the construct of EL had consistent requirements and learning expectations. Individual colleges and departments had deep discussions about major curricula and where experiential activities would enhance the student experience.

The final goal, student success, aligned with the Bradley 2017–2022 Strategic Plan and goals related to student success and academic excellence. Although enriching experiences permeate learning at Bradley University and span all aspects of a student's time at our institution, they were not required of all graduates. In addition, the pedagogical and learning expectations around these experiences varied widely. The community-wide work on the university's mission and vision through the strategic planning process helped the community understand that this core practice should not just be recommended but should in fact be required for all students to help ensure the success of all students who graduate with a baccalaureate degree.

Ensuring student success through EL also necessitated a deeper understanding of EL. According to the National Society for Experiential Education's (1998) Principles of Best Practice in Experiential Education, "most conversations about experiential learning dealt with the experience, while the learning was simply assumed to happen" (para. 1).The student success goal and stated university mission to empower students "for immediate and sustained success in their personal and professional endeavors by combining professional preparation, liberal arts and sciences, and cocurricular experiences" helped focus Bradley University on becoming an institution that not only provides enriching experiences, but also *helps students to articulate their learning effectively* and to document and share that learning as a result of those experiences (para. 1). The Bradley University 2017–2022 Strategic Plan states that the university would identify and expand the use of HIPs that contribute to the immediate and sustained success of all students. The first two of four strategic goals of the plan both reference EL, including a focus on active and reflective learning and HIPs for all students. All students who began as 1st-year students in the fall of 2019 and transfer students who began in the fall of 2020 will be able to articulate how EL enhanced their education, engaged them, and prepared them for immediate and sustained success.

Changes in Curricula

The process of approving and adopting the Bradley University EL Graduation Requirement (Figure 14.2) illustrates the many steps leading to substantial curricular change throughout campus.

Fundamental to these changes was the inclusion of seven specific curricular elements (listed in Table 14.2) required of each course seeking an "EL Tag." The curricular elements are adapted from the National Society for Experiential Education's (1998) Principles of Best Practice in Experiential Education. The curricular elements also support and align well with Kuh et al.'s (2013) eight key elements of HIPs. In addition to the seven curricular elements, guiding questions were provided to faculty and staff seeking approval for an EL Tag (see Table 14.2).

To guide curricular change, it was recommended by the Working Group that each dean and the faculty in their departments engage in conversations about which one-to-three existing experiences provided students with the best opportunity to reflect deeply on how the experience enhanced their academic learning and to modify and submit those courses for EL Tag approval. Another effort was undertaken emphasizing the interconnectedness of EL utilizing the Bradley Undergraduate Learning Experience (see Figure 14.1) as a foundation for conversation at various professional development events.

Figure 14.2. Change process in graduation requirement.

TABLE 14.2
Experiential Learning Curricular Elements and Guiding Questions to Aid Proposal Development

Curricular Elements	*Guiding Questions*
Intention The course or activity must have intentionality. Intention represents the purposefulness that enables experience to become knowledge. Learning goals/objectives, and aligned activities must be discussed and approved prior to the experience.	• What are the learning goals/objectives and aligned activities of this experience? • How will the learning goals/objectives and aligned activities be assessed at the end of the experience? • How will student and instructor approvals of learning goals/objectives and aligned activities be confirmed?
Preparedness The course or activity must be planned and structured to provide a sufficient foundation to ensure a successful experience. The student must be prepared and have the necessary knowledge to fulfill the learning goals/objectives and aligned activities that were approved and agreed upon prior to the experience.	• How will the student be prepared for this experience? • How will their preparedness be ensured, recorded, and confirmed?
Authenticity The course or activity must have a real-world context and/or be useful and meaningful in reference to an applied setting or situation. Authenticity allows the students to apply academic learning to real-world experiences. In order to achieve an authentic experience students should be engaged for a minimum of 40 hours.	• How is the experience useful or meaningful to the student in their field or discipline? • How many hours will the student be engaged in the experience? • How will the student spend their time during the experience?
Monitoring and Supervision The course or activity must have a plan for monitoring and supervising the student. Monitoring and supervising ensures the acquisition of the knowledge and the completion of the learning.	• How will students be monitored during the experience? • Who will be instructing the course or activity? • Who will be supervising the work of the student during the experience?

Curricular Elements	*Guiding Questions*
Feedback The course or activity must include structured developmental opportunities to expand the student's understanding of the context and skills of the required work.	• How will students receive feedback during the experience? • When will the student receive feedback during the experience?
Reflection The course or activity must include a reflective learning assignment that allows the student to synthesize connections among experiences, deepen an understanding of a field of study, and demonstrate a developing sense of self as a learner.	• How will the student demonstrate their learning and understandings as a result of the experience?
Assessment The course or activity must include an assessment. Assessment is a means for the instructor to verify the acquisition of the specific learning goals/objectives and aligned activities identified during the planning stages of the experience.	• How will the student learning be assessed by the instructor? • Do assessments align with stated learning goals/objectives and aligned activities? • Are both direct measures of student learning and student's reflections of their learning present?

Changes in Pedagogy

Campus-wide changes in pedagogy were required for the creation, review, and approval of an EL core practice. The work that took place during the academic year of 2016–2017 involved clarifying the language and definition of *experiential learning*. The following definition was approved by the University Senate in the spring of 2017:

> Experiential learning is a high impact practice that is at the heart of the Bradley Experience. Students will learn to apply knowledge, skills and dispositions to real-world applications within and beyond the classroom. These activities provide students with an awareness and appreciation of their growing ability to apply learning to problems that will be encountered after Bradley. Experiential learning commonly encompasses a variety of experiences that can include service-learning, study abroad, supervised research or creative production, capstone experiences, or supervised internships and practical experiences (Working Group, 2017, p. 2).

Figure 14.3. Core practice tag approval process.

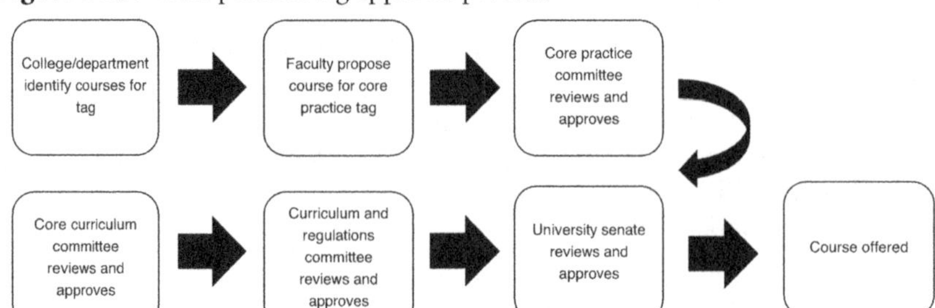

The work that took place during the summer and fall of 2017 specifically focused on developing a set of curricular elements that could be used as part of the process to review, approve, and designate courses as EL or, as they are referred to on campus, "EL Tagged" courses. Figure 14.3 indicates the steps in the process that are required for a course to receive an EL Tag.

Two key points in the approval process (see Figure 14.3), the faculty proposal and the committee review, have allowed Bradley University faculty and staff to deeply reflect on and improve their pedagogical practices, specifically those associated with reflection and assessment. Many EL Tag proposals are submitted without deep consideration for reflection and assessment. This omission activates a one-on-one conversation between a committee member and the submitting faculty member about the value of both reflection and assessment to EL and then a resubmission of the proposal with those curricular elements reconsidered.

Challenges and Successes

As with any campus-wide initiative involving change, there were many challenges to overcome. Communication, as with most change initiatives, was the primary challenge and negatively impacted the EL initiative as a result of assumptions of understandings. The Working Group assumed that the campus community was familiar with the AAC&U HIP work on which the EL construct was built and that there was awareness of terminology around reflection and assessment. The communication assumptions led to a need to provide historical context and definitions of terms. This context was provided in the draft EL Tag document as well as the guiding questions to aid proposal development and the course approval form (see Table 14.2).

Another challenge that required attention was the initial proposal's lack of focus on the benefit of the EL requirement for students. Although the value proposition for students was evident to the authors, the initial proposal did not thoughtfully and specifically describe the direct benefits to students to make it evident to the wider campus audience. The final proposal submitted to the University Senate for approval clearly identified the direct value to students and allowed the readers to understand how individual student lives would be positively impacted by the requirement. The final major challenge to implementation was a change in the financial situation of the university and the inability to hire an administrator and administrative staff member to lead and support the work of the initiative. This financial change required a realignment of work for others involved in the initiative as well as adjustments in expectations.

Although there were challenges to overcome throughout the work there were also successes to be celebrated. The alignment of the Quality Initiative to the university strategic plan, the AAC&U HIPs, and the lifetime outcomes of our students was a profound accomplishment. This alignment allowed others to share the vision of what could be possible for our institution and our students as a result of this change. The development of three tools is essential to ensuring the success of required EL at Bradley. The first, discussed earlier, was the set of curricular elements and guiding questions to assess potential EL courses. The second was a review form used to collect individual committee member reviews of potential EL courses in an asynchronous manner. This allows for more efficient committee review of course proposals. The third and final tool was a workshop provided to faculty and staff in over a dozen venues throughout 2018, 2019, and 2020. This workshop encourages faculty and staff to carefully examine the curricular elements and to draft responses to each of those elements in anticipation of submitting a course for EL Tag approval. The workshop included information on how the committee reviews the courses, typical "mistakes" in submission, and clear guidelines for each curricular element.

The adoption of required EL has provided an opportunity for Bradley University to market our institution in a new way. Enrollment Management, the office responsible for student recruitment and admission, has begun communicating the requirement as a means to differentiate our degree from that of our competitors. The Enrollment Management unit has been sending a letter to admitted 1st-year students and their parents highlighting the distinctive nature of the EL tag and its benefit to the student learning experience. Perhaps the most culture-changing achievement can be found in the collaboration between academic affairs and student affairs. This collaboration fostered a meaningful understanding and reflective appreciation of each other's work and value to the institution, which has resulted in new collaborations and opportunities for both academic affairs and student affairs.

The cultural change process of requiring EL activities as a graduation requirement at Bradley University provided the opportunity for campus administrators, faculty, and staff to investigate and debate the value of such experiences for all students, specifically those who are traditionally underserved. As a result, Bradley University has become an institution that not only provides enriching experiences but also ensures student success, helping all students reflect on their learning and articulate the learning that results from their experiences.

References

Anderson, K. L., Boyd, M., Ariemma Marin, K., & McNamara, K. (2019). Reimagining service-learning: Deepening the impact of this high-impact practice. *Journal of Experiential Education, 42*(3), 229–248. https://doi.org/10.1177/1053825919837735

Association for the Study of Higher Education. (2007). Definitions and conceptual framework. *ASHE Higher Education Report, 32*(5), 7–12.

Bradley University. (n.d.). *The history of Bradley University.* https://www.bradley.edu/about/history/

Brownell, J. E., & Swaner, L. E. (2009). High-impact practices: Applying the learning outcomes literature to the development of successful campus programs. *Peer Review, 11*(2), 26–30. https://www.proquest.com/scholarly-journals/high-impact-practices-applying-learning-outcomes/docview/216602278/se-2?accountid=14168

Coker, J. S., Heiser, E., Taylor, L., & Book, C. (2017). Impacts of experiential learning depth and breadth on student outcomes. *Journal of Experiential Education, 40*(1), 5–23. https://doi.org/10.1177/1053825916678265

Finley, A. P., & McNair, T. (2013). *Assessing underserved students' engagement in high-impact practices.* Association of American Colleges & Universities.

Hart Research Associates. (2016). Falling short? College learning and career success. *NACTA Journal, 60*(1a), 1–13. https://www.aacu.org/sites/default/files/files/LEAP/2015employerstudentsurvey.pdf

Harward, D. (2012). *Transforming undergraduate education.* Rowman & Littlefield.

Kilgo, C., Ezell Sheets, J., & Pascarella, E. (2015). The link between high-impact practices and student learning: Some longitudinal evidence. *Higher Education, 69*(4), 509–525. https://doi.org/10.1007/s10734-014-9788-z

Kuh, G. D. (2008). *High-impact educational practices: What they are, who has access to them, and why they matter.* Association of American Colleges & Universities.

Kuh, G. D., O'Donnell, K., & Reed, S. (2013). *Ensuring quality and taking high-impact practices to scale.* Association of American Colleges & Universities.

National Society for Experiential Education. (1998). *Principles of best practice in experiential education* [Standards Document].

Neill, N. O. (2010). Internships as a high-impact practice: Some reflections on quality. *Peer Review, 12*(4), 4–8. https://www.proquest.com/scholarly-journals/internships-as-high-impact-practice-some/docview/822747510/se-2?accountid=14168

Tierney, W. G. (2008). *The impact of culture on organizational decision-making: Theory and practice in higher education*. Stylus.

Trolian, T. L., & Jach, E. A. (2020). Engagement in college and university applied learning experiences and students' academic motivation. *Journal of Experiential Education, 43*(3), 317–335. https://doi.org/10.1177/1053825920925100

Working Group. (2017). *Proposal to replace the Core Practice term Integrative Learning with Experiential Learning*. Bradley University.

15

INCREASING STUDENT ACCESS AND LEARNING IN EMPLOYMENT AND INTERNSHIP EXPERIENCES

Joe O'Shea, Myrna Hoover, and James Hunt

Student employment and internship experiences are widespread in higher education. For decades, colleges and universities have supported students in work-based activities on their campuses and beyond, through federal work-study funding, internship, and campus employment programs. Done well, research suggests student engagement in these forms of experiential learning can elevate a student's academic performance and success, especially for those from underrepresented backgrounds, and help students successfully launch into employment or further education (Miller et al., 2017).

Over the years, educators consistently questioned the value and quality of these activities, and who participates. At many institutions, there is wide variation in how these programs are deployed, monitored, and assessed. These variations, unfortunately, can result in missed opportunities for students, particularly among underrepresented and lower income students, to engage in what can be high-impact practices (HIPs; Finley & McNair, 2013). Over half of U.S. college students are first generation and these students, among others, may face awareness, mentorship, networking, financial, and other obstacles that can hinder participation (Cataldi et al., 2018). More importantly, many students do not experience the growth opportunities that they often need to develop their full potential.

Addressing these inequities is a challenge for higher education, with increased pressure to improve student outcomes and respond to changing labor market needs. Many states also recognize this challenge, calling for a renewed focus on helping students prepare for and secure jobs. If improving the potential for social mobility is one of the promises of a college education, then it is incumbent upon institutions to expand career-building HIPs to all students. Because student employment and internship experiences are already common in higher education, these activities are positioned to become a vehicle for widespread HIPs. How can higher education elevate the consistency and quality of student learning in these activities and expand access to them? Many institutions, such as Florida State University (FSU), recognize this issue and are reimagining their programming to broaden participation and to align with the standards of HIPs.

Pedagogies and Practice

FSU is a large research university with a student body of about 43,000 students, 33,000 of whom are undergraduates. The student body is diverse, with nearly a third receiving Pell Grants and about the same percentage the first in their family to attend college. Institutional research at FSU, as measured through our required Graduating Senior Survey (GSS) and course registration data, finds that undergraduate engagements in experiential learning increased 153% from 2015 to 2019.

Although participation in work-based learning opportunities was widespread and many students participated in several engagements, gaps remained, with lower rates of participation from key student subpopulations. Notably, in 2014–2015, Pell Grant recipients completing the GSS indicated they participated in experiential learning at a rate approximately 2 percentage points lower than non-Pell recipients; this gap narrowed slightly under 1.5 percentage points by 2018–2019. Additionally, transfer students participated in experiential learning at dramatically lower rates than their first-time-in-college (FTIC) peers; in 2014–2015, transfer student participation was nearly 18 percentage points lower than the FTIC students, and by 2018–2019, their participation had only marginally improved.

Building on several years of efforts to expand experiential learning, in spring 2019, the FSU Faculty Senate voted to add a university-wide experiential learning graduation requirement within the liberal studies curriculum for undergraduates. Called *Formative Experience*, students must complete either one internship, undergraduate research, international study, service-learning, or significant leadership experience prior to graduation. FSU has long recognized the value of using experiential learning to advance student success and to enrich students' lives after graduation. Moreover, the university saw the requirement as a statement for higher education—that colleges and universities can provide high-quality HIPs for every student, regardless of family income or circumstance.

Reaching scale, and doing so in ways that enhance student learning, is not without challenges. FSU wanted to ensure that these experiences would be meaningful and intentional. The university established high standards, requiring substantial and sustained engagement and reflection by participating students as well as clearly defined mentoring and oversight by faculty and staff. Therefore, the implementation strategies aim to provide structure, resources, and pathways for students to engage in this form of experiential learning while maintaining strong graduation rates and ensuring that students receive the necessary financial support for their participation. FSU's institutional strategy to scale student participation and learning involves four integrated pillars that together create scaffolded pathways for students. These include (a) overcoming student information and mentorship barriers and increasing awareness of opportunities; (b) integrating more experiential learning into the curriculum so students encounter it along the way to graduation; (c) developing and scaling low-cost models of experiential learning and increasing financial assistance to students; and (d) improving tracking, evaluation, and student reflection and professional development.

Evidence of Data-Supported Equity and Quality of Research

FSU's strategies aim at increasing the number of students who engage in experiential learning, elevating quality and learning through standardized protocols, establishing new expectations for supervisors as mentors, and amplifying students' postgraduation outcomes. Although these strategies are ongoing, the early data from the GSS suggest they are increasing student participation and access.

Data from the GSS, however, have found mixed results when examining internship participation and possible correlations with postgraduation outcome data in logistic regression models that controlled for student demographics and academic performance. Although unpaid internships produced neutral or even negative results, students who completed paid internships in 2018–2019 were 1.4 times more likely to have a job offer after graduation as compared to students who did not. The more pronounced effects for paid internships mirror national research from the National Association of Colleges and Employers (NACE, 2019a) finding that students with paid internships were 34% more likely to receive at least one job offer than students who participated in an unpaid internship. In the following, each pillar of the FSU strategy is reviewed in more detail.

The First Pillar

1. *Overcoming student information and mentorship barriers and increasing awareness of opportunities.* Students often cannot or do not know how to find information about what, how, and when they should integrate these work-based learning experiences into their undergraduate careers. Addressing this involved a comprehensive university effort, starting from preorientation through graduation, with particular attention to supporting first-generation, transfer, and underserved populations.

First, this involved extensive outreach and awareness building, starting with introducing and embedding experiential learning topics in the online preorientation required for all incoming students. Discussion and planning with students continue in summer bridge programs for first-generation students, first-year and transfer seminars, student success courses, and learning communities, in which students are asked to start engaging with resources and begin to map out their experiential learning pathways. Trained peer, staff, faculty, career advisors, and mentors provide student guidance in these settings.

To help students prioritize and plan for engagements, the university developed cocurricular pathways (ProfessioNole Pathways) that provide road maps, milestones, and incentives that culminate in badging and noncredit certificates for students. These maps are integrated into academic and career advising conversations, helping students identify the skills that they can develop during college. These pathways help students plan for and integrate experiential learning into their undergraduate experience by connecting them to academic and program-specific opportunities and campus-wide engagement opportunities.

To provide additional expertise and guidance for students, the university's Career Center leveraged its extensive network of career advisors (centrally located staff who advise students on a walk-in basis) and career liaisons (career specialists housed in academic colleges). Career liaisons are located in the academic colleges to support students in that particular academic unit, "meeting them where they are." Career staff use the cognitive information processing (CIP) theory-based approach to help students create an individual learning plan based on the student's knowledge about their interests, values, and career options and learn how to use information-seeking behavior and effective decision-making to successfully find and obtain career opportunities (Sampson et al., 2004). Special attention and personalized outreach are conducted in partnership with programs that support first-generation and other underrepresented students. Dedicated career advisors provide advising and programming to both transfer students and first-generation students. The university also digitally centralized experiential opportunity listings so that all students could see and apply for positions on one platform. Before these centralization efforts, students with information access barriers and unfamiliarity with the college environment often missed out on opportunities, which also meant application pools for many positions were not as robust as they could be. The effort resulted in 95% of on-campus experiential learning and 100% of Florida part-time, paid opportunities in the centralized system receiving applications from FSU students.

Students are also encouraged to engage in the university's mentoring platform, ProfessioNole Mentors, to establish professional connections with alumni and employers in their fields of interest. This campus-wide solution enhances existing programs providing a platform for mentees to seek out mentors for advice on a variety of topics ranging from job searching to general career advice. As of early 2020, the platform had over 1,500 active mentors and nearly 1,300 active student users. Alumni affinity groups are now searchable in the mentorship platform to increase connections between students and mentors based on their background and ethnicity. Mentors from Black, Hispanic/Latinx, Asian American, and veterans alumni affinity groups are highly active, with more groups being formed.

The Second Pillar

2. *Integrating more experiential learning into the curriculum so students encounter it along the way to graduation.* Doing so can remove barriers for some students and allow students to efficiently integrate experiential learning into their academic pathways. Further embedding experiential learning in the curriculum involved scaling existing experiential learning courses; creating or revising courses, including no-cost zero-credit courses; and bolstering students' competency development through the curriculum. To increase opportunities and access, the university also leveraged the Career Center's Experience Recognition Program (ERP) zero-credit course.

The ERP course incorporates national experiential learning guidelines by providing students a structured, guided process for reflection and feedback on workplace learning and performance, and an experiential learning achievement to highlight on their résumés and portfolios. In 2019–2020, over 1,000 students completed the course. Approved by the university's governing board in 1975, this course provided cooperative education recognition for students in 53 disciplines. As co-op experiences diminished and internships increased, 35 of these courses were replaced with credit-bearing academic internship courses. In 2014, the course was broadened to accept all forms of experiential learning. In 2019, to prepare for the university's new formative experience requirement, the course was collapsed to five sections that align with internship, research, service, international, and leadership engagements.

Course enrollment requires that the student have a career-related experience that provides the student development of knowledge, skills, and competencies. Enrolled students define the intentional learning goals and the engagement responsibilities in consultation with both the course instructor and site supervisor, elevating all parties' expectations. Intentional readings related to a student's engagement type and a career readiness pathway guide them in reflection and professional development in career readiness, professional communication, résumé writing, interview preparation, diversity and inclusion, career portfolio development, and salary and job negotiations. This elective course especially attracts students from departments that do not offer distinct internship courses and/or students who want transcript recognition of their experience without incurring tuition associated with a credit-bearing course. This no-cost option opens engagement for students who may not have participated in a formative experience because of financial limitations. A Career Center professional teaches the course with assistance from a graduate assistant.

Nationally, NACE (2019b) research finds a significant gap between the career competency skills that students have developed and the skills employers desire. To further complement curricular offerings and cultivate students' professional competencies, noncredit certificate programs are being integrated into courses. Launched in fall 2019, FSU's ProfessioNole Ready program provides no-cost, university-wide, online career readiness training and badging for students to enhance their career and competency development. A resource for all students, regardless of time, location, background, diverse ability, or learning style, this curriculum features 14 modules, 38 interactive activities, and 120 videos within the university's learning management system (LMS). The learning modules based on the NACE career competencies help students effectively develop and articulate their skills and become more confident in their career decisions. In 2019–2020, more than 900 students enrolled in the program, and during the 2020 online learning period implemented due to COVID-19, engagement increased by 173%. Integrating this program into introductory departmental summer bridge, internship, capstone, seminar, and college-specific "Careers In" courses exposes students early to career readiness competencies.

The Third Pillar

3. *Developing and scaling low-cost models of experiential learning and expanding financial assistance.* The university expanded opportunities to reach the diversity of learners at the institution through leveraging on-campus internship programs, remote experiences, employer partnerships, and federal work-study funding. First, this effort involved elevating the

expectations of organizations, university partners, and the institution itself surrounding talent development. Specifically, the university administration used messaging, relationship building, and educational campaigns to partner with employers, local and statewide chambers of commerce, and others to help them see themselves as part of the university's experiential learning initiatives. The campaigns, showcasing the university's work-based learning programs, helped employers understand their role in broadening the talent pipeline and meeting their labor needs. These new expectations also meant incorporating internships into university contracts. Like most institutions of higher education, the university conducts business with major organizations, and it established a precedent of including paid internships as part of major contracts with the university. For instance, new Coca-Cola and Sodexo contracts for beverage and food supply included several paid internships as part of the contracts. The inclusion of internships signaled an institutional priority; doing business with the university meant playing a role in educating the next generation of talent.

Expanding work-based learning also meant cultivating opportunities to expose different careers to students early in their higher education journey. In fall 2016, the university formalized the FSUshadow program. The program encourages short-term (i.e., 1 day or a few days) career exposure opportunities, most commonly done during breaks in the academic calendar. These in-person or virtual lower level commitments allow for an easy way for students to connect with alumni and other friends of the university and often lead to subsequent internship positions. The Federal Bureau of Investigation, for instance, hosts dozens of students with a shadow day, including simulation of FBI investigations, and some of these students receive internships with the organization. In 2019–2020, over 600 students participated in FSUshadow, and since its inception, more than 1,200 students matched with a variety of experiences across the country; 24% of summer and fall 2019 employer hosts reported hiring or making a hiring offer to their shadowing students for either an internship or full-time position.

Increasing experiential learning opportunities also included expanding on-campus internships, leveraging the university as a learning laboratory for work-based experiential learning. In spring 2018, InternFSU, a paid, on-campus internship program, created additional internship opportunities for students regardless of financial or travel limitations. Participating students gain career-related experience; receive feedback, guidance, and mentorship from their site supervisors; and can earn academic credit or complete the ERP to meet the university's formative experience requirement. From the program's inception in spring 2018 to spring 2020, more than 529 students gained career readiness skills at more than 125 campus internship sites.

Because resources are scarce, expanding student participation also involved looking for ways to repurpose existing funding and opportunities. As such, the university leveraged work-study funding and repurposed positions to expand opportunities and deepen student learning. The university realized that converting work-study-funded positions to formative, experiential learning opportunities would present many possibilities. Many university departments and centers elevated their positions by redefining their roles and requiring students in work-study-funded positions to register for the ERP, either in the zero-credit course or the certificate option.

In addition, the university identified remote internship opportunities for students. These remote opportunities support students who cannot afford to relocate or are unable to find opportunities geographically close to the university, providing them access to opportunities throughout the globe without leaving their home community. This convenience factor also provided additional opportunities to students with care and family responsibilities who found themselves place-bound.

Finally, the university also found resources from existing budgets, donors, and other organizations to launch new scholarship funds to support experiential education for students who could not otherwise participate in them because of cost. Students can receive funding for the costs to engage in the experience as well as for potential lost income or other opportunity costs during the activity. Together, the university and its colleges distribute over US$2 million annually to support experiential learning activity.

The Fourth Pillar

4. *Improving tracking, evaluation, and student reflection and professional development.* The university worked to expand and create an infrastructure to manage experiential opportunities and record these activities. These efforts seek to ensure quality in the experiences, identify desired learning outcomes, and articulate the skills students acquire through facilitated reflection and feedback. To develop a university-wide ecosystem that not only connects students to experiential learning but also provides institutional accountability and quality, a community of faculty and staff was created to champion and facilitate student career development. The Internship Council, which includes representatives from 15 colleges, 67 departments, and four centers, meets at least three times per year to facilitate student engagement in HIPs. The council shares resources and data to track student engagement more consistently across the institution and to ensure standard elements are included in all experiences.

Until fall 2012, engagement in experiential learning was tracked through course coding and ERP data. In order to identify the number and type of experiential learning engagements across students' time in college, the university added an exit survey as a graduation requirement, resulting in success data from over 92% of the graduates. These survey data are coupled with data from a 6-month follow-up survey and institutional student data. Together, the university can track student activities and outcomes both in and beyond the classroom. These data are assessed and distributed on campus, in institutional performance dashboards for each department and through biannual meetings and briefs with each academic dean. Data are also shared off campus through promotional materials to students, governing bodies, employers, and others to highlight the university's commitment to student success.

The university also celebrates student engagement and champions excellence in these experiences through programs like the Garnet and Gold Scholar Society (GGSS), the Student Employee of the Year Award (SEOTY), and student success feature stories. The GGSS facilitates involvement and recognizes students who excel beyond the classroom by meeting program criteria in three of the five experiential learning engagement types. The SEOTY awards recognize the contributions from the more than 5,000 student employees who play an integral role in campus operations. Stories of students' successes posted online through websites and social media allow other students to learn the value of these formative experiences.

The university supports students in articulating and showcasing the evidence of their knowledge, skills, and abilities to potential employers and others through platforms like the FSU Career Portfolio, LinkedIn, and Folio, the university's badging platform. Earned badges and training from Folio can be displayed to highlight a student's achievements and artifacts of their work and proof of competence, skill development, and mastery in both academic and cocurricular work. Students are encouraged to display educational and professional content, upload images, videos (e.g., YouTube, Vimeo), PDFs, text documents, and more.

Developing a Strategy for Your Institution

As the FSU case study illustrates, expanding student participation and learning in experiential learning requires thinking comprehensively about the many barriers, challenges, and opportunities that exist. The following are four key questions to ask in developing such a strategy:

1. Assess what barriers exist on your campus for students to understand, locate, and engage in experiential learning. What are data and students telling you about participation trends and the obstacles students are facing?

2. What curricular opportunities exist to embed experiential learning, and what support is needed to do so?
3. Evaluate what internal and external partners, including alumni, exist who can provide new opportunities, funding, and mentorship. Does the institution have a compelling vision for the role of experiential learning, and how are donors and other partners responding?
4. How do you know your students are learning in experiential opportunities, and how can you amplify learning and professional development?

Over the past few years, much has been done to scale student participation in meaningful experiential learning—but much is left to do. Deeper assessment of these experiences and their impact on student outcomes long term, including postgraduation, will guide university initiatives. To continue to scale opportunities to reach more students, the university will need to continue to increase need-based funding, convert additional work-study positions into internships, leverage virtual opportunities, and develop additional external partnerships.

Higher education continues to be one of the best investments for our students and for our economy. We must fully unlock the potential of our students with the types of experiences that will empower them to be successful and make an even greater impact when they graduate. Together with business, government, research, and international partners, we can build a higher education system where every student can participate in HIPs. Doing so will help reimagine the talent-development possibilities of our country and realize even more of the promise of higher education. Until every student has the opportunity to engage in HIPs this work will not be finished.

References

Cataldi, E. F., Bennett, C. T., & Chen, X. (2018). First-generation students: College access, persistence, and postbachelor's outcomes. *Stats in Brief* (NCES 2018-421). National Center for Education Statistics. https://nces.ed.gov/pubsearch/pubsinfo.asp?pubid=2018421

Finley, A. P., & McNair, T. (2013). *Assessing underserved students' engagement in high-impact practices.* Association of American Colleges & Universities. https://www.aacu.org/sites/default/files/files/assessinghips/AssessingHIPS_TGGrantReport.pdf

Miller, A. L., Rocconi, L. M., & Dumford, A. D. (2017). Focus on the finish line: Does high-impact practice participation influence career plans and early job attainment? *Higher Education, 75*(3), 489–506. https://doi.org/10.1007/s10734-017-0151-z

National Association of Colleges and Employers. (2019a, May). *Class of 2019 student survey*. https://www.naceweb.org/store/2019/2019-nace-student-survey-report-four-year-schools/

National Association of Colleges and Employers. (2019b, March). *The four career competencies employers value most*. https://www.naceweb.org/career-readiness/competencies/the-four-career-competencies-employers-value-most/

Sampson, J. P., Jr., Reardon, R. C., Peterson, G. W., & Lenz, J. G. (2004). *Career counseling and services: A cognitive information processing approach*. Brooks/Cole.

16

HIGH-IMPACT PRACTICES IN THE CURRICULUM

Implementing and Assessing a High-Impact Practice Course Designation Program

Bradley Wilson, Brian Danielson, Jason Hilton, and Kevin McCarthy

There has been increased interest in developing high-impact practices (HIPs) for students and providing equitable access to HIPs throughout higher education (Kuh, 2008). In this chapter, we describe one approach to increasing student participation in HIPs by engaging faculty in specialized professional development designed both to broaden faculty understanding of HIPs and embed HIPs throughout the curriculum. At Slippery Rock University, a specific process of faculty professional development was established that makes use of a modified faculty learning community (FLC) structure (Cox, 2004) to support and incentivize faculty members to incorporate HIPs into their classes. Successful completion of the professional development program results in improved pedagogy, HIP course designation for the faculty member, and improved communication of HIPs to students. The HIP designation is recorded in the faculty member's section(s) of the course in our student information system.

Institutional Profile and Context

Slippery Rock University (SRU) is a teaching-oriented public regional higher education institution (Carnegie master's designation) in western Pennsylvania and is part of a 14-university state-owned system. The total enrollment is about 8,800 students, with roughly 7,400 undergraduates and 1,400 graduate students. In 2014, the language and concept of HIPs were explicitly introduced at SRU. One result was the development of a process by which faculty members could have their courses designated as incorporating HIPs in one of six areas: collaborative learning, global learning, diversity learning, service-learning, undergraduate research, and writing-intensive experiences. These six areas were seen as most amenable to direct integration into the pedagogy and content of credit-bearing courses. By embedding HIPs directly into courses, SRU attempted to address some of the equity issues relating to access to cocurricular programs that require additional time and/or money for participation, which can create barriers for underrepresented minority students, first-generation students, and students from low-income families.

First Attempt

Our initial effort at a course designation process was initiated in the fall of 2014 and launched the following year. A faculty member desiring the HIP course designation submitted an application that included their course syllabus and a brief explanation of how they were incorporating the specific HIP into their course. A small faculty committee reviewed the application using a rubric that had been developed for the purpose. This initial effort to implement a HIP course designation process met with limited success. Applications for course designation tapered off between 2015 and 2017. Initially, only 38 courses were designated as HIP. It was clear that there were barriers preventing faculty from embracing this initial process.

The first barrier was that the process itself was not faculty-friendly. With little administrative guidance or professional development support, faculty were required to develop and submit a HIP-rich syllabus and a written justification for how their course met the identified characteristics of a HIP. Rubrics were created for each of the six HIPs by a small faculty committee using the Liberal Education and America's Promise VALUE (Valid Assessment of Learning in Undergraduate Education) rubrics, developed by the Association for American Colleges & Universities. However, scoring rubrics were not consistent across the different HIPs. Second, the peer review process was opaque to the submitting faculty member. Third, the process did not always move forward in a timely fashion and was perceived by faculty as an administrative priority without clearly defined outcomes. Finally, and perhaps most importantly, it was not clear to the faculty members why they should invest the time in earning the designation, because it was not tied directly to any particular goal, outcome, or reward for the faculty member.

Second Attempt

Despite this slow start, HIP practices continued to play an important role in our strategic goals. This was manifested in other ways, such as the creation of the Office for Community-Engaged Learning (OCEL) to support service-learning within and beyond the curriculum, increased support for students to participate in short-term faculty-led international programs, and additional resources to support collaborative faculty–student research, scholarship, and creative activity. As we reconsidered the designation process, we realized that the use of FLCs could be an ideal vehicle for promoting the development of HIP-designated classes. The structure used at SRU is based on a model developed by Cox (2004) at Miami University, defining an FLC as

> a cross-disciplinary faculty and staff group of six to fifteen members (eight to twelve members is the recommended size) who engage in an active, collaborative, yearlong program with a curriculum about enhancing teaching and learning and with frequent seminars and activities that provide learning, development, the scholarship of teaching, and community building. [Miami University] FLCs offer a more structured and intensive program than other faculty groups that meet and work on teaching and learning issues, such as teaching circles (Quinlan, 1996), book clubs, seminars, or brown-bag luncheon discussion groups. . . . Multidisciplinarity and community are the elements that allow FLCs to excel in teaching and learning pursuits. An FLC is a particular kind of community of practice. (p. 8)

The structure of FLCs described by Cox (2004) allows for FLCs to contribute to a variety of goals related to teaching and learning, including building university-wide community through the scholarship of teaching and learning, broadening the evaluation of teaching and assessment of learning, increasing faculty collaboration across disciplines, and creating an awareness of the complexity of teaching and learning. These higher order goals can be achieved in addition to the specific goals of the topic of a particular FLC, which in our case would be to engage faculty in an exploration of particular HIPs, leading to the incorporation of HIPs throughout SRU programs.

At SRU, the FLC model consists of a group of faculty members from across the disciplines who engage in an active, collaborative, semester-long program with a curriculum focused on incorporating characteristics of a relevant HIP into a course taught by each participant. Each FLC is led by a facilitator and includes some combination of seminar-type meetings and activities that provide learning and development around the use of HIPs in a course, as well as discussion within the FLC meant to encourage cross-disciplinary perspectives. At the end of the semester, each faculty member who successfully completes an FLC will have modified a course to include one of six designated HIPs such that the course is deemed ready for official designation. The FLC cohort works collaboratively to approve the course, leading to investment in one another's work and a ground-up, faculty-driven process for implementing HIPs into the curriculum. At SRU, this FLC process is now required to have any course designated as including HIPs.

One key aspect of the SRU approach is the incentives connected to the FLC process, designed to target the myriad of motivations present for academics throughout their careers. Of most benefit was the opportunity to interact intellectually across departments and colleges. Many of our participants reported that the chance to think critically and constructively with their peers about bettering their own courses was not only intellectually stimulating but allowed them to gain the additional benefit of different perspectives across the FLC. At the successful completion of the FLC and the designation of a faculty member's course as containing a HIP, the faculty member was issued a letter from our Center for Teaching and Learning that acknowledged their participation and growth in the scholarship of teaching and learning. This letter serves as evidence for future performance reviews, having been worded specifically to align with local policies and procedures relating to probationary, tenure, promotion, and recurring evaluations. Finally, successful completion of the HIP FLCs was rewarded by a small increase in professional development funding (US$300), which faculty could use for future conference fees and travel. As a whole, the approach offered something for any faculty member who wished to engage.

Implementation of the new approach began in the late summer of 2017. The summer and early fall semester of 2017 were used to develop the process and to identify facilitators for each FLC. Because several of the HIP areas overlapped with cocurricular offices (notably diversity learning, global learning, and service-learning), we included as cofacilitators nonfaculty professionals in those areas. As the fall semester progressed, the FLCs attracted considerable faculty interest, with 54 faculty members beginning the process. Each FLC group had an organizational meeting near the end of the semester in preparation for the full launch of the HIP FLC process in the spring. Once in the HIP FLCs, faculty participants were encouraged to focus on one of their current classes in which to incorporate characteristics of the targeted HIP. Additionally, the FLC spent time discussing what the designated HIP could look like in a classroom setting, considering examples of HIP implementation in the literature, and exploring how best to assess student success in the area of the targeted HIP. At the conclusion of the FLC, participants achieved a HIP designation for their class based on the consensus of the

FLC via presentations to the group by each participant. The designation was specific to the type of HIP incorporated rather than a generic HIP designation for all courses (e.g., HIP-S for service-learning).

The FLC process met with rapid success. The total number of designated courses increased from 38 (fall 2018) to 140 (July 2020). Also, the number of faculty members with one or more HIP-designated courses increased from 15 (fall 2018) to 82 (spring 2020). Because multiple sections of the same course could be offered by a HIP-designated faculty member, the total number of individual classes offered increased from 19 (fall 2018) to 100 (spring 2020). Finally, the total number of students taking a HIP-designated class grew as follows: 680 (fall 2018), 1,775 (spring 2019), 2,421 (fall 2019), 2,702 (spring 2020), with an additional 540 in summer and winter sessions.

Initial Assessment Results

One of the long-term goals of the development of the new process is to collect data over time relating to the impact of HIP-designated courses. Because the courses receive an Ellucian Banner designation, they can be identified and the outcomes of students who enroll in HIP-designated classes can be compared with those who do not. Incorporating student demographic information will allow us to review the participation rates and impact on different groups: students from traditionally underrepresented groups, Pell-eligible students, and first-generation students.

One of the most common program outcomes that is measured is the correlation between participation in the program and progression to degree or student GPA. While we are still in the early stages of our process, we have done a preliminary analysis of impact on students who entered SRU as 1st-year, full-time students in the fall of 2016. The students in this cohort have had opportunities to take HIP-designated classes. It is also a cohort for which we have data on 4-year graduation rates as well as continuation to the 5th year (for those not graduating in 4 years).

The initial size of the fall 2016 cohort was 1,544. However, because the HIP-designated courses were not available until fall 2018, we compared only those students from the fall 2016 cohort who were retained until their 4th fall in 2019, because this subgroup would capture all of those students who had an opportunity to take HIP-designated classes in fall 2018–spring 2019. This subgroup consisted of 1,067 students, of which 475 students took zero HIP courses, 322 took one HIP course, and 270 took two or more (see Table 16.1).

TABLE 16.1
Comparing Outcomes of Students by HIP Course Count for All Students Retained to 4th Fall

Number of HIP Courses Taken	*Count of Students*	*% Graduating in 4 Years*	*% Retained to 5th Year*	*Average Cumulative GPA*
0	475	75.8	17.9	3.31
1	322	68.9	25.5	3.34
2+	270	64.1	31.5	3.28
Grand Total	1,067	70.8	23.6	3.31

In Table 16.1, students who took one or two+ HIP classes showed a decrease in the 4-year graduation rate, though that was offset by a higher rate of continuation to the 5th year. Combining the 4-year graduation rate with 5th year continuation shows a slight increase (though not likely statistically significant) in the number of HIP courses taken (0 HIP: 93.7%, 1 HIP: 94.4%, 2+ HIP: 95.6%). The average cumulative GPAs of the three groups of students did not vary significantly.

Subpopulation Differences

Tables 16.2, 16.3, and 16.4 reproduce the data in Table 16.1 (i.e., looking only at fall 2016 cohort students who had persisted to their 4th fall) and add in the demographic dimensions of interest: underrepresented minority (URM) status (excluding international students and students with an unknown race/ethnicity), first-generation status, and Pell eligibility. In each table and for each HIP-count group, the difference between the majority and the minority groups is indicated to facilitate analysis of the potential impact that taking HIP courses might have on intragroup differences.

These data do not show a correlation between the number of HIP courses and shrinking achievement gaps, whether measured by the 4-year graduation rate or by the cumulative GPAs of students. In fact, in each of these three tables, generally, the reverse is true. Within URM students, first-generation students, and Pell-eligible students, the achievement gap actually increases with an increase in HIP-designated classes taken. One feature that balances this result is that when both 4-year graduation and continuation to 5th year are combined, there is little difference between the various pairings. The differences thus may disappear when we look at 6-year graduation rates (which are not yet available for this cohort).

TABLE 16.2

Comparing Outcomes of Students by HIP Course Count for All Students Retained to 4th Fall by URM Status

Number of HIP Courses Taken	*URM Status*	*Count of Students*	*% Graduating in 4 Years*	*% Retained to 5th Year*	*Average Cumulative GPA*
0	Non-URM	409	78.2	16.1	3.33
	URM	59	62.7	28.8	3.16
	Difference		15.5	-12.7	0.17
1	Non-URM	291	70.4	24.1	3.37
	URM	29	55.2	41.4	3.14
	Difference		15.3	-17.3	0.22
2+	Non-URM	232	67.7	28.4	3.31
	URM	36	41.7	50.0	3.06
	Difference		26.0	-21.6	0.25
Grand Total		1,056	71.0	23.6	3.31

TABLE 16.3

Comparing Outcomes of Students by HIP Course Count for All Students Retained to 4th Fall by First-Generation Status

Number of HIP Courses Taken	*First-Generation Status*	*Count of Students*	*% Graduating in 4 Years*	*% Retained to 5th Year*	*Average Cumulative GPA*
0	Not First-Gen	318	74.5	19.8	3.32
	First-Gen	157	78.3	14.0	3.29
	Difference		-3.8	5.8	0.04
1	Not First-Gen	199	69.3	24.6	3.39
	First-Gen	123	68.3	26.8	3.27
	Difference		1.1	-2.2	0.12
2+	Not First-Gen	157	70.1	24.8	3.33
	First-Gen	113	55.8	40.7	3.20
	Difference		14.3	-15.9	0.12
Grand Total		1,056	70.8	23.6	3.31

TABLE 16.4
Comparing Outcomes of Students by HIP Course Count for All Students Retained to 4th Fall by Pell Eligibility

Number of HIP Courses Taken	*Pell-Eligible Status*	*Count of Students*	*% Graduating in 4 Years*	*% Retained to 5th Year*	*Average Cumulative GPA*
0	Not Pell-Eligible	345	78.8	14.8	3.33
	Pell-Eligible	130	67.7	26.2	3.26
	Difference		11.1	-11.4	0.08
1	Not Pell-Eligible	221	74.2	20.8	3.40
	Pell-Eligible	101	57.4	35.6	3.22
	Difference		16.8	-14.8	0.18
2+	Not Pell-Eligible	173	74.6	22.0	3.32
	Pell-Eligible	97	45.4	48.5	3.20
	Difference		29.2	-26.5	0.12
Grand Total		1,067	0.7	0.2	3.31

Preliminary Conclusions

In terms of faculty engagement and participation, the HIP FLC professional development program has been very successful. The number of faculty members with HIP-designated courses is approximately 20% of the total number of faculty members at SRU. Additionally, awareness of the program has created a better understanding of HIPs in general, beyond their implementation within the curriculum. These successes are a direct result of the use of the FLC process for learning about HIPs. The designation process enables faculty members to guide their professional development and encourages them to work with those in other departments and colleges. It also incentivizes faculty members by aligning with the evaluation process and providing support for continued scholarship of teaching and learning.

Considering the impact of taking HIP-designated classes on student success measured in terms of 4-year graduation rates or cumulative GPA, we do not have evidence of positive impact and, as just discussed, the impact on the achievement gap is slightly negative. However, before concluding that the program is not benefiting student learning, we need to consider some additional factors. First, the program has been in place for only 2 years. The cohort on which we are basing our analysis has only been able to take HIP-designated courses for four semesters and the last of those semesters was interrupted by the shift to fully online teaching due to the COVID-19 pandemic. It is too early to generalize from such a limited study population; a longer timeframe with data from additional cohorts will be more meaningful. Second, using the measures of graduation rates, persistence, and cumulative GPA implies a narrow idea of student success that does not allow for the consideration of more qualitative aspects such as enhanced learning and deeper engagement. Finally, it seems unlikely that taking one or a few classes that incorporate HIPs would have a large impact on student learning and student success. For example, global learning is a commonly cited HIP, usually understood in terms of a semester study abroad program or a significant international experience. Although taking a class that has been designated for global learning can achieve global learning outcomes to an extent, such a class is not likely to produce an equivalent impact on a student as would traveling to or living in another country and being immersed in a new culture.

One clear benefit of the program has been its success in "spreading the word" about HIPs among the faculty. Equally importantly, the program structure has given us the ability to incorporate HIP-appropriate assessment tools and processes directly into the curriculum. Many of us who are advocates for HIPs have a strong interest in looking at the impact of HIPs in a more fine-grained way—for example, by looking at specific student learning outcomes that HIPs promote and assessing student achievement with respect to those outcomes.

Through the designation process, specific learning outcomes associated with each HIP are explicitly incorporated into classes. In some cases, the learning outcomes are already part of the class, but the inclusion of a HIP strengthens the students' opportunity to achieve these outcomes and to a higher degree. For example, a political science course on campaigns and elections might have "civic engagement" as one of its learning outcomes. That learning outcome might be achieved through a group project in which groups work to study a candidate for office and create a campaign strategy and plan, culminating in a class presentation. The same course, with a service-learning HIP designation, could deepen that learning. Students might work more closely with an actual campaign, participate in organizing and staffing events, and work on "get out the vote" activities. In the HIP course, students will achieve the learning outcomes associated with civic engagement through both classroom and experiential activities, likely deepening their learning. One intriguing avenue for future research would be to compare direct assessment of student learning within HIP and non-HIP sections of the same course, or, more globally, between HIP and non-HIP courses that have the same university learning outcomes.

In addition to deepening student learning in connection with existing course outcomes, in some cases, the HIP designation leads to new learning outcomes being introduced into the class. As described earlier, undergraduate research is one of the designations at SRU, where research is understood in an inclusive way that allows for a variety of disciplinary perspectives. To achieve this HIP designation, the instructor incorporates research methods and projects into their courses. In most cases, these are courses that previously did not include research, so in achieving the HIP designation, a new learning outcome is introduced, such as "Developing expertise in research methods in the discipline." One of the goals of the Undergraduate Research FLC is to help faculty members understand different ways that research can be introduced to students in a class and how student learning in that area can be assessed.

In sum, the FLC HIP-designation program at SRU is less focused on promoting high-level university assessment targets than on promoting student learning. As we move forward, it will be crucial that we also measure specific HIP-relevant student learning outcomes in assessing the impact of HIP courses. Because the course designation process has been systematized, it is possible to ensure that assessments of particular student learning objectives are incorporated into the course design; this is an explicit component of the designation process. Having a systematized way of designating HIP courses supports a more fine-grained approach to evaluating the impact of HIP courses than the approach described earlier, thus serving as a strong complement to the higher level methods. In the final analysis, the basic goal of higher education is student learning and the assessment capabilities created through the FLC HIP process directly align with this goal.

References

Cox, M. D. (2004). Introduction to faculty learning communities. In M. D. Cox & L. Richlin (Eds.), *Building Faculty Learning Communities* (New Directions for Teaching and Learning, no. 97, pp. 5–23). Jossey-Bass. https://doi.org/10.1002/tl.129

Kuh, G. D. (2008). *High-impact educational practices: What they are, who has access to them, and why they matter.* Association of American Colleges & Universities.

17

USING ASSESSMENT DATA TO EXPAND ACCESS TO HIGH-IMPACT PRACTICES FOR EVERY STUDENT

Kimberly Yousey-Elsener and Kirsten Pagan

Measuring student participation in high-impact practices (HIPs) and its link to student success outcomes takes many years of refining methodology and enhancing practice. This chapter shares the evolution of that methodology as well as how findings continue to be used to open access and push Binghamton University to reach its 100% participation in designated HIPs goal. In 2013, Binghamton University launched its Roadmap to Premier, a strategic plan to elevate the institution as a leading public university. As part of the strategic planning process, Binghamton identified five signature HIPs: education abroad, internships, undergraduate research and creative work, community-engaged learning, and capstone/thesis, setting a goal that 100% of each undergraduate graduating cohort would participate in at least one designated HIP. These five HIPs were selected from the larger list of HIPs for one of two reasons. First, the university already had implemented some HIPs across the board (e.g., living-learning communities, writing-intensive courses); therefore, counting these would guarantee the target would be met. Second, the five selected already had some infrastructure in place via offices on campus, but there was an acknowledgment that the programs could be enhanced.

Specific university offices and/or academic programs, such as the Center for Civic Engagement, Fleishman Center for Career Development, External Scholarships and Undergraduate Research Center, and Education

Abroad, facilitated student engagement in many of Binghamton's designated HIPs. However, prior to the strategic plan, these units engaged in limited pockets of collaboration and little information was available on students' overall engagement in HIPs. In order to facilitate collaboration, the High-Impact Practices Innovations Council (HIPIC) was formed. This group brought together upper level administrators as well as staff from across the university whose offices have a role in engaging students in HIPs. Members include representatives from the Offices of the Vice President of Student Affairs and the Provost, Undergraduate Research, Career Services, Community Engagement, Education Abroad, Student Affairs Assessment, University Communications, and the University Development Office. This ever-evolving process is guided by "deep dives" into the data to ask new and relevant questions each year.

Summary of Relevant Literature

Despite studies linking HIPs with positive effects on student learning and development (Brownell & Swaner, 2009; Kilgo et al., 2015; Kinzie, 2013), there have been mixed results on directly linking participation in HIPs with retention and, therefore, graduation rates (Randall Johnson & Stage, 2018). Although the literature has yet to draw a definitive conclusion on the links between HIPs and retention/graduation, Binghamton University felt that it made sense to bring all of these concepts under the strategic plan and thereby create a direct link between HIPs and student success measured by retention, graduation, and career outcomes and investing resources to strengthen this link.

For first-destination career outcomes, the literature seems to support a more nuanced understanding. Wolniak and Engberg (2019) explained that "the relationship between high-impact experiences and early career outcomes presents a complex yet informative picture where high-impact experiences exert a relatively small and generally inconsistent influence on career outcomes in the years immediately following college graduation" (p. 848). Other work focused on specific HIPs such as service-learning, internships, and capstones showed positive influences on job placement after college (Callanan & Benzing, 2004; Saltikoff, 2017). Even with complex and sometimes contradictory empirical evidence, the university set off to strengthen its HIPs via a data-informed approach. Looking specifically at Binghamton's data, Handy Twang (2020) found positive relationships with participation in at least one of the five HIP experiences to career placement (employment or graduate school) as well as starting salary.

Identifying Gaps in Equity

The first question asked by HIPIC was *How many people are participating in HIPs?*—or, from a strategic planning mindset, *Is the university meeting the goal of 100%?* In order to answer this question a reliable dataset was needed. When Binghamton University launched its Roadmap to Premier, the institution adopted a cocurricular involvement platform (Binghamton initially purchased Engage, or CollegiateLink, by Campus Labs and then migrated to CampusGroups in 2019) to centralize student experiences and become the primary tracking tool for HIPs. The advantage of using an involvement platform versus a database is that it serves multiple constituencies on campus through three distinct access levels. Level 1 applies to the casual student user, who can do the following: identify specific clubs/organizations and events that interest them, interact with said groups, and log experiences (e.g., participation in an internship or research opportunity) on their individual cocurricular transcript (CCT). They may also monitor their progress through specific group-created curricula/tracks. Level 2 consists of group administrators, typically student club/organization officers or university personnel, who may use the system in the following ways: market group activities/events, communicate with members, and/or track student/cohort progress through a curriculum/track. Level 3 includes system-wide administrators, such as assessment staff, who ensure integrity of the records through routine maintenance and by conducting bird's-eye view reporting to respond to various constituencies. The system's ability to not only track event attendance and club members but also cocurricular experiences provided a strong foundation for tracking HIPs.

Once a platform was adopted, the challenge of getting data into the system began. The processes evolved over time, especially to address three key challenges: (a) identifying and validating experiences, (b) obtaining buy-in from campus partners, and (c) maximizing efficiencies. The initial focus was on gathering data from partner offices and the university's student records system, as opposed to relying on individual students to self-report. The decision to gather and vet experiences ensured that, first, each record met the institution's criteria for a given HIP and, second, it quickly maximized the volume of data available to inform decision-making. Experiences are validated via a two-step collaborative effort: The individual office or organization determines the quality of the experience; then the assessment office serves as the gatekeeper for whether or not an experience is loaded into the data system and how it is counted in the overall dataset. By nature of being for-credit (with specific criteria) and/or validated via offices sending rosters, this process ensured that a level of quality was maintained in a relatively efficient manner. This process continues to evolve to this day as experiences change, partnerships evolve, and opportunities are created. Although this seems like a simple process, it took years of building relationships, combing academic courses to identify those that qualified as HIPs, and refining systems for continuously uploading data into the involvement platform, referred to locally as "B-Engaged."

Overall Participation

By 2015, the university had consistent and reliable data with which to answer the first question: *How many students in each graduating cohort are participating in HIPs?* (Table 17.1).

This initial data told the first story. As cohorts grew by 33%, from 2015 to 2019, the percentage of those who participated in at least one HIP ranged from a low of 83% in 2016 to a high of 86% in 2018 and 2019. Therefore, the sheer numbers of students who participated in one or more HIPs also grew. Efforts to increase access to HIPs were working, but still needed to grow with the cohort size in order to see a jump beyond 86%.

Participation by HIP

With tracking systems in place, HIPIC's second question was easily answered: *Which HIPs are students participating in?* (Table 17.2). Most notably, participation in both community-engaged learning and undergraduate research and creative work grew by over 60%. This increase is likely explained by a combination of greater numbers of students and experiences as well as more robust data collection methods.

TABLE 17.1
Graduating Seniors Who Participated in at Least One HIP

	Total Seniors	*Seniors Having at Least One HIP*	
Cohort Year	*n*	*n*	*% of Cohort*
2015	2,000	1,704	85
2016	2,590	2,146	83
2017	2,417	2,042	84
2018	2,586	2,215	86
2019	2,659	2,279	86

TABLE 17.2
Graduating Seniors' Participation by HIP

High-Impact Practice	*2015*	*2019*	*% Change*
Education Abroad	230	268	17
Capstone/Thesis	624	922	48
Community-Engaged Learning	480	788	64
Undergraduate Research and Creative Work	442	719	63
Internship	1,233	1,534	24

Nonparticipation

By 2018, these basic metrics demonstrated that although focusing on HIPs was increasing participation and access, the average participation rate was around 85%, not the 100% target. This led to the next question: *Who are the nonparticipants?* This question was asked in order to begin to identify barriers to access. Known as the first deep dive into the data, a quantitative approach was used by exploring student demographic variables (i.e., school, major, cumulative GPA, admission type [1st-year/transfer], sex, nationality [international/domestic], race, NCAA athlete status, Educational Opportunities Program participant status), financial aid status (PELL/TAP recipient) and, finally, career outcomes at 6 months after graduation. Findings indicated that nonparticipants

- had lower employment/graduate education placement rates compared to the overall university;
- were mostly (90%) enrolled in the college of arts and sciences;
- had lower GPAs compared to participants; and
- were more likely to receive Pell/New York State Tuition Assistance Program (TAP) Grants.

Some emerging trends also suggest higher proportions of nonparticipants among transfer students, males, and international students relative to their populations at Binghamton.

HIPIC used this data to begin to open access via three important first steps. The first step was to offer more funding sources. Although there was some funding available for HIP experiences, these resources were often difficult for students to find and relied on students having strong networks between advisors, faculty, and other offices and often led to students jumping from one office to another. To improve access to funding, the university created a website with a centralized list of all funding sources and how to access them. This eliminated the reliance on word-of-mouth knowledge of funding and made it easier for students to quickly access funding sources. In addition, funding was increased via fundraising efforts. The University Development Office was charged with adding HIPs as a focus area for fundraising efforts and found much success in alumni and others wanting to help students access HIPs. This funding went directly back into increasing available funds and expanding the centralized list of funding available to students.

Second, the departments involved in HIPIC began expanding programs/partnerships in the college of arts and sciences. Given the wide variety of academic disciplines in this college, it was no surprise that the majority of nonparticipants were part of this school. Unlike the professional schools that embedded many HIPs into the curriculum, the diverse curricular paths in the arts and sciences led to a much less centralized approach. Although not a surprise, having the data helped to form partnerships that connected students and faculty with HIPs. These programs included career counselors in residence with specific academic departments; providing resources for faculty to receive training, support, and funding for creating community-engaged courses; and expanding undergraduate research beyond the STEM fields.

Third, HIPIC members began improving ways students initially access HIPs during their 1st year of study. The most visible of these include career development programs/retreats geared toward helping students "kick-start" their career development as well as expanding the 1st-year undergraduate research program beyond STEM fields to include students with an interest in humanities and social sciences. However, there was still more to learn, which led HIPIC to ask two additional questions: *Is there a natural sequence among HIPs for those who do participate?* and *What are the barriers to students not participating in HIPs?*

Sequence

In fall 2019, the question of sequence became a focus for an additional deep dive into the data. The premise is that by knowing students' natural progressions, intentional paths could be developed that mimic what is already occurring. Whereas the first HIPs reports looked "backward" from the point of graduation, the sequencing project explored students' actual participation in HIPs, looking "forward" from entrance year through the students' 4th year. The paths of 11,192 new 1st-year, first-time students who were admitted between the 2014–2015 and 2017–2018 academic years were explored.

TABLE 17.3
Participation in HIPs by Class Year

	Year 1	*Year 2*	*Year 3*	*Year 4*	*Total*
Count	4,159	4,829	5,407	4,582	18,977
%	22	25	28	24	100

When combined, HIPs were distributed in roughly equal proportions across the 4-year span. That is, approximately 25% of 18,977 grand total HIP experiences occurred each year (Table 17.3).

As a result of this exploration, the following trends were identified:

- Undergraduate research and creative work experiences (31%) occurred during the participant's 1st year.
- Community-engaged learning experiences (45%) also occurred during the participant's 1st year, followed closely by the 2nd year.
- Internship experiences (43%) occurred during the participant's 3rd year.
- Education abroad experiences (52%) also occurred during the participant's 3rd year.
- Capstone/thesis experiences (55%) occurred during the participant's 4th year.

The results of this analysis were sent to HIPIC members right before the university shifted its focus in response to the COVID-19 pandemic. Although the HIPIC committee had not met to discuss how to use these findings as of this publication, individual offices began using it to plan experiences for the following academic year. For example, the Center for Civic Engagement (CCE) looked at this data through the lens of their shifting work with faculty. As their efforts to support faculty in designing community-engaged learning (CEL) courses ramped up, they were seeing more faculty focus on designing experiences for upper level courses. The CCE talked about how that shift might lead to future data also shifting away from students having CEL experiences early in their academic experiences, which may change how students engage with the community. As they are working with more faculty, the results from this analysis have helped them stay more in tune with creating a balance of offerings across multiple years at the institution. In addition, the undergraduate research office appreciated that this was the first time they had quantitative evidence that more students were participating in research during their 1st and 2nd years. This data played a role in a proposal for the

Beckman Scholars Program that would allow them to focus on recruiting 1st- and 2nd-year students for the fellowships rather than upperclassmen. The data helped to show that some Binghamton students would be prepared after their 1st year to undertake such a prestigious research fellowship.

Barriers

The 2018 nonparticipant project (NPP) indicated that participating in HIPs matters when it comes to graduate outcomes, which Handy Twang (2020) later confirmed. Despite identifying who was not participating, the NPP did not provide information on why. Although educated guesses could be made, more evidence was needed. In spring 2020, a deep dive began into barriers to participation. Initially focus groups were designed, but that soon shifted to an open-ended survey format due to the university's response to COVID-19. The survey was sent to May 2020 graduating seniors who were enrolled in the School of Arts and Sciences and had not completed a HIP as of fall 2019. A little over 200 people responded to the survey. Although not as strong as a response rate as we would have liked, the survey yielded more responses than we would have been able to gather via focus groups and had enough responses to create trustworthy themes. This project provided initial groundwork for identifying barriers. It was clear that students were weighing the value of having a HIP experience against structural barriers, such as needing to work for financial income, family needs, being home for the summer, and academic demands of their majors. Students also shared that when they tried to apply for opportunities it was hard to start the process and they were not selected due to lack of experience.

Next Steps

With each additional deep dive into the data, the university learned how to reduce barriers and increase access to HIPs. Although the first look at nonparticipation did not identify traditional underserved student populations as the primary "who," it did identify compounding factors, such as income and GPA, that are known to often disproportionately affect Students of Color and first-generation college students. Each deep dive continues to expand conversations around how each of these data projects combined to give better clues as to how to increase access. For example, the sequencing project showed that many 1st-year students participate in undergraduate research through the 1st-year research programs. But the nonparticipant survey showed that students find it hard to get the process started, a few identifying research as one area where if they did not participate during their 1st year, it was harder to access opportunities in later years. Which leads to the question *How might more first-generation Students of Color and transfer students get involved in 1st-year research programs?* As deep dives are continued, each layer of data helps us in implementing change in order to increase access. Offices such as the Fleishman Center for Career Development and Student Transition and Success, which works with transfer students, are particularly interested in learning the answer to this question in order to enhance efforts moving forward.

The ability to track participation data centrally has allowed Binghamton University to explore participation at a higher level than individual units could achieve on their own. In addition, a centralized group, HIPIC, brings together campus leadership, directors of offices related to each HIP, and the data team to coordinate efforts, ask larger questions, put the data to use, and take steps to increase access. This group has taken on raising funds to support students who have financial barriers to participating, creating a centralized website where students can learn about experiences and find funding, implementing changes to programs that help connect experiences for students, and asking more questions of the data in order to continue the work. Future questions are waiting to be explored: *What does the sequence look like by academic discipline (e.g., business or engineering in contrast to arts and sciences)? Should student employment be added as a HIPs category? How can we help students with the first step and at the same time reduce structural challenges that make the first step difficult? What support structures helped those low-income and students with lower GPAs who participated in a HIP? How can support structures be made more available to students?*

As Binghamton University continues to explore pathways to success in engaging in HIPs, these and more questions will continue to arise. As a university, we are fortunate to have an evolving dataset that can grow and be harvested in the pursuit of reaching the 100% goal set forth in the strategic plan. When embarking on the journey of tracking/assessing HIPs, the following steps have been key to Binghamton's success and may be helpful to others:

- *Begin with an equity mindset.* When the intention from the start is to serve an institution's complete student body, resource allocation and program development will follow suit.
- *Get clear.* Why are HIPs important to your institution/your students? Is the goal simply to jump into the latest trends with appearances or to offer well-intentioned life-changing experiences?
- *Develop a concrete and concise framework.* Will you focus on tracking (and assessing) all 11-plus HIPs, or will you focus on a core few that best match your institution's mission and culture?
- *Take an inventory.* Who's already collecting and keeping what? Are there redundancies?

- *Invest in relationships.* Maintaining relationships with your colleagues from across the institution will ensure you're "looped in" as your institution develops new HIP programs.
- *Secure a champion.* Foster buy-in from a senior leader. Having this type of political support is helpful for breaking down obstacles, particularly in the early stages.
- *Include student voices.* Although collected data are great for answering "what" questions, go to the source when you need to know "why."

Although Binghamton University has a good problem on our hands (i.e., trying to get the last 15% of students to participate in HIPs), our team of educators maintains an attitude of positive restlessness, striving to make HIPs achievable for all.

References

Brownell, J., & Swaner, L. (2009). High-impact practices: Applying the learning outcomes literature to the development of successful campus programs. *Peer Review, 11*(2), 26–30. https://www.proquest.com/scholarly-journals/high-impact-practices-applying-learning-outcomes/docview/216602278/se-2?accountid=14168

Callanan, G., & Benzing, C. (2004). Assessing the role of internships in the career-oriented employment of graduating college students. *Education + Training, 46*(2), 82–89. https://doi.org/10.1108/00400910410525261

Handy Twang, A. (2020). *High-impact learning experiences and post-graduate outcomes: Exploring the influence on employment, continuing education and salary* [Manuscript submitted for publication]. Center for Civic Engagement, Binghamton University.

Kilgo, C., Sheets, J., & Pascarella, E. (2015). The link between high-impact practices and student learning: Some longitudinal evidence. *Higher Education, 69*, 509–525. https://doi.org/10.1007/s10734-014-9788-z

Kinzie, J. (2013). Taking stock of capstones and integrative learning. *Peer Review, 15*(4), 27–30. https://www.proquest.com/scholarly-journals/taking-stock-capstones-integrative-learning/docview/1506113339/se-2?accountid=14168

Randall Johnson, S., & Stage, F. K. (2018). Academic engagement and student success: Do high-impact practices mean higher graduation rates? *The Journal of Higher Education, 89*(5), 753–781. https://doi.org/10.1080/00221546.2018.1441107

Saltikoff, N. (2017). The positive implications of internships on early career outcomes. *NACE Journal.* https://www.naceweb.org/job-market/internships/the-positive-implications-of-internships-on-early-career-outcomes/

Wolniak, G., & Engberg, M. (2019). Do "high-impact" college experiences affect early career outcomes? *The Review of Higher Education, 42*(3), 825–858. https://doi.org/10.1353/rhe.2019.0021

18

TRACKING HIGH-IMPACT PRACTICE PARTICIPATION AND STUDENT SUCCESS WITH FIDELITY ACROSS A COMMUNITY COLLEGE SYSTEM

Heidi Leming

The College System of Tennessee, under the Tennessee Board of Regents (TBR), comprises 40 institutions, including 13 community colleges and 27 colleges of applied technology. Since 2013, Tennessee's Drive to 55 legislative initiative has sought to increase the percentage of citizens with postsecondary degrees and certificates to 55% by 2025. Curricular improvements for the TBR System have been done in concert with statewide policy reform, including two college access programs that have boosted college enrollment for traditional high school graduates (TN Promise) and adult learners (Reconnect; see Figure 18.1).

The TBR Completion Agenda prioritized several strategies to achieve student success goals, including providing academic foci, corequisite remediation, accessible online learning, guided degree and transfer pathways, and high-impact practices (HIPs). Under the priority strategy titled "Community, Belonging, and Inclusion," the TBR Office of Student Success has directed a scaling plan for HIPs that furthers the access and equity work outlined in the Completion Agenda. From the beginning, this work has been underpinned by the Association for American Colleges & Universities' (2011) Liberal

Figure 18.1. Timeline of major initiatives and milestones.

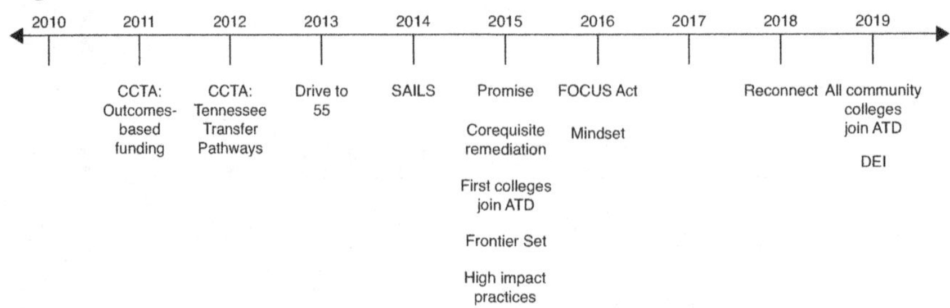

Education and America's Promise vision and essential learning outcomes, while being supported and supplemented by grants from both the Gates Foundation Frontier Set and the Lumina National Association of System Heads (NASH) TS3 HIPs program, as well as by system-wide participation in the Achieving the Dream network.

The Community, Belonging and Inclusion Priority Strategy recognizes that there is a growing body of research that suggests that noncognitive factors are hugely influential in the transition into postsecondary education and persistence to success. Recent work by Duckworth and Yeager (2015) for the Carnegie Foundation and research by Headden and McKay (2015) has shown that traits such as academic perseverance, grit, (one's ability to persevere and strive for long-term goals), and a sense of belonging play a powerful role in student success and completion. The greatest impact on student success appears to stem from students' total level of campus engagement, particularly when academic, interpersonal, and extracurricular involvements are mutually reinforcing (Pascarella & Terenzini, 2005).

Through the use of taxonomies that provided minimum definitions of practice for a set of identified HIPs, the system sought to systematically code student participation in the student information system in order to assess the impact on various student completion metrics and to see if a particular set of practices appears to be more effective in closing equity gaps. The goal was to identify those practices that seem to make the biggest difference for specific groups of students and to scale those practices for the benefit of all. The work in Tennessee illustrates how creating a framework for consistent and reliable data collection on student participation in HIPs provides evidence as to how quality implementation and scaling are possible across multiple institutions, supporting statewide college completion reform efforts.

Project Background

Beginning in 2015, the TBR System worked with six universities and 13 community colleges to include HIPs in the core structure of TBR's Momentum Year approach to the curriculum, which included four key components:

1. *Academic foci.* Students are guided to identify a specific major and career focus upon enrollment that aligns their career interests with a chosen academic degree or transfer pathway. Research investigating the effect of early engagement in focus area courses to student success in the TBR system showed incoming 1st-year students who successfully completed at least 9 hours in their focus area during their 1st academic year showed a dramatic increase in graduation rates over those who did not (Denley, 2016).
2. *Corequisite remediation.* While maintaining academic rigor, the TBR system has worked with faculty to redesign gateway math and English courses through a corequisite remediation model that has been implemented at scale. The adoption of corequisite instruction in partnership with the use of HIPs across the system is a strategy to increase retention while also closing skills gaps for underserved populations.
3. *Guided pathways.* As a measure to support student academic focus areas, TBR institutions have developed default degree maps for each degree program and for each of the 56 Tennessee Transfer Pathways (TTP). The TTP degree maps, or guided pathways, were constructed to ensure that students who change from one pathway to another experience minimal credit loss. Within these guided pathways students are advised to attempt at least 9 hours of credit in their academic focus area within the 1st year.
4. *HIP taxonomies.* The taxonomies were created by faculty committees to provide minimum definitions of practice for each HIP to be used in course coding and statewide data tracking and analysis processes. The staged milestones within each taxonomy also serve as institutional implementation and self-evaluation tools that help identify areas for growth (TBR, 2016).

The research report by Kuh (2008), *High-Impact Educational Practices: What They Are, Who Has Access to Them, and Why They Matter*, identified a set of teaching and learning practices that have been widely implemented and that show evidence of effectiveness in fostering completion. The practices identified in Kuh's research guided the choice of initial HIPs that the TBR system would address in the first phase of scaling efforts across the system. At inception, the plan to raise awareness and use of HIPs included convening faculty from each university and community college to develop taxonomies of practice for six initial HIPs. The development of the taxonomies assisted in increasing faculty understanding of the value of HIPs, while also providing a tool that institutions could use in the initial assessment of where they were in the institutionalization of the practice on campus. Each taxonomy creates a structure that outlines three "milestones" of development of the HIP at the institution. The minimum definition of practice also allows for consistent coding in the student information system so that the TBR system office could analyze the effect of student participation in the designated HIP courses. The taxonomies have since been revised to reflect only community college–centric language. Most recently, the system began developing taxonomies for student participation in experiences outside of credit-bearing courses.

System Approach to Scaling HIPs

With the introduction of TN Promise in 2015, many access barriers that had existed in Tennessee were removed with the introduction of "free community college," and a renewed interest in addressing equity gaps in student completion took center stage. According to data retrieved from Complete College Tennessee (2017), achievement gaps at many institutions had narrowed, particularly among Hispanic students, but institution graduation rates for Black students remained well below the rate of their peers (see Figure 18.2).

At the start of this work, the system taught over 8,000 different courses to more than 1 million student-course enrollments. However, more than half of those enrollments were in about 30 of those classes. Further analysis of those classes shows that the courses also play a critical curricular role in the overall learning structure of the system—successful learning in those classes disproportionately leads to further success; lack of success in those classes leads to failures elsewhere. That analysis has informed the system's course revitalization initiative, including use of HIPs, for the classes with the most influence on the curriculum. The structural curricular analysis suggests that changes in these classes will reach across the student body quickly and will also influence success across the breadth of the curriculum.

Although the literature around HIPs nationally has either looked at National Survey of Student Engagement or individual course-level data, the TBR system set out to deploy a scaling model for HIPs that can connect student participation in a high-impact designated course to information on the individual student academic record. This system-level approach provides a

Figure 18.2. Graduation rates by race and system level.

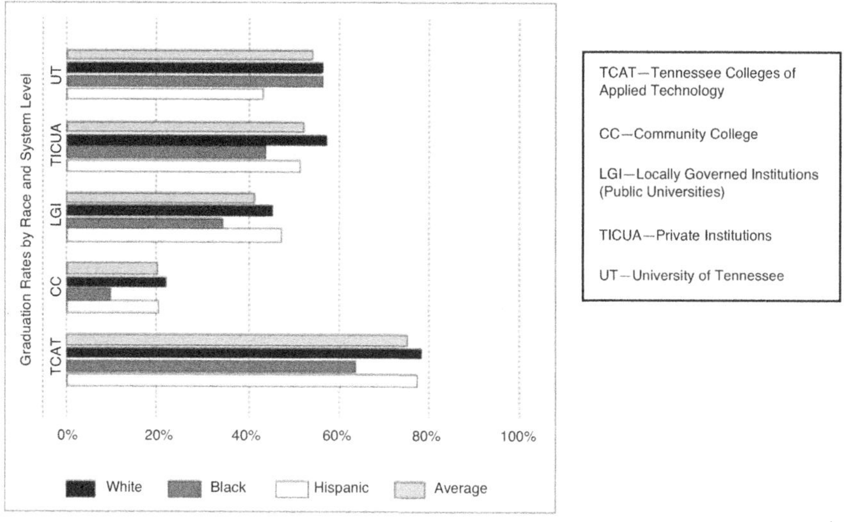

sizeable number of student records to analyze and allows the system to compare similar types of students across institutions in Tennessee. The ability to extract these data across all colleges also supports the institutions that may be limited in their capacity to do a deeper analysis of the HIP data.

System taxonomies help ensure that a minimum definition of practice is followed in the coding of credit-bearing courses that include a designated HIP. Because all colleges in the TBR system use the same student information system, the data has allowed the system to identify which HIPs students most frequently participate in, at what point in the academic pathway they engage in the practice, and how the success rates of different student demographics compare for each HIP. This analysis is a central feature of the completion agenda as TBR seeks to close equity gaps. As of 2018–2019, the data collected through the student information system shows that approximately 30% of students are engaged in at least one HIP. Since the initial data collection began, this is nearly a 10% increase over previous years (see Figure 18.3).

Early analysis supported the hypothesis that first-year seminar courses are the first HIP that the majority of students encounter as they begin their college career, which was encouraged in TBR policy by allowing institutions to add up to three additional credit hours in programs of study to require the first-year seminar course. Learning communities and service-learning courses rank second and third most popular, with more than 8,500 students participating in each (see Figure 18.4).

Figure 18.3. Percentage of students enrolled in at least one HIP.

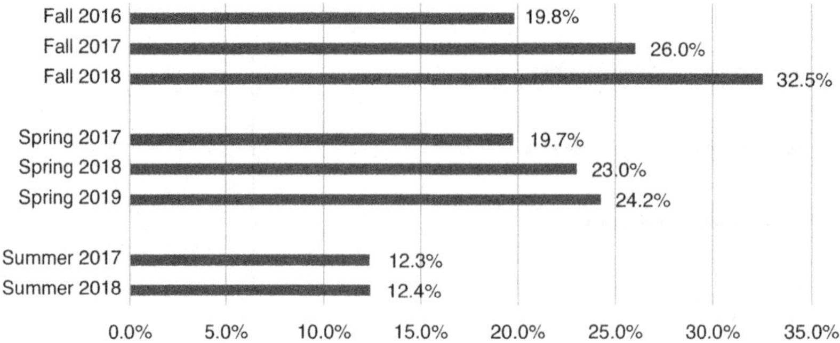

Figure 18.4. Percentage of students enrolled by HIP type, 2018–2019.

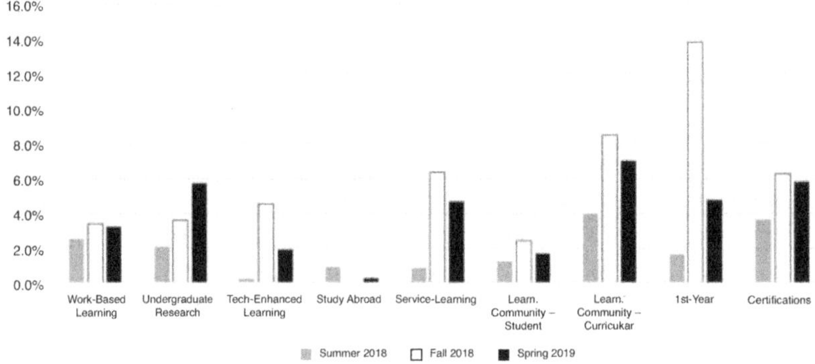

The TBR System also developed an assessment guide to support institutions in ensuring quality in HIP-designated courses. In collaboration with faculty across the state, the TBR Office of Student Success created the quality assurance tool to serve as a template for institutions to use in crafting their own approval processes for HIP-coded courses. The guide includes minimum definitions of all TBR-coded HIPs, HIP quality dimensions, an implementation form for faculty creating HIP courses, a postcourse exit form for faculty to evaluate the effectiveness of the HIP course, and a rubric for quality assurance evaluators of the HIP course. The HIP Assessment Guide recommends that all HIP classes be evaluated following the first semester of initial implementation and again every 3 academic years the course is offered (TBR, 2019). The assessment tool is now required as part of the grant funding cycle for course revitalization funds from the TBR System Office.

The goal for the TBR System has always been to ensure that regardless of where a student attends college in Tennessee, every student will experience at least three HIPs before they graduate. As such, attention has been paid to embedding HIP courses in the academic pathways for every student so that it is in the fabric of the common student experience. In the 2018 and 2019 calendar years, the Lumina NASH TS3 HIPs grant enabled five TBR community colleges to pilot scaling HIPs across degree and transfer pathways. These efforts culminated in September 2019 with a gathering of faculty representatives from all 13 community colleges, who worked together in discipline teams to develop best practice plans to embed three HIP courses into each of the related degree and transfer pathways.

Throughout the scaling efforts and pilot work, the TBR System has supported the promotion and advancement of faculty training on how to develop robust student learning outcomes, conduct appropriate assessment, and ensure quality implementation of HIPs. Initially, faculty learning communities led by the system for each practice were created to allow cross-institutional best practice sharing with faculty on particular pedagogical approaches. These faculty champions then were charged with creating campus-based faculty learning communities to continue to build a network of HIP faculty learning opportunities. As faculty champions were developed, the system moved to provide annual support through statewide and regional conferences. In the first 4 years of the scaling plan, faculty training was funded entirely by grants. Thus, sustainability of faculty learning is now moving into strategic training and support for directors at teaching and learning centers at each institution. The goal is to foster campus ownership and responsibility for faculty learning on how to strengthen and expand HIPs into all academic programs.

Early Evidence

As a system, the vision for this work has been to collect data from our student information system from all the TBR institutions on student participation in courses designated as containing a HIP and then use that data to identify areas for growth, detect promising practices that can be scaled, and ensure equity in experiential learning opportunities. With the initial coding in place, analysis of student participation, disaggregated by race, ethnicity, and other demographic variables, will provide insight into what practices appear to have greater effects in closing equity gaps and encouraging student persistence and degree completion. Although it has taken several years to implement consistent coding practices at the institutional level, the TBR System has begun to take a deeper dive into specific practices and has analyzed institutional data on student participation in HIP-designated courses. Early analysis done by the TBR System Office has shown that of the 30% of our students who do participate in a HIP-designated course, the distribution by type of student is fairly consistent (see Table 18.1).

Deeper analysis by specific HIP designation shows where student participation gaps may exist within particular types of pedagogical experiences. For example, in examining service-learning and work-based learning–designated courses, TBR was able to identify that Black student participation is lower than the system average in work-based learning courses, but low-income students exceed the system average in participation in service-learning courses (see Table 18.2). The finding prompted further examination of how faculty do outreach to Black students to engage in internship or apprenticeship opportunities and examination of additional barriers students may be facing that impact their participation.

Overall, HIP participation leads to higher retention compared to those who do not participate across all populations, but the effect varies by student type and their academic needs. Because approximately 66% of first-time 1st-year students are also in learning support, there is interest in examining the effects of student participation in particular types of HIPs in combination with other curricular reform efforts like corequisite courses. For example, of the first-time 1st-year students who participate in a first-year experience course, students who are also in a learning support course

TABLE 18.1
Student Participation in HIPs by Population

		Any HIP		*Any HIP, Not FYE*	
	Total	*Count*	*%*	*Count*	*%*
System Total	89,078	28,972	33	24,357	27
Black	14,308	4,891	34	3,363	24
Hispanic	4,986	1,806	36	1,501	30
White	64,217	20,537	32	17,999	28
Other	5,567	1,738	31	1,494	27
Female	53,627	17,673	33	14,822	28
Male	35,439	11,298	32	9,534	27
Adult (Age 25+)	24,673	7,546	31	6,712	27
Nonadult	64,405	21,426	33	17,645	27
Pell Recipient	32,093	13,829	43	11,250	35
Non–Pell Recipient	56,985	15,143	27	13,107	23

TABLE 18.2
Student Population Participation by Practice

	Service-Learning	*Work-Based Learning*
System Total	6%	3%
Black	5%	1%
Hispanic	8%	2%
White	7%	4%
Other	6%	3%
Female	6%	4%
Male	6%	2%
Adult (Age 25+)	5%	5%
Nonadult	7%	3%
Pell Recipient	9%	4%
Non–Pell Recipient	5%	3%

(corequisite) have a higher retention rate than their peers who also take a learning support course (see Figure 18.5). This analysis can be done at the institutional level and has prompted further qualitative examination on the topics covered in the first-year seminar at each campus to identify how course content or pedagogical approaches in the course may change the success rate of students.

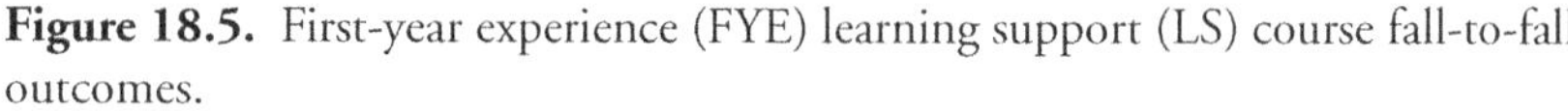

Figure 18.5. First-year experience (FYE) learning support (LS) course fall-to-fall outcomes.

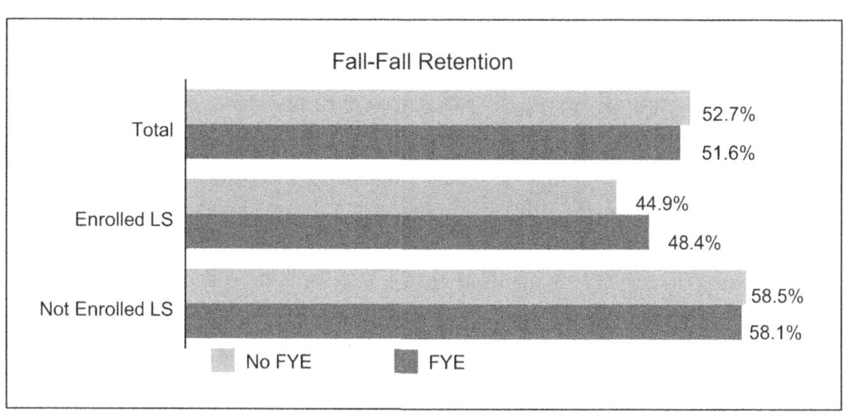

Effects on Student Success

Through the system's involvement in several national grant-funded initiatives, the opportunity to engage with third-party evaluators has allowed for validation of initial findings by the TBR System institutional research team. In December 2017, a third-party evaluator for the Lumina NASH HIPs project, DVP-Praxis Ltd. (2019), designed a mixed-methods evaluation plan with two overarching research questions:

1. To what extent did student participation in HIPs expand during the initiative overall and particularly for African American, Latinx, and American Indian student populations?
2. What are the educational outcomes for students who participate in HIPs, and are these outcomes different for students who do not participate in HIPs?

As part of its multifaceted approach to answering these questions, DVP-Praxis (2019) analyzed TBR System data from five of the 13 Tennessee community colleges. Students were considered to have participated in a particular HIP if they were flagged as participating in either the fall 2017 term or the spring 2018 term, or both. In order to gauge HIP participation across an entire academic year, the sample was restricted to students enrolled in the five institutions in both the fall 2017 term and the spring 2018 term—a total of 19,230 students. There were five key findings from the DVP-Praxis (Valentine & Price, 2021) research report:

1. Across the five Tennessee colleges, nearly one-third (31%) of all students participated in at least one HIP during the 2017–2018 academic year.
2. The bulk of HIP participation occurs during the 1st year of enrollment, with lower HIP participation for continuing students. Forty-four percent of 1st-year students participated in a HIP in academic year 2017–2018; this was primarily driven by participation in first-year experiences (36%), followed by learning communities (13%) and service-learning (9%).
3. Notable racial/ethnic differences emerge when comparing overall HIP participation rates for 1st-year and continuing students—African American and Latinx students are more likely than White students to participate in a HIP during their 1st year in college but White students are more likely to participate in subsequent years.
4. For 1st-year students, higher HIP participation by African American and Latinx students is driven by their much higher participation in first-year experiences and in learning communities.

5. For continuing students, higher HIP participation by White students is driven by their higher participation in certifications and work-based learning, and to a lesser extent by their higher participation in service-learning and undergraduate research.

The TBR research team has an ongoing assessment plan for the HIP-coded courses to identify strengths and weaknesses in the data collection and to connect data with emerging research on particular pedagogical approaches. Furthermore, as the TBR System Office does further analysis, findings are disseminated to campus leadership for consideration and institutional research staff are encouraged to work with academic affairs and faculty to do analysis at the course level. The data analysis done at the system level also provides year-over-year comparisons that can track growth of HIP offerings, increases in student participation, and changes to equity gaps.

Lessons Learned From Scaling Efforts

Taking a system approach to the work has yielded several benefits for the member institutions. First, the system can facilitate the spread of ideas and strategies from one campus to another and identify pilot campuses to take the lead in working out solutions to common problems. Through the governance structure in place within TBR and the support of grant-funded positions at the TBR System Office that coordinate professional development and learning events, campuses have developed the habit of learning from each other. Second, the system approach builds upon capacities that have been developed either through the system office (like faculty learning, data analysis, and grant support) or scaling best practices identified at the institutional level to all institutions in the system. The leadership and coordination provided by the TBR Office of Student Success has also fostered communities of practice that are continuously supported and reinforced to ensure that the central focus is not lost as new initiatives are introduced.

The strategy to embed HIPs into degree pathways has provided connectivity between the equity goals, use of HIPs, and the overall completion plan. These efforts were supported by grant funding that enabled pilot work and provided a template for how this can be done in other pathways moving forward. Using this scaffolded approach to educate and prepare all TBR stakeholders to be champions of student equity and success, the system has experienced continued improvement. This success includes participation of more than 400 faculty in learning communities and annually attracting more than 200 faculty to its statewide HIP conference. In addition to growing faculty awareness and support in the use of HIPs, the student record data show that student participation is increasing, and we can see early evidence of the effect of student participation on their academic success and persistence.

Future Directions

Even with these achievements, the TBR System knows that additional work is needed. Greater intentionality with faculty development efforts is ongoing. In working through the scaling efforts, system administrators found that faculty respond best to (a) gathering and discussing ideas at face-to-face events, (b) using "champion faculty" to help spread excitement about HIPs with a "bottom-up" approach, (c) supporting efforts with quantitative evidence on why HIPs work, and (d) providing resources such as incentivized course redesign, student engagement grants, faculty development opportunities, and technology platforms to help everyone scale effectively.

Continuous attention must also be paid to educating students about what HIPs are, the benefits of participating in a HIP-designated course, and transparency of student learning outcomes in all courses. As a first step, the system has created HIP badges for inclusion in course catalogs and on course syllabi so students can more readily identify courses with these experiences. Marketing materials have also been created for institutional use as they expand their own HIP offerings. Furthermore, work is already underway to implement a complete student record that would illustrate student learning outcomes in the HIP-designated courses as well as out-of-class experiences. Together with Lumina, the American Association of Collegiate Registrars and Admissions Officers, and the National Association of Student Personnel Administrators, the TBR Office of Student Success is currently developing an electronic "warranty card" that students can share with employers. The warranty card documents the specific skills and competencies achieved in technical certificate and degree programs and guarantees to employers that the students have earned these skills. The future goal is that the pilot on the warranty card will be expanded to include an electronic diploma connected to the academic transcript for all degrees conferred and would include cocurricular activities and competencies in addition to curricular achievements.

The work done within the Tennessee system illustrates the efficiencies and capacity building that is possible when whole systems look to scale best practices in teaching. The ability to engage multiple stakeholders in developing common definitions and taxonomies, coordinate state-level resources for faculty development, and systematically gather data to direct the scaling efforts have together acted as a "force multiplier" that allows the state to push boundaries within a quick timeframe. Through TBR's pilot efforts, the system has been able to test particular strategies and then use the data to make the case for why the work needed to go to scale across all institutions. This particular model is something that other states could learn from if they want to move the work beyond a single institution.

References

Association of American Colleges & Universities. (2011). *The Leap vision for learning: Outcomes, practices, impact and employers' views.* https://www.aacu.org/sites/default/files/files/LEAP/leap_vision_summary.pdf

Complete College Tennessee. (2017). *Beneath the surface: The state of higher education in Tennessee* [Report]. Author. https://educationdocbox.com/College_Life/76144683-Beneath-the-surface-the-state-of-higher-education-in-tennessee-the-state-of-higher-education-in-tennessee-1.html

Denley, T. (2016). *Choice architecture, academic foci, and guided pathways* [Technical brief]. Tennessee Board of Regents.

Duckworth, A., & Yeager, D. (2015). Measurement matters: Assessing personal qualities other than cognitive ability for educational purposes. *Educational Researcher, 44*(4), 237–251. https://doi.org/10.3102/0013189X15584327

DVP-Praxis Ltd. (2019, February). *Tennessee Board of Regents baseline report on participation in high impact practices* [White paper].

Headden, S., & McKay, S. (2015). *Motivation matters: How new research can help teachers boost student engagement.* Carnegie Foundation for the Advancement of Teaching. https://www.carnegiefoundation.org/resources/publications/motivation-matters-how-new-research-can-help-teachers-boost-student-engagement/

Kuh, G. D. (2008). *High-impact educational practices: What they are, who has access to them, and why they matter.* Association of American Colleges & Universities.

Pascarella, E., & Terenzini, P. (2005). *How college affects students: A third decade of research.* Jossey-Bass.

Tennessee Board of Regents. (2016). *High impact practices taxonomies.* https://www.tbr.edu/student-success/tbr-high-impact-practices

Tennessee Board of Regents. (2019). *High impact practice (HIP) quality assurance & coding: A guide for faculty and academic administrators.* https://www.tbr.edu/sites/default/files/media/2020/01/TBR%20HIP%20QA%20and%20Coding%20Packet_1.pdf

Valentine, J., & Price, D. (2021). *Scaling high-impact practices to improve community college student outcomes: Evidence from the Tennessee Board of Regents* [Issue paper]. Lumina Foundation. https://www.luminafoundation.org/resource/scaling-high-impact-practices-to-improve-community-college-student-outcomes/

PART FOUR

ASSESSING OUTCOMES

Various forms of applied and experiential learning are not "high impact" until we have gathered data and evidence that clearly demonstrate their impact on student learning and success. This entire volume was compiled with the explicit goal of elevating and showcasing examples of high-quality scholarship and assessment of high-impact practices (HIPs). The contributors to chapters in our preceding three sections, "Advancing Equity," "Assuring Fidelity," and "Achieving Scale," provide evidence of their work at the program, unit, campus, and/or system level. We invite educators and practitioners to use these chapters as examples when gathering evidence of "impact" of their own student programming, to identify and close equity gaps, and to shape future scholarly work in the field.

In compiling this volume, we identified several pieces that appear to be taking research and assessment to the next level, bringing rigorous research designs and sophisticated quantitative techniques from the social sciences and educational research to the study of HIPs. We wish to feature this work in this fourth and final section. A persistent methodological issue in our efforts to understand and empirically investigate the influences of HIPs on measures of student success and learning is our lack of a control group. We typically study only students who participate in HIPs, and we know there are significant equity gaps in student participation, especially from traditionally underserved student populations (e.g., first-generation, racially minoritized, low income). How can we truly isolate the impact of participating in a form of applied and experiential learning when we know academically successful students from higher income backgrounds are more likely to seek out these opportunities?

Conducting an experimental design, with random assignment to an experimental group (e.g., participation in HIPs) and a control group (e.g., nonparticipation in HIPs) is the only way to truly isolate the impact of the experience on the intended student success measure. However, setting up an experimental design is not a feasible option for most HIPs. Two studies in this section offer examples of how one might mitigate this methodological issue. The contributors of chapter 19 use a quasiexperimental design with logistical regression modeling to empirically investigate the impact of a university-wide ePortfolio initiative to promote metacognition and student learning at the University of North Texas. And in chapter 21, a team from three separate institutions demonstrates how propensity score matching, a statistical procedure that provides a quasicontrol or comparison group, can be used to isolate the impact of student participation in experiences like undergraduate research, study abroad, service-learning, and learning communities on various student success measures. In chapter 20, a pair of contributors discuss efforts at Utah Valley University to develop an internal engagement survey to measure student outcomes and success among their 41,000 students. This research effort showcases the development of a survey instrument and employs structural equation modeling to measure engagement at the course level and its impact on student success.

Although some of the statistical techniques may be complex and outside one's comfort zone, we believe each of these pieces can be used to stimulate new and exciting conversations with your institutional research (IR) office, faculty in related disciplines, and assessment staff, exploring how similar research might be conducted on your own campuses. These professionals can help you to assess the data you have, the data you might need, and how you might be able to analyze the information in ways that can help you tell a powerful story. We also hope that the chapters in this section will serve to stimulate additional research and assessment efforts within the field through replication and refinement.

Discussion Questions

- We can assess the effectiveness of HIPs using primary data collection (e.g., gathering your own data, such as surveys and interviews) or through secondary data analysis (e.g., institutional data from your institutional research office). What data do you have access to, within your program, department, unit, or at the institutional level? How might you use these data to evaluate and assess the impact of your program on student learning and success? What data are missing that you might need to collect?
- We know that students with financial and social capital are most likely to participate in HIPs. How do you know if these experiences are equitably accessible? How can you distinguish between the benefits of these experiences compared with other confounding factors?
- Another barrier to the assessment of HIPs are self-selection effects. To what extent are your data based on students choosing to participate in a specific HIP experience? How might this bias any findings you might see in your data? Do the examples presented in this section offer some possibilities for overcoming this limitation? If so, how?
- What kind of relationship do you have with your institutional research office, faculty in related disciplines, and assessment staff? What are some ways you might build upon your existing relationship, or establish a deeper partnership? How might you use the chapters in this section to begin a conversation with these researchers?

19

HIGH-IMPACT PRACTICE CONNECTIONS AS CATALYSTS FOR EQUITABLE RETENTION

Meena C. Naik, Adam N. Wear, Scott Peecksen, Regina Branton, and Mike Simmons

High-impact practices (HIPs) have become necessarily ubiquitous for institutions of higher education, but systematically leveraging these activities effectively to support institutional outcomes surrounding student success increases their value. Innovative HIP adjustments supporting the equitable retention and persistence of at-risk and historically underserved students increase both the challenge and the value of those practices. The University of North Texas (UNT) considered how best to accomplish this innovation at scale and implemented a university-wide ePortfolio strategy linked to coordinated learning outcomes to support metacognitive practices encouraging connection and generalization of learning in a distributed, faculty-driven approach.

HIPs and Retention

Student success initiatives can be done for the sake of providing a service or to intentionally introduce opportunities meant to reduce the attrition of at-risk students. Done well, these initiatives support educational attainment, deeper learning, and student preparation for experiences extending far beyond postsecondary education. Tinto's (1993) theory of student departure asserts increasing social and academic integration encourages the development of a sense of belonging for students, thereby supporting their retention. Extending Tinto's work focusing on students who are historically underserved, Hunter et al. (2010) suggested that in addition to intentional interaction between the student and the institution, these strategies support students in finding greater direction and an understanding of future goals (e.g., major, career, etc.). These approaches promote self-efficacy or self-belief, as well as students' motivation and overall academic success (Hunter et al., 2010). Taken together, institutional commitments that prioritize programs meant to engage students, improve access to cocurricular experiences, and promote services supporting student transitions ultimately influence student persistence and retention by increasing the frequency of interaction between students and the academic and social structures of the educational institution (Huber, 2010; Kuh et al., 2013). Coincidentally, these characteristics represent hallmark qualities of HIPs (Kuh et al., 2013).

All-encompassing strategies by which students can be better engaged and supported are challenging to conceptualize. Kuh (2008) argued HIPs offer an avenue by which to engage students in activities that foster essential learning and engagement. At their best, HIPs facilitate deeper learning across curricular and cocurricular experiences, while promoting collaboration with faculty and peers and supporting structured opportunities to integrate learning (Kilgo et al., 2015; Kuh et al., 2013). Simply offering these experiences is not enough. Coordinating these experiences to better consider the needs of students as they matriculate while supporting connections across experiences (generalization of learning) is essential for effective implementation of HIPs (Kinzie, 2013; Kuh et al., 2013). Kuh (2010) pointed to reflection and synthesis as a way this generalization of learning can occur. Furthermore, Finley and McNair (2013) noted Hispanic and Black students who engage in HIPs demonstrate disproportionately higher outcomes with their GPAs and are more likely to be retained when compared to their White peers. Moreover, the authors also note those same underserved students do not necessarily seek out these experiences or self-select into the programs at the same rate as their counterparts.

To that end, UNT sought to coordinate HIPs in an institutionally distributed manner by using ePortfolios, the 11th HIP, as a centralized pedagogical tool meant to integrate other HIPs such as service-learning, internships, and undergraduate research (Eynon & Gambino, 2017). Given this method of use, ePortfolio is more effectively termed a "meta-HIP" (Eynon & Gambino, 2017). Accordingly, UNT offers a model by which connections across HIP learning experiences are supported by leveraging, embedding, and integrating ePortfolio pedagogy, ultimately encouraging students to generalize and contextualize otherwise discrete learning opportunities.

UNT Connect and ePortfolio Meta-HIP

UNT, located north of the Dallas–Fort Worth Metroplex, is a large Tier 1, doctoral-granting, public university with an annual enrollment of approximately 40,000 students. UNT is also a minority- and Hispanic-serving institution (HSI) and, therefore, has a vested interest in ensuring students who are historically underserved receive the appropriate support and resources to engender further success. In 2016, UNT launched the Career Connect project to support undergraduate education by identifying and strengthening existing HIPs and connecting them through general learning outcomes in the form of employer-valued marketable skills (NACE, 2020).

As a first step in this effort, UNT launched a university-wide ePortfolio, working with faculty to embed this meta-HIP into existing service-learning, internships, and other HIPs to work as a catalyst for students to engage in metacognitive reflection and to support the collection of artifacts of student learning (Eynon & Gambino, 2017). These artifacts serve as evidence of employer-valued skills and learning outcomes, as defined by national standards, such as oral and written communication, critical thinking, and teamwork as defined by national standards set by the Association for American Colleges & Universities (AAC&U, 2017). Together, these learning experiences generate "Connect Activities" that help students collect evidence of generalized skills in a single repository, with notes, artifacts, and facilitated reflections meant to allow for deeper connection and earlier thinking about the relevance and value of these learning experiences. UNT faculty and staff participate in a Connect Activity when they integrate ePortfolio as a meta-HIP into their course or program, identify evidence of skill proficiency, and evaluate student learning artifacts against common, AAC&U-adapted valid assessment of learning in undergraduate education (VALUE) rubrics.

UNT Connect anchors HIPs for the institution and the students by taking advantage of existing assessment and teaching structures and activities. The broad goals are to support institutional planning, instructional quality, and design and encourage students in the process of contextualizing learning. Given the role HIPs play for underserved and at-risk students, UNT Connect supports equitable engagement and retention practices. This effort allows students to better integrate a variety of cocurricular experiences with their curricular experiences and outcomes while connecting this learning to future careers through demonstrations of employer-valued marketable skills.

Scaling Up

UNT Connect grew the reach of Connect Activities through three major approaches: universal ePortfolio access, pedagogical practices, and innovative digital credentials. First, to increase access, ePortfolio was made available for all students and was embedded into existing learning experiences with required ePortfolio components to facilitate use. Integrating ePortfolio technology into the learning management system (LMS) was an essential step to reduce technology confusion for faculty and staff, resulting in an overall increase in student usage. This streamlining increased use in courses and cocurricular activities by nearly 200% from Year 1 to Year 2 of implementation of the Connect Project.

Next, UNT Connect emphasized growth at scale by way of mass faculty and staff adoption of HIP experiences paired with ePortfolio to increase the likelihood those students who were most at risk would pass through one of these opportunities. To encourage this growth, UNT Connect provides ongoing, robust development opportunities for faculty to revise their courses with the intention of integrating ePortfolio pedagogy, engaging in community-based practices, and further developing service-learning HIPs within their courses or learning experiences. These development opportunities have supported the launch of more than 30 service-learning partnerships and helped UNT to demonstrate its institutional purpose and value to the surrounding community. To support further implementation, UNT Connect partnered with staff and other departments on campus. Although the Career Center is a direct entry point into internships, the partnership with student affairs allows for direct integration with a variety of service-learning opportunities and living-learning communities.

Whereas these strategies support breadth, UNT Connect has also developed an ePortfolio implementation structure inclusive of interdisciplinary skill assessments, integrated with UNT's LMS and ePortfolio systems, and tied to each student's ePortfolio project. Any student who participates in a Connect Activity submits evidence collected from their experience into projects within their ePortfolios. Each of these projects contains an AAC&U-adapted VALUE rubric accessible through the grading view of the LMS. Students can link otherwise discrete curricular and cocurricular experiences through common skill assessments and reflection within their ePortfolios. Finally, as students are rated as proficient or higher on an AAC&U-adapted rubric, the ePortfolio triggers digital credentials, or badges. Each digital badge holds information about the activity completed and serves as evidence of skill proficiency to facilitate student recognition of value across diverse learning experiences they gain while also offering validation for any external viewers.

Testing Equitable Impact and Success

UNT Connect offers a scalable model to coordinate and grow HIPs on campus by leveraging technology and taking the process to as many classrooms and through as many cocurricular events as possible. With the imperatives of UNT being an HSI and minority-serving campus, Connect hopes to actively reach those students who are most at risk and offer an intervention to mitigate their risk by universally extending these practices and ePortfolio to the majority of undergraduate students. The question is twofold. First, is there a scalable method to extend ePortfolios from a tool available to students to a tool intentionally embedded into students' university experiences with other HIPs that positively impacts their learning? Second, as a result of the more accessible and integrated presence of HIPs, are there positive and equitable impacts on academic outcomes among student groups least likely to be retained at the university?

Methodology and Samples

Before considering the impact of ePortfolios and HIPs on student outcomes, UNT first had to scale the process and adoption of both coordinated HIPs via ePortfolios and the use of standard rubrics for skills assessments. As we achieved success, we shifted attention to outcomes and impact. To consider the impact, we evaluated outcomes for students participating in Connect Activities during the fall 2017 and spring 2018 semesters using causal inference and quasiexperimental designs. Using established empirical outcomes indicating early positive impacts on academic outcomes for participating students, we replicated the causal inference and quasiexperimental designs but instead focused on targeted student subgroups (Peecksen et al., 2020).

We conducted quasiexperimental research designs with data from two samples of treatment (or Connect) and control students from the fall 2017 and spring 2018 semesters (see Table 19.1). Two samples of students participated in Connect activities during fall 2017 (n = 870) and spring 2018 (n = 551) semesters. Students in the fall 2017 sample were 19 years old (SD = 2.09) on average, compared to an average age of 22 years old (SD = 4.83) for spring 2018 students. The majority, 64%, of students in the fall 2017 sample were 1st-year students (n = 560) whereas roughly 21% were 1st-year students (n = 114) in the spring 2018 sample.

From there, we utilized a matching method to create control groups for both samples. In general, matching is a nonparametric method that processes data, controlling for potential pretreatment confounding control variables by minimizing the difference between the treatment and control groups.

TABLE 19.1
Descriptive Statistics of Demographic Data for Samples

	Fall 2017 Sample		*Spring 2018 Sample*	
	Control (%)	*Connect Engaged (%)*	*Control (%)*	*Connect Engaged (%)*
Race/Ethnicity				
White	44.84	44.37	48.57	46.46
Hispanic	24.99	26.9	28.23	30.49
African American	17.61	17.93	10.12	10.34
Asian/Pacific Islander	7.75	7.01	7.66	7.62
Non-Resident Alien	2.76	2.18	2.93	2.9
Other	2.05	1.61	2.49	2.18
Classification				
Freshman	64.42	64.37	20.05	20.69
Sophomore	24.53	24.48	18	18.33
Junior	8.87	8.97	15.32	14.34
Senior	1.69	1.72	44.98	45.01
Postbaccalaureate	0.49	0.46	1.65	1.63
Pell-Eligible				
Yes	36.45	37.93	35.19	34.3
No	63.55	62.07	64.81	65.7
Sample Size	N = 3,846	N = 870	N = 2,728	N = 551

Specifically, we used coarsened-exact matching (CEM), which serves to enhance the estimation of potential Connect effects on student retention and cumulative GPA while reducing covariate imbalances between participating and control students (Iacus et al., 2012). We matched fall 2017 and spring 2018 Connect students with control students by demographic characteristics such as ethnicity, class, Pell eligibility, and age as indicators for socioeconomic status and minoritized status.

Analysis Plan

To predict retention, we ran logistical regression models where treatment status, several demographic variables (e.g., ethnicity, gender, age, classification, first-generation status), and the matching variables (i.e., presemester cumulative GPA and Pell Grant eligibility) were used as independent variables or predictors. To predict cumulative GPA the following semester, we used the same predictors in an OLS regression model. We ran these models for both samples representing diverse student populations, and for several subgroups to preliminarily test equitable impacts on student outcomes as a result of participating in a Connect activity.

A logistical regression model (Equations 1 and 2) was used to predict retention. *Ret* equaled 1 when the student (x) was retained. CC indicated student x participated in the treatment during fall 2017 or spring 2018. GPA_1_DEM symbolizes presemester variables of achievement (e.g., beginning-of-semester GPA) and demographic variables.

$$P_r\,(Ret_x = 1)\ \frac{exp(Y_x)}{1 + exp(Y_x)} \tag{1}$$

$$Y_x = \alpha + CC_x\,\beta + GPA\_1\_DEM_x\,\delta \tag{2}$$

Equation 3 defines the linear regression model used for predicting beginning-of-the-following-semester GPA or GPA_2 with predictor variables from Equation 2.

$$GPA\_2_x = \alpha + CC_x\beta + GPA\_1\_DEM_x\,\delta \tag{3}$$

Results for the entire sample and at-risk subgroups for both semesters are presented in in Tables 19.2 and 19.3 in our results.

TABLE 19.2

Estimated Impact on GPA and Retention (Fall 2017 Sample)

	Δ *Expected GPA*	Δ *Probability Retention to Spring 2018*	Δ *Probability Retention to Fall 2018*
All Groups	0.12^{***}	0.04^{**}	0.04^{*}
First Gen	0.07	0.05	$0.07^{\dagger}$
Non–First Gen	0.16^{***}	0.02	0.02
Female	0.13^{**}	0.02	0.00
Male	0.12^{**}	0.05^{*}	0.07^{**}
Black	0.29^{***}	0.06	0.05
Hispanic	0.00	0.03	0.02
White	0.13^{**}	0.03	0.07^{**}

$^{***}p < 0.001$; $^{**}p < 0.01$; $^{*}p < 0.05$; $\dagger p < 0.10$.

TABLE 19.3
Spring 2018: Sample Estimated Impact on GPA and Retention

	Δ *Expected GPA*	Δ *Probability Retention to Fall 2018*
All Groups	0.07^{***}	0.08^{**}
First Gen	0.08^{**}	0.01
Non–First Gen	0.05^{**}	0.12^{***}
Female	0.09^{***}	$0.05_{\dagger}$
Male	0.05^{*}	$0.13^{\dagger}$
Black	0.04	0.09
Hispanic	0.05^{*}	0.01
White	0.07^{***}	0.14^{***}

$^{***}p < 0.001$; $^{**}p < 0.01$; $^{*}p < 0.05$; $\dagger p < 0.10$.

Results

We approached this work wanting to determine if we could effectively scale HIPs and ePortfolio practice at a large institution. After increasing reach, we explored whether we could track an equitable impact on student outcomes resulting from practices encouraging deeper metacognitive reflection, generalization of learning, and recognition of skill attainment for those students least likely to persist at the university.

First, scale is increasingly important in both supporting a culture of HIP integration at the university and creating opportunities that are accessible to the students for whom impact can be tested. Although all students had access to the system, not everyone made use of that access. Only 8,108 students created ePortfolio accounts during the 1st year of implementation. Through targeted advertising, increasing the number of activities related to the initiative, and integrating the ePortfolio system with the LMS, usage has scaled to 23,577 active ePortfolio users creating 50,209 projects and 7,787 digital portfolios. In addition, UNT Connect has seen a 340% increase in staff and faculty accounts from Year 1 to Year 3, hosting 1,002 faculty and staff users as of July 2020.

As noted in Tables 19.2 and 19.3 (see results for "All Groups"), participation in Career Connect in fall 2017 and spring 2018 predicted (a) higher cumulative GPAs (i.e., 0.12 points higher and 0.07 points higher for treatment students, respectively; $p < 0.001$) the following semesters and (b) higher rates of spring 2018 and fall 2018 retention (i.e., about 4 percentage points higher and 8 percentage points higher for treatment students, respectively; $p < 0.01$) the following semesters (Peecksen et al., 2020).

Improved success measures across the board are always beneficial, but we believe the ePortfolio provides an opportunity for the equitable application of HIPs. To understand the impact of HIPs, the treatment and control populations were grouped by gender, ethnicity, and first-generation status for analysis.

Results from the subgroup analyses indicate similar impacts of fall 2017 Connect participation on spring 2018 cumulative GPA among non-first-generation students (0.16 points higher for treatment students; $p < 0.001$), females (0.13 points higher; $p < 0.01$), males (0.12 points higher; $p < 0.01$), Black students (0.29 points higher; $p < 0.001$), and White students (0.13 points higher; $p < 0.01$) compared to matched control students. This subgroup analysis also revealed three retention impacts from fall 2017 Connect participation among males (5 and 7 percentage points higher for spring 2018 and fall 2018 retention, respectively; $p < .05$), among White students (14 percentage points higher in fall 2018 retention; $p < 0.01$), and among first-generation students (7 percentage point difference; $p < 0.10$).

Similarly, the subgroup analysis for spring 2018 treatment students revealed significant impacts on GPA for first-generation students (0.08 points higher; $p < 0.01$), non-first-generation students (0.05 points higher; $p < 0.01$), females (0.09 points higher; $p < 0.001$), males (0.05 points higher; $p < 0.05$), Hispanic students (0.05 points higher; $p < 0.05$), and White students (0.07 points higher; $p < 0.001$). Subgroup analyses also indicated significant differences in fall 2018 retention rates among spring 2018 non-first-generation treatment students (12 percentage points higher; $p < 0.001$) and White students (14 percentage points higher; $p < 0.001$) and borderline significant differences in fall 2018 retention rates for females (5 percentage points higher; $p < 0.10$) and males (13 percentage points higher; $p < 0.10$). These results indicate clear improvements from participation in Connect Activities, along with promising findings toward equitable impacts on student outcomes.

Discussion and Implications

UNT Connect implemented at scale ePortfolio as a meta-HIP in a large research university to create intentional and accessible HIPs for as many students as possible. We will continue to explore the causal impacts of this type of coordinated approach on student academic success and retention, focusing particularly on students who are historically underserved and less likely to persist at the university. The growth in faculty, staff, and student use of ePortfolio as a meta-HIP alongside existing HIPs led to 23,577 active ePortfolio users by the end of the 3rd implementation year. By embedding ePortfolio into existing university courses, including selected general education courses, learning experiences, and cocurricular programs, the barrier to reach students who are most likely to benefit is greatly reduced.

Using the ePortfolio with assessments of employer-valued skills provides a net for connection and generalization. Results support that participation in Connect Activities improves student GPA outcomes. From here, we turn our attention to those who would benefit most from this type of programming in search of an equitable intervention and student success initiative. Early findings suggest a potential equitable and accessible method to support students because the overall GPA outcomes for historically underserved students were above that of matched control samples. It is possible, and analysis in future semesters can affirm this, as fidelity in the implementation of Connect Activities increased, positive outcomes increased for more of those students most at risk for attrition.

Considering semester-over-semester retention outcomes, impacts were generally positive for Connect students when compared to students not engaging in Connect. The data show an interesting outcome with first-generation students, suggesting potential (borderline significant) impacts on retention from engagement in a Connect Activity in the fall and significant impacts on GPA from spring 2018 engagement. This may be a result of discomfort with technology and the use of ePortfolio tools during the first term, particularly because the fall sample represents more college 1st-year students who are new to the experience. The first term of engagement with Connect may not offer enough time to develop fluency in using the technology and managing a rigorous learning experience, but by the second term (spring 2018 for the fall 2017 sample), students may be more able to engage effectively. Other activities on campus (e.g., TRiO Student Support Services), although not Connect engaged, may still utilize the ePortfolio to discuss career readiness and marketability, further increasing relevance to traditionally underserved and underrepresented students.

Recommendations

Collecting and collating visible benefits from HIPs within a sustainable university-wide structure has proven to be a beneficial task, although not a simple one. To encourage the implementation of similar projects at this scale, we offer the following recommendations.

1. *Define your purpose.* UNT Connect was designed for the purpose of providing students with a clearer understanding of the employer-desired skills they are regularly gaining as part of their education and a way to

signal skill attainment to employers. Equitable impact on retention and GPA are an important byproduct of the process, but not the sole focus of the work.

2. *Garner institutional support.* Developed as the university's SACSCOC Quality Enhancement Plan (QEP) and now part of UNT's 2020 strategic plan, UNT's commitment of technological support, grant funding, and staff resources to the project has been and remains a necessity for a project of this scale. In addition, recruiting and developing faculty participants in multiple departments builds the foundation for universal use.
3. *Don't reinvent the wheel.* The general education core courses at UNT were already assessed on the adapted AAC&U VALUE rubrics, and the standards had been reviewed and agreed upon through the faculty governance processes. Because many of the VALUE rubrics assess skills sought after by employers, basing the Connect activities around these rubrics opened a path for both the student and the university to provide longitudinal evidence of skill attainment.
4. *Develop partnerships supporting technology.* The value of partnering with technology providers from the beginning cannot be overstated. Finding vendors who are excited about the project and willing to be flexible with adjustments and system integrations prevent major hurdles in the development and marketing of the product. This brings us to the last point.
5. *Train every stakeholder.* Students need to find value in the process. If that value is maligned from faculty, staff, administration, parents, or employers, the difficulty of the project increases exponentially. With these principles in mind, the hope is to widen the reach to every student on campus, ensuring valuable access to HIPs during their college experience.

Connect's main purpose is to support student connection and generalization of learning by linking HIP activities to transferable learning outcomes in a manner that signals those outcomes to students. Using technology to support scalable approaches to affirm, validate, and empower student learning, Connect is supporting this broad range of students and has seen that HIPs are holding up under assessment. Implications of early findings offer promising outcomes suggesting disproportionately positive outcomes for students who were already at risk for poor academic outcomes, regardless of demographic background. Further, with equity in mind, Connect's impact is showing positive influences on GPA.

References

Association of American Colleges & Universities. (2017). *On solid ground, VALUE report.* https://www.aacu.org/publications-research/publications/solid-ground-value-report-2017

Eynon, B., & Gambino, L. (2017). *High-impact ePortfolio practice: A catalyst for student, faculty, and institutional learning.* Stylus.

Finley, A. P., & McNair, T. (2013). *Assessing underserved students' engagement in high-impact practices.* Association of American Colleges & Universities. https://www.aacu.org/assessinghips/report

Huber, B. (2010). *Does participation in multiple high impact practices affect student success at Cal State Northridge?* https://www.csun.edu/sites/default/files/MultHIPOverviewFinal.pdf

Hunter, M., Tobolowsky, B., Gardner, J., Evenbeck, S., Pattengale, J., Schaller, M., & Schreiner, A. (2010). *Helping sophomores succeed: Understanding and improving the second year experience.* Wiley.

Iacus, S., King, G., & Porro, G. (2012). Causal inference without balance checking: Coarsened exact matching. *Political Analysis, 20*(1), 1–24. https://doi.org/10.1093/pan/mpr013

Kilgo, C. A., Sheets, J. K. E., & Pascarella, E. T. (2015). The link between high-impact practices and student learning: Some longitudinal evidence. *Higher Education, 69*(4), 509–525. https://doi.org/10.1007/s10734-014-9788-z

Kinzie, J. (2013). Taking stock of capstones and integrative learning. *Peer Review, 15*(4), 27–30. https://www.proquest.com/scholarly-journals/taking-stock-capstones-integrative-learning/docview/1506113339/se-2?accountid=14168

Kuh, G. D. (2008). *High-impact educational practices: What they are, who has access to them, and why they matter.* Association of American Colleges & Universities.

Kuh, G. (2010). Forward: High-impact practices retrospective and prospective. In J. Brownell & L. Swaner (Eds.), *Five high-impact practices* (pp. 5–11). Association of American Colleges & Universities.

Kuh, G. D., O'Donnell, K., & Reed, S. (2013). *Ensuring quality and taking high-impact practices to scale.* Association of American Colleges & Universities.

National Association of Colleges and Employers. (2020). *NACE Job Outlook 2020.*

Peecksen, S., Branton, R., Branch, A., Simmons, M., & Naik, M. (2020). *Improving university students' success through high-impact practices* [Manuscript submitted for publication]. Career Connect, University of North Texas.

Tinto, V. (1993). *Leaving college: Rethinking the causes and cures of student attrition* (2nd ed.). University of Chicago Press.

20

MEASUREMENT AND EVALUATION OF HIGH-IMPACT PRACTICES WITHIN A CENTRALIZED MODEL

Rasha M. Qudisat and Frederick H. White

In 2008, Kuh asserted that although assessment of certain high-impact practices (HIPs) was occurring at many universities, the utilization of these practices "was unsystematic, to the detriment of the student" (p. 9). In an attempt to address Kuh's specific concerns, we have learned that three major questions must be addressed in organizing student engagement opportunities. First, how do we implement a university-wide program? Second, once we have a program, how do we measure and assess it? Third, how do we maintain consistency in this program so that the quality of the engagement is available to every student?

At Utah Valley University (UVU), we have made significant progress in addressing these questions, although the third still presents challenges. As a result, this chapter provides a centralized model for addressing HIPs at an institutional level; introduces a unique type of measurement and evaluation; and shares initial findings and suggests that such an approach provides actionable data that can lead to changes at the course, department, college, and institution levels. More specifically, we offer an overview of our strategies and the development of UVU's Five Pillars of Student Engagement as one stratagem toward addressing Kuh's concern of an unsystematic approach, which does more harm at times than good to our students' education.

Centralized Model

UVU is an open-enrollment institution with more than 41,000 students enrolled as of fall 2019. As a comprehensive teaching university, UVU addressed the daunting challenge of retaining and graduating our students by establishing an Office of Engaged Learning (OEL) in 2010. UVU had been recognized at that point with Carnegie designations as both a community-engaged and curricularly engaged institution. As an institution, UVU had fully embraced a commitment to student engagement, beyond a branding slogan. The questions that we faced in moving from theory to practice were those stated previously: How could we go beyond commitment and move to a campus-wide plan that was measured and assessed, while maintaining quality and consistency across the university?

This is what we have learned over the years: When faced with 11 HIPs, do not to try to address all 11 immediately. We selected those that were already well established and, therefore, were easier to implement (see Figure 20.1). It did not mean that we were not doing most of them in other areas of the university, but we needed to select specific HIPs to include in the first stage

Figure 20.1. UVU's Five Pillars of Student Engagement and associated organizational structure.

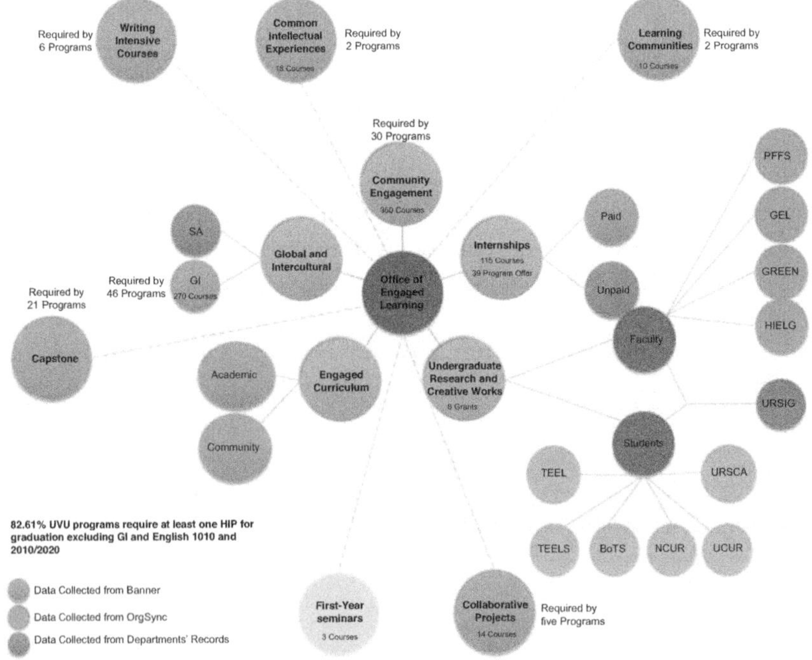

of our university-wide plan. Unlike many universities, UVU has developed a very centralized administrative and governing model. This was helpful when selecting our HIPs. For some other universities that use a decentralized governing model, this may take some time to organize. The first steps, however, were to identify our HIPs and how to administer them within our university's governing structure.

In 2017, UVU officially launched the Five Pillars of Student Engagement, organized and supported by OEL: (a) global and intercultural experiences, (b) internships, (c) community engagement (including academic service-learning), (d) undergraduate research and creative works, and (e) engaged curriculum (our measurement and assessment pillar). Most of these areas had previously reported in some way to OEL, but by defining them as specific pillars, it gave a level of coherency as to "why?" that had been missing. In order to strengthen this approach, UVU created director-level or higher positions for each one of these pillars. From an administrative standpoint, assessment, measurement, and consistency demand a centralized approach, with individuals dedicated to the complex problems that come along with university-wide initiatives. At the launch of the Five Pillars of Student Engagement, we had five directors (or higher), one for each pillar, who reported directly to the associate vice president for engaged learning.

At UVU, we took the approach that each one of the schools and colleges could embrace at least one of the pillars for their programs without significantly disrupting their curriculum. It was suggested that once they designated one or two pillars, then each school or college must strengthen those existing efforts. This worked very well. Business embraced internships and community engagement; social sciences and humanities selected study abroad programs and increased their internship opportunities; sciences was deeply committed to faculty-led undergraduate research; arts was invested in undergraduate creative works; and University College continued their efforts with internships and expanded their global and intercultural programming; technology and computing, education, and public safety all had substantial, long-standing experience with community engagement and internships. Every dean, more specifically, was interested in strengthening the engaging curriculum of the classroom, and this is where we may have made our most significant innovations.

Having the university as a whole understand and support the plan for HIPs was very important. However, equally significant was the data to track and measure efforts. Without data and regular updates on progress, the coherence of our efforts could be lost in the multitude of issues that arise each semester. At UVU, each pillar director addressed the Academic Affairs Council once a semester and the President's Leadership Council once a year.

Therefore, the five pillars remained a part of the ongoing discussion about university development.

Baseline for Measurement

In order to establish a baseline, the director of the engaged curriculum conducted a comprehensive study of our existing efforts and curricular programming (see Figure 20.2). As measured in August 2017, out of the eight colleges, there were 46 overarching programs, which encompassed all of the degrees offered. Of the 46 programs, every program required a global/intercultural (G/I) course as well as English 1010 and 2010/2020 courses for graduation. These courses fulfilled two of the 11 HIPs (i.e., diversity/global learning and writing-intensive courses). Therefore, all programs had at least two HIP requirements to graduate; however, not every program encompassed every HIP. First-year seminar courses were not required for any program to graduate. Only two programs required common intellectual experience courses and learning community courses to graduate. Five programs required collaborative project courses, and six programs required writing-intensive courses. A minority of programs required a capstone project or course. Thirty-eight programs required at least one HIP. Many programs included optional courses that were HIP in nature, including internships. This answered in large part the first question. UVU had defined its Five Pillars for Student Engagement, had gained campus-wide acceptance, and had established a baseline for future measurement and assessment.

An Engagement Instrument

In response to the need to measure and evaluate academic engagement, specifically students' experiences in the classroom, we created an in-class engagement instrument, SEGO, which measures, assesses, and tracks academic and community engagement, even beyond the definition and practices of the 11 HIPs. This instrument was developed in house as a partial spin-off from a Title III grant. The name SEGO was selected because the sego lily is the state flower of Utah and the flower's structure seemed to mirror our own three-dimensional engagement model. Referencing the research of Hung et al. (2006), we identified the main factors of engaged learning, searched for reliable and valid instruments from scholarly literature, and expanded the original conceptual model in order to create a reliable instrument that measured academic and community engagement within the classroom (see Figure 20.3).

Figure 20.2. HIPs dashboard—created based on UVU's course catalog, August 2017. See note on Figures 20.1, 20.2, 20.4, and 20.6 at end of this chapter.

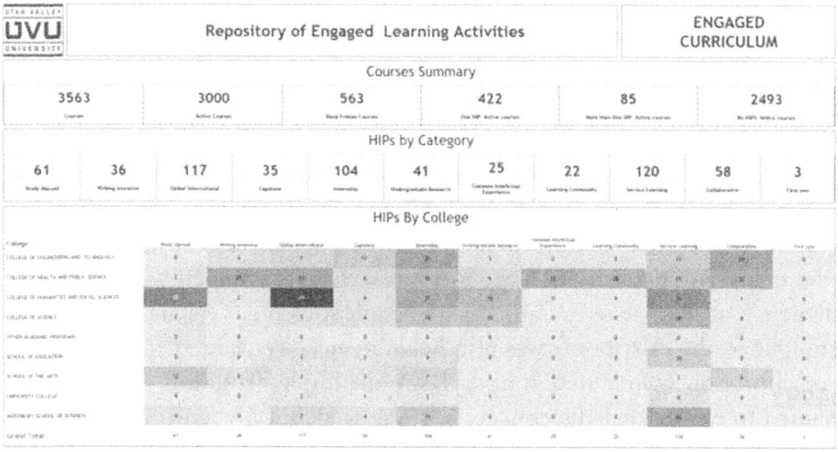

The first version of SEGO used a participatory approach and relied on a 200-item survey that was reviewed in fall 2016 by our Engaged Learning Committee. Furthermore, as we piloted the instrument in select courses, we also collected feedback from the faculty who administered the survey and from the student respondents. With this data, we used an exploratory factor analysis (EFA) replication procedure (Osborne & Fitzpatrick, 2012) to confirm the model as hypothesized. Using the EFA criteria, we eliminated from the instrument any redundancies, badly worded questions, and highly correlated items. This procedure was performed for every factor.

The goal for the evaluation instrument was to create a survey that asked students basic questions about the activities and assignments of a course that we deemed significant for academic and community engagement. For example, *Did the course involve input from a client or professional expert?* represents

Figure 20.3. Main factors of engaged learning.

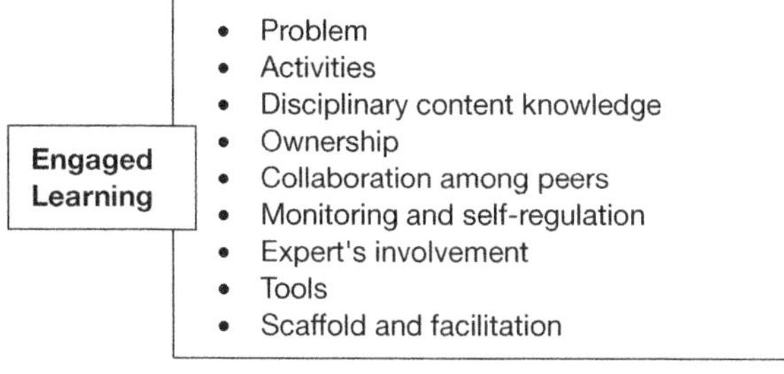

the client interaction factor; *Did a course require a presentation?* represents the active collaborative learning factor. We understood that some courses were designed to rate higher on community engagement, and some would be focused on academic engagement. The point was to ask those students who were taking the course if the intended design (how it was represented in the catalog or the syllabus) was what was experienced inside and outside of the classroom.

Once we had created the measurement model and understood the relationship between faculty, students, and engaged curriculum, we made some important decisions for implementation. In order to avoid conflict with those who may think that SEGO was a measure of faculty competence, the faculty element was held at zero. Similarly, the student element (what abilities they brought to the classroom) was also held at zero. We wanted to concentrate our efforts on course design and classroom implementation. After all, we wanted to ensure that the course itself was academically and/or community engaged as originally designated.

SEGO plotted courses on an *x-y* continuum, which was divided into four quadrants: high academic, high community/high academic, low community/low academic, high community/low academic/low community. The academic engagement factor was measured within the following categories: theory and knowledge, application and skills, collaboration, learning tools, content, and context of the course as designed. Community engagement was measured by community involvement (as a result of the course design) and professional interaction. Some courses, by design, were high on one factor, but not on the other. The analysis showed that higher level courses were higher on academic and community engagement than lower level courses.

Additionally, we used the measurement model to create a structural model, to verify the prospective link between academic engagement, community engagement, and our students' course success and retention (see Figure 20.4). The structural equation model (SEM) showed that there was a positive effect of academic engagement on course success, which meant that the higher academic engagement that the students experienced, the better their chances for curricular success (see Figure 20.5). This finding only further solidified Kuh's (2008) suggestion for a systematic approach to student engagement. We could now measure the impact of HIPs within individual courses and assess their influence on student retention and higher rates of completion.

We also investigated structure invariance between groups (gender, ethnicity, and employment). Because every college is different, a SEM was created for each college separately, investigating the effect of academic engagement on course success and retention. Once we had the raw data,

Figure 20.4. Structural model.

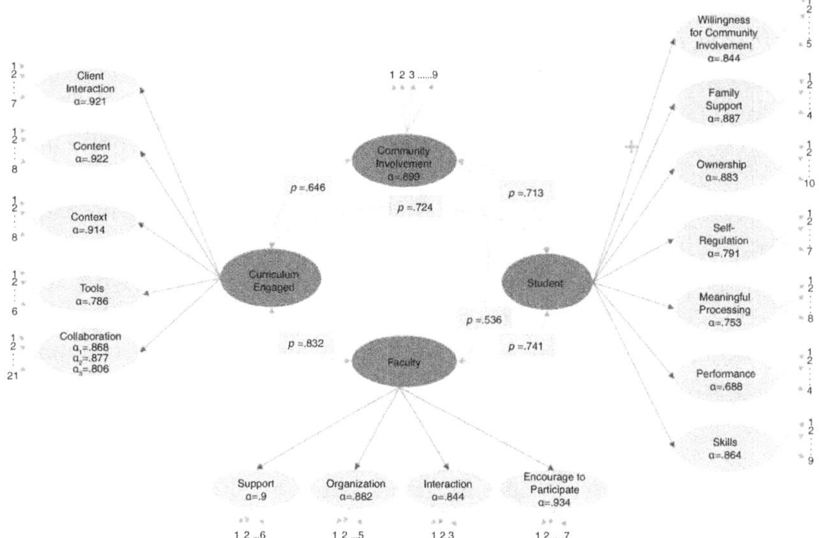

Figure 20.5. Measuring academic engagement.

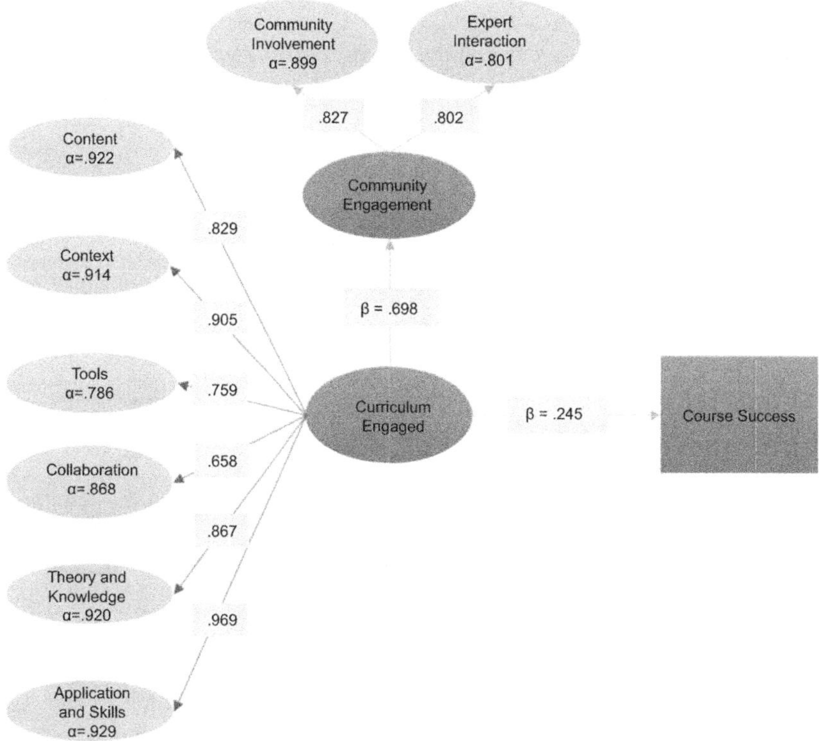

we could correlate much more than what we had originally anticipated and could focus on certain student groups to ensure that a course design did not dis/favor any subgroup. For example, we could compare if part-time students scored a course similarly to full-time students. We could also look at how a course was scored by female students or first-generation students and compare that to the course score to gain an understanding of how a course might impact subgroups.

Due to these decisions and after refining the measurement instrument further, SEGO finally consisted of a 45-item survey, which took about 10 minutes to complete. Optimally, colleges would administer the survey every semester in a course, to maximize the response rate among students, with the intention of eventually designating courses as high, medium, or low engaged. The purpose of this model was to locate courses within the academic and community engagement definition, which could be used in course selection by students in curricular and program design by departments, for accreditation by administrators, and more. In doing so, OEL was only tasked with measurement and assessment. As will be discussed in the following, the Office of Teaching and Learning (OTL) would then play a vital role in addressing with faculty any noted discrepancies in a course in order to improve the course design.

The SEGO Dashboard provides an in-depth view of student engagement at the course level and pays special attention to class demographics

Figure 20.6. SEGO Dashboard display.

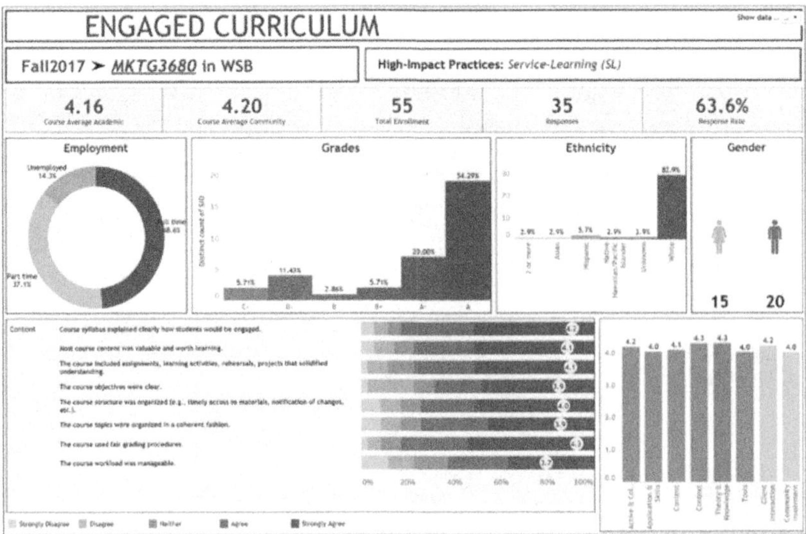

(gender, ethnicity, employment, and grades). Figure 20.6 is one example of the display for the course MKTG3680, offered by the Woodbury School of Business, representing the survey data for fall 2017. The dashboard shows the course's HIPs designation (i.e., s-l) in the upper right corner, as well as the mean academic and community engagement scores, enrollment, demographics, and mean scores of academic and community engagement by factors in the lower right corner. By clicking on a specific factor, it is possible to see the items of that factor with their mean scores. As a result of our efforts and in recognition of our initial successes, UVU has sought a patent for SEGO and has also begun to explore commercialization options.

Student Success

Once SEGO was established, we began to further investigate the relationship of engagement to student success. We needed to test the theory that multiple HIPs were beneficial among our own student population as an open-enrollment institution. Our findings mirrored the published research (Bonet & Walters, 2016; Brownell & Swaner, 2010; Gipson & Mitchell, 2017; Johnson & Stage, 2018; Kilgo et al., 2015; Sweat et al., 2013), but we were also concerned with finding the appropriate HIP, at the right intensity, at the right time in our students' education, that would have a significant, positive effect on retention, persistence, and success. Understanding the level of engagement at various stages in our students' education was imperative for course evaluation and review, program design, and policy development.

Using student identification numbers, we began to classify students who had experienced multiple engaged opportunities at UVU. The repository data could then be united with the course-level data in order to measure all 11 HIPs in varying degrees. In our model, the 11 HIPs shared the concept of "engagement," and based on the expectations that HIPs are to be highly engaged on some level and type, we measured them using SEGO. The premise was that when combined and organized in the proper sequence, HIPs significantly raised graduation rates. This supposition offered a practical question as well—*How can we accurately measure and assess multiple HIPs combinations?*

Once again, we looked at our own data to find out how our students had benefited from a collective impact approach. For example, the graduation rate among UVU students who participated in the collective impact of study abroad, G/I, and academic service-learning courses was 72%. For those who participated in some, but not all three, it was 43%, and for those who did not take advantage of any of these options, it was 6%. Admittedly, because taking a G/I course is now a graduation requirement, this probably explains the drastic decrease in graduation rates for those who did not participate in any of these three engagement opportunities.

Therefore, we further investigated the 2017 cohort in order to identify the effect of four pillars of engagement participation as collective impact, which might provide predictors for persistence for 1 academic year. The population selected was 14,152 full-time UVU students enrolled in fall 2017. We posed three research questions. The first concentrated on independent variables such as student level, ethnicity, gender, economic status (Pell Grant eligibility), total OEL pillars enrollment, program type (STEM, non-STEM), and high school GPA. The other two questions were only focused on OEL participation and did not account for other independent variables.

What are the predictors of students' academic performance (GPA)? Significantly, UVU is an open-enrollment university. Our motto has been "Come as you are" and high school GPA had not been used as a predictor of success. Results of the linear regression model indicated that the student level ($\beta = .195, p < .000$), ethnicity ($\beta = .112, p < .000$), gender ($\beta = -.093, p < .0001$), economic status ($\beta = -.054, p < .000$), and total OEL pillars enrollment ($\beta = .036, p < .000$) are predictors for a student's cumulative GPA. Prior preparation (i.e., high school GPA) was not a predictor of academic success.

Does OEL enrollment in the Five Pillars of Student Engagement *(global and intercultural experiences, internships, community, engagement, undergraduate research and creative works,* and *engaged curriculum*) predict persistence? Based on the first research question's findings (i.e., that OEL pillar enrollment predicts GPA) and that it was this factor that we in OEL could manage/develop, we focused the second research question only on the number of pillar enrollments (i.e., the intensity of HIPs). Results indicated that the number of participated OEL pillars is a significant predictor for students' persistence; each additional OEL pillar participation increases the odds of persistence by 47%, and the critical value of OEL participation to persist to the next semester is four OEL pillars.

Which interaction of OEL pillars predicts best student persistence? Once we knew the answer to the first two questions, we wanted to find the best combination of OEL pillars. Out of six 22-OEL pillar interactions, only two proved to be significant predictors of students' persistence: service-learning with G/I experiences and service-learning with research. A combination of service-learning and G/I courses will increase the odds of persistence by 63% and a combination of service-learning with research courses by 95%. This finding supports the previous study we conducted on the 2009 cohort, which concluded that service-learning has the most effect on students' graduation and academic performance. As a summary, we created the Collective Impact Dashboard, which provided descriptive information about participation in service-learning, G/I experiences, undergraduate research, and internships.

HIPs Quality Evaluation

Now we turn to our third question: *How do we maintain consistency in this program so that the quality of the engagement is available to every student?* Not all HIPs are equal in quality. Not all engaged experiences are equally impactful. Not all sections of the same course are as effective at academic engagement. This is where we are in the process of the Five Pillars of Student Engagement. We envision a circular continuum: The faculty is responsible for the curriculum, OEL is responsible for measuring and assessing engagement, and OTL addresses identified deficiencies in curricular design, method of instruction, or any other structural issue. All of this should benefit the student's educational experience by providing greater coherence across the curriculum. In an ideal situation, all sections of a course designated as high academic, high community engaged would score into these quadrants. This does not mean that the content is at issue, but maintaining course design and delivery methodology (as described in the course syllabus) is the issue so that students in all sections have a similar experience on the level of engagement.

As an example, we have data on the effectiveness and consistency of effort on our G/I courses, using the Assessment of Intercultural Competency (AIC) instrument. The G/I team revised the instrument to be applicable to UVU G/I objectives. Intercultural competency is a second-order factor that measures skills, attitude, awareness, and knowledge. We collect longitudinal data on intercultural competency to assess the improvement levels between semesters and track sections to pinpoint any outliers. Improvement of intercultural competence is measured retrospectively and after the class; AIC improvement ranged between 19% in spring 2018 and 27% in fall 2018. The average improvement over four semesters was 23%. As a result, chairs, deans, and administrators will be able to review programs and courses to keep track of engaged learning and plan strategies for improvement. Still, much more must be done to institutionalize the process loop of faculty, students, OEL, and OTL in order to achieve quality and consistency with our engagement opportunities.

At UVU, development, management, and implementation of SEGO were institutionalized under the Office of Engaged Learning. Eventually, the engagement instrument will be used in all classes across campus to assess the level of engagement in courses at the institution. The SEGO Dashboard will become a tool for administration, faculty, and staff to assess and improve student engagement across the institution and to maintain the quality of HIPs.

It is planned that the SEGO evaluation instrument will be administered in spring 2022 for the first time to every student in every course across the university. The 45-question survey will be given two-thirds of the way through the semester. Participation will be a required assignment in all classes. Faculty will not be involved in the administration of the survey, which will be delivered through Canvas. The data from the survey will then be used to populate the SEGO Dashboard; access will be given to every dean, department chair, and faculty member, depending on their level of responsibility. The SEGO Dashboard will provide actionable data that can lead to changes at the class, department, college, and institution levels.

In summary, a centralized model for addressing HIPs at an institutional level has been advantageous for UVU. The development of an engaged instrument (SEGO) has offered a unique type of measurement and evaluation that has been used (in limited scope) by various entities within the university to make meaningful changes at various levels of the institution. In the future, SEGO will need to be tested in other university environments and at other universities in order to confirm a wide applicability and optimal usage for decision-making. Armed with this information, faculty can work to improve their courses, administrators can better employ HIPs throughout the university curriculum, and internal and external decision-makers can potentially address issues of equity within our higher education system.

References

Bonet, G., & Walters, B. (2016). High impact practices: Student engagement and retention. *College Student Journal, 50*(2), 224–235. https://academicworks.cuny.edu/cgi/viewcontent.cgi?referer=https://scholar.google.com/&httpsredir=1&article=1101&context=kb_pubs

Brownell, J. E., & Swaner, L. E. (2010). *Five high-impact practices: Research on learning outcomes, completion and quality*. Association of American Colleges & Universities.

Gipson, J., & Mitchell, D. (2017). How high-impact practices influence academic achievement for African American college students. *Journal Committed to Social Change on Race and Ethnicity, 3*(2), 124–144. https://doi.org/10.15763/issn.2642-2387.2017.3.2.123-144

Hung, D., Tan, S. C., & Koh, T. S. (2006). Engaged learning: Making learning an authentic experience. *Engaged Learning With Emerging Technologies*, *25*(1), 29–48. https://doi.org/10.1007/1-4020-3669-8_2

Johnson, S. R., & Stage, F. K. (2018). Academic engagement and student success: Do high-impact practices mean higher graduation rates? *Journal of Higher Education*, *89*(5), 753–781. https://doi.org/10.1080/00221546.2018.1441107

Kilgo, C. A., Ezell Sheets, J. K., & Pascarella, E. T. (2015). The link between high-impact practices and student learning: Some longitudinal evidence. *Higher Education*, *69*(4), 509–525. https://doi.org/10.1007/s10734-014-9788-z

Kuh, G. D. (2008). *High-impact educational practices: What they are, who has access to them, and why they matter*. Association of American Colleges & Universities.

Osborne, J. W., & Fitzpatrick, D. C. (2012). Replication analysis in exploratory factor analysis: What it is and why it makes your analysis better. *Practical Assessment, Research & Evaluation*, *17*(15), 1–8. https://doi.org/10.7275/h0bd-4d11

Sweat, J., Jones, G., Han, S., & Wolfgram, S. M. (2013). How does high impact practice predict student engagement? A comparison of white and minority students. *International Journal for the Scholarship of Teaching and Learning*, *7*(2), 1–26. https://doi.org/10.20429/ijsotl.2013.070217

21

USING PROPENSITY SCORE MATCHING TO ASSESS HIGH-IMPACT PRACTICES OUTCOMES

Angela Byrd, Heather A. Haeger, Wendy Lin, A. Sonia Ninon, and Steven S. Graunke

The factors that predict student success in higher education are often the same factors that predict a student's participation in engaged learning (EL) or high-impact practices (HIPs; Finley & McNair, 2013). Assessing the efficacy of EL then becomes problematic. Differences in student outcomes may merely be reflective of accessibility and equity. If the HIP occurs later in students' academic careers, gauging impact becomes even more challenging: Participants must have already been persisting and retained to have participated. Consequently, the ability to demonstrate the individual effects of HIPs on student outcomes relies on the ability to parse out the effects of confounding sociodemographic and academic variables and minimize self-selection bias. Propensity score matching (PSM) is one statistical method that can help researchers reduce the impact of confounding effects and control for self-selection in order to demonstrate the important impact of HIPs on student success.

Summary of Relevant Literature

Many quantitative researchers tend to consider randomized experimental studies ideal. A truly random experimental design allows researchers to better control the effects of confounding variables where any participant has an equal chance of being assigned to a "treated" or "untreated" (i.e., "control") group. Many statistical procedures used for quantitative research in higher education also depend on randomized assignment as a fundamental assumption. However, given the known benefits of EL, it is neither realistic nor ethical to randomly assign HIPs participation. Instead, higher education professionals must assess the impact of academic support programs on student success through quasiexperimental studies. In situations where students cannot be randomly assigned, it is difficult to tease out the effects of selection bias and confounding factors from actual program effects. PSM, based on the causal effect model introduced by Rubin (1974), could be used to minimize selection bias and allow causal inferences to be made (Rosenbaum & Rubin, 1983, 1984). Using PSM, researchers can create a control group by matching participants with one or more nonparticipants who had equal or similar probabilities of participation. Differences between the treated and matched control subjects are therefore less influenced by selection bias than in most quasiexperimental designs.

Methodology

The propensity score is defined by the predicted probability that a subject will be assigned to a group, based on conditions that exist at the time of group assignment. In evaluating HIP outcomes, it is the probability that a student would have been a participant. One commonly used technique for estimating a propensity score is logistic regression (Stuart, 2010), where a binary outcome (program participation = Yes/No) is predicted given a series of predictor variables:

$$\text{Logit}(y) = a + b_1 x_1$$

Once propensity scores are calculated for each participant and nonparticipant, one or more nonparticipants with exact or similar propensity scores are selected as comparable controls. The average outcome among controls is used to estimate the expected outcome for their matched treated subject. The difference between each treated subject and matched pairs are used to estimate the effect of the intervention program, known as the average treatment effect for the treated (ATT).

The quality of matching is assessed by comparing the balance of covariates in the control and treated group before and after matching. Methods include examining differences in the distributions of the variables between the treated and control groups (Ho et al., 2007), standardized differences in the variables between the treated and control groups (Stuart, 2010), and percentage reductions of absolute differences.

Lastly, the underlying assumption of PSM is that all the confounders are accounted for in the model. This assumption can be tested by sensitivity analysis, which considers how strong the unobserved covariates would have to be in order to negate the conclusion of the study (Liu et al., 2013). A more in-depth description of sensitivity analysis appears later in the chapter.

Pedagogies and Practices: Investigating HIPs Using PSM

Several institutional researchers and assessment professionals have used PSM to assess the effects of HIPs on their campuses. A few illustrative examples are described in the following sections.

Service/Community Engagement

The Sam H. Jones Scholarship (SHJ) is a community service scholarship offered by the Indiana University–Purdue University Indianapolis (IUPUI) Center for Service and Learning (CSL) and awarded to students with prior service to their high school, campus, or community. Not only does SHJ offer financial awards to support continued involvement in meaningful service, leadership, and social advocacy, but participants also enroll in a service-learning course that includes rigorous reflection activities and learning assessment. These practices have been shown to effectively increase personal growth and personal self-efficacy (Sanders et al., 2015).

CSL staff asked for assistance in assessing the effectiveness of the SHJ Scholarship program in facilitating student success. Preliminary analyses showed that SHJ participants from fall 2017 were more likely to be female, attending full time, have lower unmet financial need, and were more academically prepared compared to their peers. Such differences were a source of confounding, which could obscure the impact of the program on student success. Using PSM, every SHJ participant was matched with a nonparticipant who shared similar demographic, financial, and academic characteristics. Results indicated that the SHJ program resulted in a significant increase in fall-to-fall retention (8.8 percentage point increase in fall-to-fall retention at IUPUI and 7.9 percentage point increase in fall-to-fall retention as a result of participating in the SHJ program). Participants earned a significantly higher semester GPA. The program greatly benefited students from an underrepresented group, as underrepresented students showed an 11% increase in retention (96% for participants compared to 85% for matched nonparticipants). These results provide further evidence that the SHJ program could positively impact retention. That said, sensitivity analysis suggested that there exists some student characteristics that were not accounted for in the original model. Students who engage in community service are likely different from their peers in terms of social-psychological aspects, personality, and motivational characteristics, or if they have experienced difficult life circumstances (such as poverty; Snyder & Omoto, 2009). These may be important data points to collect and include in future analyses.

Undergraduate Research

A great deal of previous research has illustrated the benefits of undergraduate research (UR; Hathaway et al., 2002; Hunter et al., 2007; Kuh, 2008; Kuh et al., 2010; Russell et al., 2007). Unfortunately, those studies have not demonstrated a causal relationship between UR and student success because they rely on self-reported learning, sample data from single institutions, do not control for student characteristics, or use inappropriate comparisons. This study built upon previous research by using a quasiexperimental design across five public institutions to examine the relationship between participating in UR and likelihood of graduating along with time-to-graduation. PSM was used to simulate random assignment to treatment and comparison groups across five universities. This PSM model matched students who participated in undergraduate research with similar peers in terms of gender, ethnicity, prior academic performance, socioeconomic status, parental education, and major. Logistic regressions were used on this matched sample to test the impact of UR on 4-year and 6-year graduation rates while controlling for student background characteristics and prior academic performance. Results show that 89% of undergraduate researchers graduated in 6 years or less and were significantly more likely to graduate in 4 and 6 years ($p < 0.01$) than their matched peers. These findings suggest that institutions may specifically invest in UR as a tool to increase their students' graduation rates.

Residential-Based Learning Communities

Brower and Inkelas (2010) defined *living-learning communities* as "residential housing programs that incorporate academically based themes and build community through common learning" (Brower & Inkelas, 2010, para. 4). Nationally, research has been done to investigate the diversity and impact of learning communities through the National Study of Living-Learning Programs, which occurred in 2007. Inkelas et al. (2018) developed a comprehensive research-based model for residential-based learning communities (RBLCs) that synthesized the experiences of multiple campuses from the National Study of Living-Learning Programs. This model is not only helpful for designing and delivering living-learning programs (LLPs) but it also provides valuable insight into assessing the status of those communities and can be utilized as a framework for program review.

The most recent analysis of the RBLC experience at IUPUI began in the Fall 2019 semester. The researchers wanted to examine the impact of participation in one of the 14 RBLCs at IUPUI on student retention and academic performance measured by term and cumulative GPAs. PSM was used to identify a set of Fall 2018 full-time beginning 1st-year students seeking a bachelor's degree who did not participate in the RBLC experience with similar demographic and academic characteristics as those who participated. Students who did not participate were selected based on degree-seeking status, campus location (Indianapolis compared to a satellite campus), course load, race/ethnicity, residency status, gender, age, first-generation status, best SAT score, Pell Grant, receipt of Indiana's 21st Century award, receipt of other institutional need-based aid, and major. Logistic regression models were then conducted using the matched dataset.

Results show the 1-year retention rate at all IU campuses was 91% for the RBLC students compared to 76% for the non-RBLC students. The 1-year retention rate at IUPUI was 89% for the RBLC students versus 73% for the non-RBLC students. Students with an RBLC experience also had higher first-semester and cumulative GPAs than their counterparts without an RBLC experience. Further assessment, review, and evaluation have been planned to determine why there is such a wide gap in retention rates, in addition to the impact of RBLCs beyond retention and GPA.

Study Abroad

Internationalization and global learning have been a focus of growth throughout the past decade at Western Kentucky University (WKU). In 2013–2014 WKU was ranked 19th in the nation among similar institutions for its number of students studying abroad (IIE, 2019). However, the demographic and academic characteristics of WKU students who studied abroad were not representative of the student population. At-risk students (Pell-eligible, underrepresented minorities, and first-generation college students) were only half as likely to study abroad as their counterparts. These disparities are not unique to WKU. Due to its academic, social, and economic demands, study abroad (SA) is not always accessible to all students. As "study abroad students aren't representative of all students," our tendency is to attribute any of its positive outcomes to "the elite academic status of those who typically choose to study abroad, and not to the study abroad experience" itself (Sutton & Rubin, 2004, p. 74). Nonetheless, SA participation has been shown to have a positive impact on student retention and completion rates as well as GPAs—especially for marginalized and at-risk students (Malmgren & Galvin, 2008; Sutton & Rubin, 2004; Willett et al., 2013). In 2018, interest in evaluating the accessibility and efficacy of study abroad programs led WKU's Office of Institutional Research to examine the effects of study abroad participation on 6-year graduation rates.

Study abroad participation at WKU requires that students be enrolled and perform well academically. This created an analytical problem in that enrollment in later terms is a better predictor of graduation than enrollment in earlier terms. Consequently, it was necessary to look at the *timing* of study abroad participation (rather than participation in general)—and to control for retention and academic performance at that same point in time. PSM was used to create control groups of nonparticipants who had comparable characteristics of students who had studied abroad by the end of their 2nd, 3rd, or 4th academic year. Control variables used included race, gender, Pell Grant eligibility, first-generation status, and cumulative GPA (as a proxy for retention and academic strength). Logistic regression provided estimates of the individual effects of study abroad participation on the predicted probability of a student graduating within 6 years. Results showed that study abroad participation by the end of students' 2nd academic year improved predicted 6-year graduation rates by 6% overall, by 15% for Pell-eligible (low-income) students, and by 8% for first-generation college students. Study abroad participation had the greatest effect on graduation rates for at-risk and lower performing students. WKU's division of Global Learning and International Affairs now has a focus on making study abroad more accessible, which is underscored by the incorporation of these findings into the university's 10-year strategic plan metrics.

Quality of Research

Before considering the use of PSM in the assessment of HIPS, researchers should first consider which types of programs are appropriate for the methodology. In addition, as with any statistical technique, it is important to check the assumptions to make sure the results are valid.

Research Question Development

Rosenbaum and Rubin (1983) suggested that PSM be used to create matched samples when the pool of potential control subjects is large and a wide variety of variables could be potentially confounding. Given the limited availability of resources to extend participation in HIPs, as well as the many documented ways in which HIP participation is not equitably distributed, almost any evaluation of the effectiveness of HIPs would fit these criteria (Finley & McNair, 2013). That said, because effective use of PSM involves dividing samples into subclasses, small sample sizes can lead to inaccurate estimates and incorrectly derived groups (Fan & Nowell, 2011). Researchers should limit PSM to the evaluation of HIPs when a sufficient number of students have participated, though there is not currently consensus on what that number should be.

Checking Assumptions

PSM is designed to create matched pairs that have equal or similar chance of receiving treatment. When some unknown confounders exist, matched pairs created by the PSM procedure might not be comparable. Rosenbaum and Rubin (1983) mentioned that it would be virtually impossible to create a perfectly matched comparison group even using PSM. This is why it is critical to use sensitivity analysis in order to determine if there are unaccounted sources of variation.

Sensitivity analysis considers if hidden bias is strong enough to alter the conclusion of the study. Sensitivity analysis can be performed using Wilcoxon's signed rank test for matched pairs. The degree of hidden bias from unobserved confounders is measured by Γ. Under the ideal situation where no unobserved confounds exist and all subjects have a similar chance of receiving treatment, $\Gamma = 1$. Suppose $\Gamma = 2$; this means one subject is 2 times more likely to receive treatment than the other due to some unobserved confounds. For each $\Gamma > 1$, the sign rank test provides an interval of *P*-values reflecting uncertainty due to hidden bias. The sensitivity analysis searches for a tipping point that alters the study conclusion. For instance, if the study conclusion changes for Γ very close to 1, the study is highly sensitive to hidden bias and we conclude that some unobserved confounders exist.

Using PSM at Your Institution

Although the statistical components of PSM are complex, its usage and applicability are not. The following tips can help any educator or researcher use this method:

1. *Collect and clean the data.* There is no limit to the emphasis that should be placed on collecting complete and accurate HIP-related data. It is critical to not only track HIP participation but also the type, timing, and outcome(s) of participation. If there is even a marginal chance that a variable will be counted/evaluated later, it must be captured. Relevant

data should be on record within the unit(s) administering the program(s). If variables change over time, it is best practice to capture "snapped" data (i.e., data "as of MM/DD/YYYY") regularly.

2. *Utilize existing institutional data.* Researchers can work with their institution's information technology (IT) or institutional research (IR) divisions to develop a framework for recording and warehousing HIPs-related data. Additionally, IT and IR may help append relevant demographic and academic variables for research purposes, such as entry term, institutional GPA, time-to-degree completion, and other data. IR professionals can also identify and track cohorts of students, which is important when evaluating the impact of HIPs on retention, persistence, and graduation rates.
3. *Learn about the participants.* Communication within and across institutions can help identify ways HIPs participants differ from nonparticipants. After compiling a comprehensive dataset, data exploration and visualization can help reveal any variables that are heavily skewed. Checks should also be made for multicollinearity and confounding variables.
4. *Apply the method.* Statistical software programs SAS, Stata, SPSS, and R each have built-in procedures for PSM. Software-specific support and documentation are the best resources for learning those procedures. With such software, the researcher can use variables that may contribute to HIP participation and outcome to calculate the propensity score, match participants with nonparticipants, and perform additional analyses of outcomes between groups.
5. *Consult experts if you need help.* As noted elsewhere in this book (see chapter 5, this volume), PSM is an increasingly common technique in assessment and institutional research beyond just the evaluation of HIPs. If you are uncomfortable with statistics or unfamiliar with PSM techniques, we recommend reaching out to your institutional research office or other professionals on campus who are able to help.

Evidence of Data-Supported Equity

PSM and other matching methodologies are important in order to understand patterns of structural inequalities in access to HIPs and to determine the impact of these practices while accounting for advantage and privilege. First, PSM requires identifying how the population of students who participated in the HIP differ from other students who did not. In testing the differences between participants and nonparticipants, we can identify equity gaps in access to participation. For example, in creating a PSM model to assess UR at five different universities, we found that patterns of access were different at each institution. The only common factor that predicted participation at each university was prior academic performance (first-year GPA). Patterns of unequal participation for students of color and first-generation students were present at some universities and not others. PSM requires an analysis of these patterns; we can take that information a step further by not only identifying gaps but working to determine why they persist and how to reduce or eliminate them.

Second, PSM allows for more accurate assessment of the impact of HIPs while accounting for differences in student populations and in the privileges (or disadvantages) those populations have experienced. For example, students that have experienced privilege in the educational system because of their race and/or socioeconomic status are more likely to engage in HIPs and are more likely to score higher in many traditional educational metrics because of that same privilege (Kinzie et al., 2008). Understanding both structural inequities in engagement in HIPs and the impact of these programs beyond perpetuating privilege is crucial for understanding the real impact of these practices.

References

Brower, A. M., & Inkelas, K. K. (2010). *Living-learning programs: One high-impact educational practice we now know a lot about.* Association of American Colleges & Universities. https://www.aacu.org/publications-research/periodicals/living-learning-programs-one-high-impact-educational-practice-we

Fan, X., & Nowell, D. L. (2011). Using propensity score matching in educational research. *Gifted Child Quarterly*, *55*(1), 74–79. https://doi.org/10.1177/0016986210390635

Finley, A., & McNair, T. (2013). *Assessing underserved students' engagement in high impact practices.* Association of American Colleges & Universities. https://eric.ed.gov/?id=ED582014

Hathaway, R. S., Nagda, B. A., & Gregerman, S. R. (2002). The relationship of undergraduate research participation to graduate and professional education pursuit: An empirical study. *Journal of College Student Development, 43*(5), 614–631. https://www.researchgate.net/profile/Biren_Nagda/publication/234625388_The_Relationship_of_Undergraduate_Research_Participation_to_Graduate_and_Professional_Education_Pursuit_An_Empirical_Study/links/5452ea260cf2cf51647a4e9f.pdf

Ho, D. E., Imai, K., King, G., & Stuart, E. A. (2007). Matching as nonparametric preprocessing for reducing model dependence in parametric causal inference. *Political Analysis*, *15*(3), 199–236. https://doi.org/10.1093/pan/mpl013

Hunter, A. B., Laursen, S. L., & Seymour, E. (2007). Becoming a scientist: The role of undergraduate research in students' cognitive, personal, and professional development. *Science Education, 91*(1), 36–74. https://doi.org/10.1002/sce.20173

Inkelas, K. K., Jessup-Anger, J., Benjamin, M., & Wawrzynski, M. (2018). *Living-learning communities that work: A research-based model for design, delivery, and assessment.* Stylus.

Institute of International Education. (2019). *Institutions by total number of study abroad students* [Dataset]. https://www.iie.org/opendoors

Kinzie, J., Gonyea, R., Shoup, R., & Kuh, G. D. (2008). Promoting persistence and success of underrepresented students: Lessons for teaching and learning. In J. M. Braxton (Ed.), *The Role of the Classroom in College Student Persistence* (New Directions for Teaching and Learning, no. 115, pp. 21–38). Jossey-Bass. https://doi.org/10.1002/tl.323

Kuh, G. D. (2008). *High-impact educational practices: What they are, who has access to them, and why they matter.* Association of American Colleges & Universities. https://www.aacu.org/node/4084

Kuh, G. D., Kinzie, J., Schuh, J. H., & Whitt, E. J. (2010). *Student success in college: Creating conditions that matter* (G. D. Kuh, Ed.; 1st ed.). Jossey-Bass.

Liu, W., Kuramoto, S. J., & Stuart, E. A. (2013). An introduction to sensitivity analysis for unobserved confounding in nonexperimental prevention research. *Prevention Science, 14*(6), 570–580. https://doi.org/10.1007%2Fs11121-012-0339-5

Malmgren, J., & Galvin, J. (2008). Effects of study abroad participation on student graduation rates: A study of three incoming freshman cohorts at the University of Minnesota, Twin Cities. *NACADA Journal, 28*(1), 29–42. https://doi.org/10.12930/0271-9517-28.1.29

Rosenbaum, P. R., & Rubin, D. B. (1983). The central role of the propensity score in observational studies for causal effects. *Biometrika, 70*(1), 41–55. https://doi.org/10.1093/biomet/70.1.41

Rosenbaum, P. R., & Rubin, D. B. (1984). Reducing bias in observational studies using subclassification on the propensity score. *Journal of the American Statistical Association, 79*, 516–524. https://doi.org/10.1017/cbo9780511810725.018

Rubin, D. B. (1974). Estimating causal effects of treatments in randomized and nonrandomized studies. *Journal of Educational Psychology, 66*(5), 688–701. https://doi.org/10.1037/h0037350

Russell, S. H., Hancock, M. P., & McCullough, J. (2007). Benefits of undergraduate research experiences. *Science, 316*(5824), 548–549. https://doi.org/10.1126/science.1140384

Sanders, M., Van Oss, T., & McGeary, S. (2015). Analyzing reflections in service learning to promote personal growth and community self-efficacy. *Journal of Experiential Education, 39*(1), 73–88. https://doi.org/10.1177/1053825915608872

Snyder, M., & Omoto, A. M. (2009). *Who gets involved and why? The psychology of volunteerism.* City University of Hong Kong Press.

Stuart, E. A. (2010). Matching methods for causal inference: A review and a look forward. *Statistical Science, 25*(1), 1–21. https://doi.org/10.1214/09-sts313

Sutton, R. C., & Rubin, D. L. (2004). The GLOSSARI project: Initial findings from a system-wide research initiative on study abroad learning outcomes. *Frontiers: The Interdisciplinary Journal of Study Abroad, 10*(1), 65–82. https://frontiersjournal.org/index.php/Frontiers/article/view/133/115

Willett, T., Pellegrin, N., & Cooper, D. (2013, December 21). *Study abroad impact* [Technical report]. http://globaled.us/cccsoar/project-report.asp

AFTERWORD

The HIPs Just Keep Coming!

George D. Kuh

There are no shortcuts to helping students realize high levels of learning and personal development. The eminent developmental psychologist Nevitt Sanford (1968) got it exactly right when he declared challenge and support to be the cornerstones of effective educational practice. Through recursive iterations of challenge and support, educators put students in situations that cultivate the habits of the mind and heart that, over time, enable them to deepen their learning, develop resilience, transfer information into action, and generate alternative approaches to managing complex issues and problems.

Such capacities are needed to fashion constructive responses to rapidly evolving circumstances facing every form of human endeavor. Workplaces, societal institutions, and the world order are only going to get more complex to navigate. Now more than ever, people must be informed, responsive, and responsible, equipped with the knowledge, proficiencies, and dispositions to be economically self-sufficient, intellectually alert, and socially and civically engaged throughout their lifetime.

What kind of educational system and experiences will adequately prepare the current and coming generations to survive and thrive? How can colleges and universities in particular ensure that all students acquire the cross-cutting skills that employers value (AAC&U, 2021)—critical thinking, written and oral communication, teamwork, digital literacy, and using what one has learned in real-world settings?

Toward this end, and much simplified, the major tasks for undergraduate education today are ensuring students learn how to

- reflect—think about their thinking and experiences in and out of the classroom, on and off the campus;
- apply—transfer and use what one has learned in different settings that present novel challenges and opportunities; and

- integrate—connect and grasp the relevance of what they are learning from different courses, out-of-class experiences, and life beyond the institution.

There are many roads to the top of this mountain. Among the more promising is *for every college student* to participate in one or more high-impact practices (HIPs), especially those with a substantial experiential component. Indeed, one of the most noteworthy benefits of HIPs participation are the salutary effects students from historically underserved populations realize. That is, those first in their family to attend college, the academically underprepared, and those from racially minoritized populations who do at least one HIP tend to get a boost in their performance.

In this chapter, I discuss several areas that need attention to advance HIPs work, complementing ideas presented in many of the chapters in this book. To contextualize these thoughts, I first remind us of what it is about HIPs that make them developmentally powerful. Understanding how and why HIPs enrich the student experience is necessary for designing, implementing, and scaling HIPs; this in turn yields insights into what is required to increase the odds that all students benefit to optimal degrees from their participation. I also suggest how the animating features of HIPs can inform the search for and verification of other undergraduate experiences with the potential to confer benefits comparable to HIPs.

What Makes a HIP a HIP?

As emphasized throughout the chapters in this book, HIPs are now well established as a set of highly engaging activities linked with multiple indicators of student success in college. The array of positive outcomes associated with HIPs participation is not surprising, because—*when done well*—they are composed of eight educationally effective features (Kuh, 2008; Kuh et al., 2013; Kuh et al., 2017):

1. Performance expectations set at appropriately high levels
2. Significant investment of time and effort by students over an extended period
3. Interactions with faculty and peers about substantive matters
4. Experiences with diversity, wherein students are exposed to and must content with people and circumstances that differ from those with which students are familiar
5. Frequent, timely, and constructive feedback

6. Periodic, structured opportunities to reflect and integrate learning
7. Opportunities to discover relevance of learning through real-world applications
8. Public demonstration of competence

Standing alone, each of these features has a solid empirical foundation to qualify as a good practice in undergraduate education (Brownell & Swaner, 2008; Chickering & Gamson, 1987; Eynon & Gambino, 2017; Mayhew et al., 2016; Pascarella & Terenzini, 2005; Watson et al., 2016).

What makes a HIP unusually impactful is the bundling of these practices, in that the experience incorporates all of these features to varying degrees. The "officially approved" list of 11 HIPs promulgated by the Association of American Colleges & Universities (AAC&U) suggests there is a limited, specified set of practices that warrant the HIP label. However, considering each of the individual features in the context of a learning and teaching setting makes it plain that these features can be used in any classroom, laboratory, or studio. This opens up the happy prospect that to broaden and deepen learning we should infuse HIP-like features in a range of activities inside and outside the classroom in addition to those currently on the HIPs list. More about this later.

For now, consider two axiomatic principles about student engagement that account for high levels of learning and personal development in college. First, what matters most is *what students do*, especially the time and effort they devote to educationally purposeful activities. As Pascarella and Terenzini (2005) put it: "Because individual effort and involvement are the critical determinants of college impact, institutions should focus on the ways they can shape their academic, interpersonal, and extracurricular offerings to encourage student engagement" (p. 602).

Second, and equally important, is *what colleges and universities do*—using effective educational practices throughout the institution to induce students to do the things that research shows contributes to their learning and personal development. That is, "the greatest impact appears to stem from students' total level of campus engagement, particularly when academic, interpersonal, and extracurricular involvements are mutually reinforcing" (Pascarella & Terenzini, 2005, p. 647). In other words, educationally effective institutions intentionally design and implement policies and practices that channel student energy toward the highly engaging activities and behaviors that are linked with desired outcomes—grades, persistence and completion, student satisfaction, and gains across a range of desired learning and personal development outcomes (Chickering & Reisser, 1993; Kuh et al., 2010; McNair et al., 2016).

It's more complicated than this, of course. Some effects of college are conditional (Mayhew et al., 2016). For example, women generally tend to score higher compared with men on the National Survey of Student Engagement (NSSE). Similarly, students who live on campus are more engaged than commuters, as are students enrolled full time compared with their counterparts attending part time. Although these relative differences hold for students who participate in HIPs, the benefits associated with their participation tend to be substantially greater than their peers who do not do one or more HIPs (Finley & McNair, 2013).

In addition to this enviable pattern of outcomes, HIPs participation is particularly promising for cultivating dispositional attributes essential for success during and after college (Kuh et al., 2018). These include

- interpersonal competencies (e.g., expressing information to others, interpreting others' messages and responding appropriately);
- intrapersonal competencies (e.g., self-management, conscientiousness, flexibility, resilience); and
- neurocognitive competencies (e.g., crystallized and fluid intelligence).

Whatever their possible limitations (Harper, 2010; Kinzie et al., 2021), the overwhelming evidence that HIPs participation generally is associated with unusually positive benefits makes it all the more important that efforts to scale participation in an equitable manner become a high priority for all institutions.

Even so, almost always, someone at the institution will argue that HIPs are too resource intensive in terms of time and money to try to make them available to all students. The most persuasive rejoinder is to emphasize the expected return on investment in terms of revenue captured from increased student persistence and completion rates (Wellman & Brusi, 2013), along with evidence showing greater learning gains associated with HIP participation that employers and family members value. It also is worth emphasizing that not every faculty or staff member has to be directly involved with a HIP. However, their support is important to create and sustain a campus culture that values and rewards HIPs and HIP-like experiences.

Scaling HIPs

The need to scale HIPs has been painfully obvious since the first national report (Kuh, 2008). As noted earlier, although all students benefit, those from historically underserved populations often benefit even more in relative terms, receiving a bump in their performance. However, the sad reality is that such students are less likely to participate in a HIP. These disparities existing within most institutions are both unfortunate and difficult to correct. What is required for a college or university to achieve parity across students from various backgrounds?

The surest and likely most cost-effective way to scale HIPs in an equity-sensitive manner is to *require student participation* in at least two HIPs (ideally more), one in the 1st year and another later as part of the student's major field. This is not as far-fetched as it may first appear.

For example, when well designed, a first-year experience program, which many colleges and universities offer, is a good first step toward this goal, especially if a learning community or writing-intensive seminar or service-learning component is embedded. To extend HIP participation beyond the 1st year, consider the SUNY system, which requires all students to complete at least one "applied learning experience" (SUNY, n.d., para. 1), activities that have many of the earmarks of a HIP. The University of Wisconsin System (2021) does something similar, as does Hendrix College (n.d.), Luther College (2021), and a host of other liberal arts colleges. Given that at many institutions a substantial number of students do independent research, an internship, or a culminating experience later in their program of study, it is not much of a reach to expect every academic program to make such an accommodation. Indeed, one can persuasively argue that it is a breach of academic ethics for an academic program to allow a student to graduate without a culminating experience that demands students demonstrate what they have learned and can do as a result of studying a particular field or discipline. To gain momentum in this regard, it would be instructive to know how many institutions now require in some form participation in one or more HIPs.

Of course, getting to the point at which an institution requires HIP participation will take concerted effort over time, beginning with marshaling interest and support for HIPs. Most colleges and universities include something in their strategic plan about giving students opportunities to translate their learning to real-world settings so they can see the relevance and value of their studies. Regularly referring to the strategic plan as a rationale for HIPs participation is a direct pathway to obtaining governing board support, as that group owns the strategic plan and counsels the president.

Intrusive academic advising looms large in scaling HIPs. Every advisor–student interaction should include a discussion about *when*, not if, the student will do a HIP. This along with including two or more HIPs as requirements for degree completion is the most efficacious way forward to ensure that available HIPs "opportunities" (a vacuous term in this context) are converted into *equity-oriented participation*.

As noted earlier, HIPs or HIP-like features can be bundled and infused into any classroom, lab, or studio. Examples of such efforts are wide-ranging—from an introduction to literacy course (Gilchrist, 2021) to a liberal arts seminar (Snow, 2018) to an engineering design course (Pusca & Northwood, 2018). Capital Community College in Connecticut is using a Title V grant to embed HIPs into entry-level courses (LaPierre-Dreger, personal communication, February 16, 2021).

Such courses are more likely to attain the desired ends if instructors use backward design (Wiggins & McTighe, 2005) and universal design principles (Burgstahler, 2015), such as aligning course outcomes with program and institutional learning goals; designing assignments that elicit the desired outcomes; valuing diversity, equity, and inclusion; and using multiple instructional methods accessible to all students. Also important is adopting a mindset that sees the classroom as a locus of community building (Tinto, 1997), whereby students are invited to help shape the course through sharing reciprocal expectations and personal interests. Toward this end, cultivating a culturally sensitive, community-oriented classroom requires structured, educationally purposeful activities that intentionally prompt students to spend time with classmates (online, inside, and outside of class) and connect in meaningful ways with positive role models (peers, tutors, staff, others).

One more critical step is selecting the appropriate HIP(s) and HIP features to emphasize. Among the more promising are creating a learning community by linking two or more classes, or perhaps developing a standalone course that is writing or inquiry intensive, or including a service-learning or community-based project, or requiring collaborative assignments and projects, or some combination.

For any innovation to take root, leadership matters. The SUNY system took a top-down approach, with the chancellor's office leading the way. Even the New York governor's office asserted its support for such a requirement. To convince academic administrators and faculty members of the value of HIPs participation, evidence is key, of which there is a good deal. However, that does not mean everyone is familiar with or convinced by the extant data. Thus, some internal champions at various levels of the organization must take up and pursue the cause with an appropriate degree of zeal in a manner congenial with the campus culture.

Students, alumni, and employers also are very important to scaling HIPs; their testimonies often are among the most articulate and persuasive about the value of such experiences. Featuring HIPs and their importance in campus and alumni publications is essential for introducing and reminding people why investing in and scaling HIPs are priorities.

One more approach to encourage scaling is to create an outside-in demand for HIPs. Advocates would do well to enlist the support of colleagues who interact with students before they matriculate and continue such a campaign through the early days of college. Consider these multiple efforts toward this end:

- Inform high school counselors and teachers about the value of HIPs.
- "Sell" HIPs to parents and other family members. The NSSE (2021) *Pocket Guide to Choosing a College*, which describes HIPs and their value, can be useful toward this end.
- Feature HIPs in materials for prospective students.
- Promote HIPs in new student registration and orientation.

Implementation Fidelity

Scaling HIPs in the absence of careful attention to design and implementation fidelity can be an exercise in mediocrity as well as a poor investment of institutional resources. For this reason, reverberating throughout many of the chapters in this book is the importance of intentionally implementing the engaging features of HIPs in a way that is consistent with their design, student needs and capabilities, and campus culture. This is why whenever extolling the virtues of HIPs, one must (again) be mindful of doing HIPs well.

As others have said in this book and elsewhere, just because an activity has the same name as those that appear on the AAC&U HIPs list does not ensure the experience will be high impact. Evidence is needed to demonstrate that students engage with the features that characterize a HIP. Similarly, outcomes data are essential for ensuring that students benefit from their participation in the intended ways.

Collecting the evidence will almost certainly require intrainstitutional collaborations among assessment office staff, institutional research and effectiveness office staff, faculty members, student affairs staff, students, and others. In this regard, Finley (2019) provided an excellent framework for assessing the quality of HIPs.

One often overlooked step is addressing two "implementation with integrity" questions (Bryk et al., 2015):

1. What do we need to do to get *this HIP* to work well *here*? Just because, for example, a certain learning community structure works well in one institutional context does not mean the same approach will be effective

in another. Campus culture, student attitudes and interests, instructor characteristics, and many other variables can affect implementation and impact. Careful thought must be given to tailoring a given HIP to the local, immediate context.

2. How well is this HIP working, *for whom*, under *what circumstances*? As Kinzie et al. (2021) demonstrated, although HIPs participation generally benefits all students, their perceptions of those benefits may vary. Good practice demands periodically examining the quality of implementation of various HIPs and the effects of HIP participation disaggregated by student background characteristics. Participation patterns can also be revealing. For example, if a disproportionately small number of women are conducting independent research in a given program, or very few students from low-income backgrounds are securing paid internships, what are the proximal causes of such disparities and what might the institution do to respond?

Next Generation HIPs

The circumscribed list of HIPs is largely an artifact of the NSSE. That is, five of the 11 HIPs appeared on the inaugural 2000 NSSE questionnaire as a cluster of items labeled "enriching educational experiences" and a sixth was a question about participating in a service-learning course. The data NSSE collected over the years about these activities and the persistent, consistent patterns of high engagement and self-reported learning gains associated with HIPs participation stand in stark contrast to the single institution and sometimes anecdotal information available about some other HIPs, such as writing-intensive courses and common intellectual experiences.

It stands to reason that one does not become an excellent (or even competent) writer by completing a single writing-intensive course. Much more likely is that one's writing will improve substantially by completing three or more such courses!

In the same vein, what constitutes a high-impact common intellectual experience? Does a set of coenrolled courses such as a learning community count? How many courses in common does it take to claim the experience is "high impact"? Moreover, where are the data to buttress such a claim?

Consider, too, first-year seminars that vary widely in their structures, delivery, and so forth. Which one is likely to be high impact—an 8-week, no-credit orientation to college course taught by an adjunct instructor or a 15-week, discipline-based, writing-intensive seminar taught by a senior faculty member supported by a peer preceptor? Both are labeled first-year seminar. Caveat emptor. Equally important, more work is needed to determine whether these widely differing student experiences are associated with benefits comparable to other HIPs.

The field also needs to attend to a related matter—activities in which students participate that potentially confer benefits comparable to an officially endorsed HIP, but are deemed less worthy. This is due largely to the absence of a robust national dataset to confirm the virtues that NSSE provided for six HIPs. Kuh et al. (2017) posed a short list of likely qualifiers—cultural and performing arts, campus publications, employment, organizational leadership, and intercollegiate athletics to name a few. Especially promising are efforts to leverage educationally purposeful peer interactions such as peer tutoring, mentoring, and advising. For example, a creatively designed technology platform has been shown to increase the equity-focused reach and impact of peer tutoring. Additional research is needed to determine whether peer tutoring and other promising efforts warrant designation as HIPs (Kuh et al., 2021).

Last Words

Many factors affect student success in college, with some of the most influential occurring long before a student matriculates to a postsecondary institution. Family circumstances, economic status, quality of K–12 schooling, and many other considerations position students for success in college, including the kinds of educational activities in which they will engage. Although HIPs show unusual promise, they are only one albeit important piece of the student success puzzle (Kuh et al., 2007).

In addition to the equity-sensitive scaling of HIPs, colleges and universities must employ many other educationally effective policies and practices to foster higher levels of student accomplishment. Among them are widespread use of engaging pedagogical approaches and mandating the use of demonstrably effective policies and practices throughout the institution (Kuh et al., 2007, 2010). The latter include embedding ongoing orientation in entry-level courses, stopping late registration, deploying effective early warning systems, and designing assignments requiring reflection and integration coupled with feedback (lots of timely, pointed feedback).

Taken together, the chapters in this book are an important contribution to an ever-expanding HIPs literature. Even so, more good work is needed. For example:

- What are the incentives and barriers to scaling and effectively implementing HIPs and HIP-like activities?
- What kinds of faculty and staff development activities are needed to do HIPS and HIP-like activities at scale?

- Which HIPs can be modified and adapted for virtual environments with fidelity?
- What are the characteristics of a "done well" framework for guiding and evaluating HIPs implementation with integrity (e.g., Brownell & Swaner, 2009; Eynon & Gambino, 2017)?
- Are certain HIP features more or less important for a particular HIP to optimally benefit students from different backgrounds?

The unforgiving fiscal and human resource pressures on colleges and universities are here to stay, fueling initiative fatigue and severely straining the bandwidth for innovation, including scaling HIPs. These circumstances are not new. However, they usher in an unparalleled sense of urgency, which may compel many institutions at long last to do the most difficult thing—decide what they will stop doing to implement and scale high-quality HIPS and other demonstrably effective learning and teaching approaches.

And so we come full circle, recognizing that there are no shortcuts to ensuring all students realize high levels of achievement and personal development. To pretend otherwise is educational and political folly, and a recipe for mediocrity. Our students and American society deserve and need better.

References

Association of American Colleges & Universities. (2021). *How college contributes to workforce success: Employer views on what matters most*. https://www.aacu.org/sites/default/files/files/research/AACUEmployerReport2021.pdf

Brownell, J. E., & Swaner, L. E. (2008). *Five high-impact practices: Research on learning outcomes completion and quality*. Association of American Colleges & Universities.

Brownell, J. E., & Swaner, L. E. (2009). Outcomes of high-impact educational practices: A literature review. *Diversity and Democracy, 12*(2). https://www.aacu.org/publications-research/periodicals/outcomes-high-impact-educational-practices-literature-review

Bryk, A. S., Gomez, L. M., Grunow, A., & LeMahieu, P. (2015). *Learning to improve: How America's schools can get better at getting better.* Harvard University Press.

Burgstahler, S. (Ed.). (2015). *Universal design in higher education: From principles to practice* (2nd ed.). Harvard Education Press.

Chickering, A. W., & Gamson, Z. F. (1987). Seven principles for good practice in undergraduate education. *American Association for Higher Education Bulletin*, 3–7. ERIC. https://eric.ed.gov/?id=ed282491

Chickering, A. W., & Reisser, L. (1993). *Education and identity* (2nd ed.). Jossey-Bass.

Eynon, B., & Gambino, L. (2017). *High-impact ePortfolio practice: A catalyst for student, faculty, and institutional learning.* Stylus.

Finley, A. (2019, November). *A comprehensive approach to assessment of high-impact practices* (Occasional Paper No. 41). University of Illinois and Indiana University, National Institute for Learning Outcomes Assessment (NILOA). https://www.learningoutcomesassessment.org/wp-content/uploads/2019/11/Occasional-Paper-41.pdf

Finley, A., & McNair, T. (2013). *Assessing underserved students' engagement in high-impact practices.* Association of American Colleges & Universities.

Gilchrist, S. B. (2021, April). *It's HIP to be square: Instruction, high-impact practices, and the framework.* Virtual presentation to the annual meeting of the Association of College and Research Libraries, Chicago, IL, United States.

Harper, S. R. (2010). An anti-deficit achievement framework for research on students of color in STEM. *2010*(148), 63–74. https://doi.org/10.1002/ir.362

Hendrix College. (n.d.). *Academics: The Odyssey Program.* https://www.hendrix.edu/academics/odyssey/

Kinzie, J., Silberstein, S., McCormick, A. C., Gonyea, R. M., & Dugan, B. (2021). Centering racially minoritized student voices in high-impact practices. *Change: The Magazine for Higher Learning, 53*(4), 6–14. https://doi.org/10.1080/00091383.2021.1930976

Kuh, G. D. (2008). *High-impact educational practices: What they are, who has access to them, and why they matter.* Association of American Colleges & Universities.

Kuh, G. D., Citty, J., Hudson, J. E., Jr., Iruoje, T., Mladic, J., & Qureshi, S. (2021). Right before our eyes: Making peer interaction matter more for all students. *Change: The Magazine for Higher Learning, 53*(4), 15–21. https://doi.org/10.1080/00091383.2021.1930977

Kuh, G. D., Gambino, L. M., Bresciani Ludvik, M., & O'Donnell, K. (2018). *Using ePortfolio to document and deepen the dispositional learning impact of HIPs* (Occasional Paper No. 32). University of Illinois and Indiana University, National Institute for Learning Outcomes Assessment. http://learningoutcomesassessment.org/documents/Occ%20paper%2032Final.pdf

Kuh, G. D., Kinzie, J., Buckley, J. A., Bridges, B. K., & Hayek, J. C. (2007). *Piecing together the student success puzzle: Research, propositions, and recommendations* (ASHE Higher Education Report, Vol. 32, No. 5). Jossey-Bass.

Kuh, G. D., Kinzie, J., Schuh, J. H., Whitt, E. J., & Associates. (2010). *Student success in college: Creating conditions that matter.* Jossey-Bass.

Kuh, G. D., O'Donnell, K., & Reed, S. (2013). *Ensuring quality and taking high-impact practices to scale.* Association of American Colleges & Universities.

Kuh, G. D., O'Donnell, K., & Schneider, C. G. (2017). HIPs at ten. *Change: The Magazine of Higher Learning, 49*(5), 8–16. https://doi.org/10.1080/00091383.2017.1366805

Luther College. (2021). *High-impact learning.* https://www.luther.edu/academics/high-impact-learning/

Mayhew, M. J., Rockenbach, A. N., Bowman, N. A., Seifert, T. A., Wolniak, G. C., Pascarella, E. T., & Terenzini, P. T. (2016). *How college affects students: Vol. 3. 21st century evidence that higher education works.* Jossey-Bass.

McNair, T., Albertine, S., Cooper, M. A., McDonald, N., & Major, T., Jr. (2016). *Becoming a student ready college: A new culture of leadership for student success.* Jossey-Bass.

National Survey of Student Engagement. (2021). *A pocket guide to choosing a college: Questions to ask on your college visit.* https://nsse.indiana.edu/support-resources/students-parents/pocket-guide/english.html

Pascarella, E. T., & Terenzini, P. T. (2005). *How college affects students: Vol. 3. A third decade of research.* Jossey-Bass.

Pusca, D., & Northwood, D. O. (2018). Implementation of high-impact practices in engineering design courses. *World Transactions on Engineering and Technology Education, 16*(2), 108–114. http://www.wiete.com.au/journals/WTE&TE/Pages/Vol.16,%20No.2%20(2018)/02-Northwood-D.pdf

Sanford, N. (1968). *Where colleges fail: A study of student as person.* Jossey-Bass.

Snow, H. K. (2018). High-impact practices, universal design and assessment opportunities in liberal arts seminars. *ASIA Network Exchange: A Journal for Asian Studies in the Liberal Arts, 25*(2), 117–135. http://doi.org/10.16995/ane.284

State University of New York. (n.d.). *The State University of New York Applied Learning Plan.* https://www.suny.edu/media/suny/content-assets/documents/applied-learning/SUNY-Applied-Learning-Plan.pdf

Tinto, V. (1997). Classrooms as communities: Exploring the educational character of student persistence. *Journal of Higher Education, 68*(6), 599–623. https://doi.org/10.1080/00221546.1997.11779003

University of Wisconsin System. (2021). *UW System High Impact Practices Initiative.* https://www.wisconsin.edu/hips-initiative/

Watson, C., Kuh, G. D., Rhodes, T., Penny Light, T., & Chen, H. (2016). ePortfolios: The eleventh high-impact practice. *International Journal of ePortfolio, 6*(2), 65–69. http://www.theijep.com/pdf/IJEP254.pdf

Wellman, J., & Brusi, R. (2013). *Investing in success: Cost-effective strategies to increase student success.* Association of American Colleges & Universities.

Wiggins, G., & McTighe, J. (2005). *Understanding by design* (expanded 2nd ed.). ASCD.

EPILOGUE

Shaun Harper

I was a PhD student at Indiana University when George Kuh and his talented team of researchers created and launched the National Survey of Student Engagement (NSSE). Professor Kuh was my dissertation advisor at that time. I somehow knew then that the survey would become what it is now. NSSE responded to a timely need for data about how college students spend their time and the extent of their engagement in activities, programs, and experiences that have been empirically proven to produce positive educational outcomes. Over an impressively short time period, George, my dear friends Jillian Kinzie and Brian Bridges, and other scholars in the Indiana University Center for Postsecondary Research brilliantly evolved one great idea into a multifaceted suite of useful surveys, student engagement tools, and institutional transformation experiences. I am not at all surprised that thousands of colleges and universities have benefited from these contributions—NSSE and everything associated with it were destined to succeed from the start. This is just one of many reasons why I am among the proudest graduates of the Indiana University Higher Education and Student Affairs program.

One of the most praiseworthy innovations of the work emanating from NSSE was the identification of what is now known as high-impact practices, the topic of this important book. Throughout my career, unfounded claims pertaining to college student success have persistently troubled me. Specifically, student affairs professionals, faculty members, and institutional leaders claiming without evidence that certain programs and approaches lead to the production of student outcomes. "We know we make a difference in students' lives, we just know" was never good enough for me. "How do you know and what data do you have to confirm this presumption" are questions I have frequently posed to well-intended colleagues on campuses over the past 2 decades. NSSE data on high-impact practices disrupted this. Suddenly, our industry had trustworthy evidence collected via rigorous quantitative survey instruments to confirm what actually leads to the production of extraordinary educational outcomes for college students. This book showcases how the concept has evolved, what colleges and universities have done to conduct deeper assessment and develop more tailored HIP work, and specifies what must be done to actualize the potential of these practices.

I assert that equity is what remains to be done to fully actualize HIPs. Equitably delivering on the promise of high-impact practices requires at least five conceptual, methodological, behavioral, and implementation shifts. Here, I write about these specifically through the prism of racial equity.

First, there is a one-sidedness in how we understand these practices. It is all about the production of positive outcomes. I understand, at least in part, why this is the case: We already have so much bad news about practices and conditions that lead to student attrition, disengagement, academic failure, and other negative outcomes. In a similarly one-sided fashion, I spent the first 14 years of my faculty career studying Black and Latino male student success in high school and in higher education. I convinced myself and many others that we already knew much (not everything, but lots) about what undermined educational success for boys and young men of color. Thus, I studied and only documented positive factors. I am thinking differently now about the similarity of my early career research approach and the ways high-impact practices are typically conceptualized, studied, and institutionalized. This shift, for sure, is informed by my longer-standing scholarship on campus racial climates.

In qualitative studies that I have conducted since 2005, college students of color almost always describe horrifying experiences that they and I would absolutely deem "high impact." For example, on all but one campus where I have done qualitative climate assessments, one or more Black students talked about the devastating experience of being called the N-word by white peers or employees of the institutions they were attending. Others talked about being the only student of color in their major, on their residence hall floor, or in a campus club. The racial microaggressions, stereotypes, low expectations, and tokenization that occur for them in these spaces incontestably have negative effects on their success. How can I say this so declaratively? Because students of color consistently tell me so. Being a student activist whose mental wellness and grades suffer because of engagement in protests against campus racism has a high impact. These and many other experiences described to us in qualitative interviews over the years have been corroborated by data from the National Assessment of Collegiate Campus Climates (NACCC), my center's quantitative survey that has been administered to more than two million undergraduates since 2019. Racial equity requires us to understand, in a multidimensional way, everything that has an extraordinarily high impact on success for students of color in higher education, not only the positive factors.

In addition to appreciating and exploring the bidirectionality of HIPs, racial equity also necessitates recognizing that students of color are experts on their own experiences. I totally respect and believe that doing research with a faculty member, studying abroad, and participating in meaningful service-learning opportunities, for example, are incontestably high-impact experiences. All the research associating HIPs with beneficial outcomes say so in the most believable ways. Notwithstanding, I think we should ask students of color which experiences have the highest impact on their successes and failures. As it pertains to academic achievement, for instance, they may offer a much different list of practices, programs, policies, relationships, and cultural forces. Doing an internship in one's field may not be at the top of their lists. Having a same-race faculty mentor may be what an academically successful Latina student puts first on her list. The integration of Indigenous epistemologies across the curriculum may be what an Indigenous student says ignited and sustained high levels of engagement for him in his courses. The methodological shift I am calling for here is a qualitative exploration and documentation of what students of color deem high impact. It is shortsighted to presume that factors identified by a predominantly white cadre of higher education researchers impact students across all racial and ethnic groups the exact same way.

Even though I just argued that students of color are very likely to name a much more extensive list of HIPs, let's assume for a moment that I am mistaken and that they identify the same set of experiences that have been empirically proven in the student engagement literature. Evidence about students' participation in HIPs from NSSE, as well as college and university data, have long made clear that students do not have equitable access to those experiences. This is certainly true when data are disaggregated by race and ethnicity. But the inequities are even more pronounced at the intersections: lower-income students of color, trans and gender nonbinary students of color, and students of color with disabilities, to name a few. These realities require professionals who work at colleges and universities to make equity, not equality the aim as they attempt to deliver on the promise of high-impact practices.

Pursuing equity rather than equality is essential. Equality is advertising applications for learning community participation in ways that conceivably reach all students—everyone seemingly has equal opportunity to see the announcement posted on residence hall bulletin boards, on social media, and in various spaces throughout the student union building. Yet, this approach has failed to ensure that students who have been long underrepresented in learning communities become less underrepresented. If Asian American and Pacific Islander (AAPI) students are one such group, equity would entail partnering with AAPI student influencers, AAPI faculty and staff, the AAPI cultural center, and AAPI student organizations to aggressively disseminate the call for applications. Some flyers would picture AAPI students who participate in learning communities, along with quotes about their experiences. Administrators who are interested in equity would also conduct focus group interviews with AAPI students who are in learning communities to determine what compelled them to apply for engagement in this high-impact experience; they would use what they learn to equitably appeal to other AAPI students who may not view this particular experience as a valuable use of their time. Conversely, focus groups with nonparticipants might help program administrators understand why and how their learning community marketing and recruitment efforts lack cultural resonance with AAPI students. Institutions must discard the erroneous "if we build it and market it to everyone in the exact same ways, they all will come" assumption. This is one reason why we continue to see inequitable rates of participation in HIPs.

I have had the enormous privilege of working with hundreds of colleges and universities that span every geographic region of the United States. I have said some version of this on just about every campus at which I have spoken or consulted: We must shift the onus of engagement and success from students to institutional actors. I have also repeatedly made this same point in several things I have published. But yet, institutions continue to behave in the same ways year after year—I can now say decade after decade. What specifically do faculty, staff, and administrators do to equitably engage students in high-impact practices? How do we know? Which professionals are more likely than are others to contribute to student success in these extraordinarily powerful ways? What is the race of these persons? How do we reward them? And how do we hold those who do too little accountable? What did the people who work in the internships, learning communities, and study abroad offices do differently this year than they did last year and the year before that to attract a more diverse slate of student participants in their programs? Do white faculty routinely and equitably invite Black, Indigenous, and Latinx students to conduct research with them? If so, then what is it about these professors that make this form of engagement unappealing to these particular student groups? These are just some of many questions that institutions should, but often fail to ask themselves. We must concern ourselves more with what employees do to engage students, especially diverse collegians. Doing so would signify a long overdue behavioral shift for colleges and universities.

Privileging students who would benefit most from HIPs is the final shift I am calling for here. A middle-class student who routinely traveled internationally with family members for several years prior to enrolling in college would probably benefit less from an overseas study abroad experience than would a lower-income classmate who has never been on an airplane. Ideally, every student would have full access to HIPs, but few campuses have the capacity and resources to offer these experiences to everyone. Hence, I insist on placing students who are not typically engaged in HIPs at the front of the line and making every strategic effort to connect them with these experiences. That would be equity.

For 3 years, the research center I direct studied this approach taken by North Carolina Central University (NCCU), a public historically black institution. Disaggregated 1st-to-2nd year persistence data revealed that Black men who were admitted to the university with high school GPAs below 2.5 were least likely to persist. Those are the students for whom NCCU administrators created the Centennial Scholars Program, a multidimensional learning community. Fifty-seven Black male 1st-year students were in the inaugural cohort; all but one returned for sophomore year. Across the first three cohorts, the 2nd-year persistence rate steadily hovered around 90%. When my research team and I visited the campus, both the president and vice president of the NCCU Student Government Association were Centennial Scholars; several others held campus leadership roles and were engaged in a wide array of HIPs. Providing a first-year experience that is typically reserved for honors students to those who most needed the centralized resources, common courses, academic support, luxury residence hall, and multidimensional programming not only impacted the 350 Black men in the first three cohorts of Centennial Scholars, but it also drastically improved NCCU's overall 1st-to-2nd year persistence rates.

Although I was not one of the graduate assistants who worked in the IU Center for Postsecondary Research when my advisor and other scholars created what has since become one of higher education's most important surveys, I have always felt like part of the NSSE family. One of the first peer-reviewed journal articles I published as a faculty member used NSSE data; I cowrote it with a trio of friends who worked for the survey at that time. While it measures entirely different things and serves a different (yet complementary) purpose, the NACCC is very much influenced by what I learned from my NSSE academic family members over the years. My hope is that higher education professionals will take these tools we have created, push to expand the assessment of their own practices, and use this information in equitable, strategic ways that accelerate and ultimately sustain student success. This new book is another incredibly useful contribution to the student engagement and assessment literature. Inequity is our past and present. We must embrace the shifts I have presented here to deliver on the promise of a more equitable future.

EDITORS AND CONTRIBUTORS

Editors

John Zilvinskis is assistant professor of student affairs administration at Binghamton University, State University of New York. By training, he is a survey researcher who studies the engagement of college students and his research has been published in *Research in Higher Education*, *The Review of Higher Education*, the *Journal of College Student Development* and the *Journal of Diversity in Higher Education.* His inquiry into high-impact practices (HIPs) emerged during his work at the National Survey of Student Engagement (NSSE) with the dissertation titled *Measuring Quality in High-Impact Practices.* This research has informed his agenda to study the equity and access of HIPs using data from NSSE and Community College Survey of Student Engagement. In his scholarship, Zilvinskis employs critical quantitative methods, such as avoiding deficit-framed research questions and disaggregating data, to model rigorous research design.

Jillian Kinzie is associate director of the Center for Postsecondary Research and interim codirector of the National Survey of Student Engagement at Indiana University. Her scholarship focuses on institutional assessment practice and outcomes assessment, teaching and learning in higher education, and college student learning, development and success. She has been conducting HIP assessment and research and studying what institutions do to improve quality and equity since HIPs were first named. She investigates the ways HIPs can be more intentionally incorporated into the curriculum, particularly as the bookends of all undergraduates' experiences, encouraging educators to create signature, integrated, applied, culturally relevant HIPs that prepare students more effectively for life and work.

Jerry Daday is a professor of sociology and the executive associate dean in the Institute for Engaged Learning (IEL) at Indiana University–Purdue University Indianapolis (IUPUI). He works with a team of faculty and staff striving to ensure the equitable progression of IUPUI's 20,000 undergraduate students through pathways of scaffolded engaged learning experiences beginning in the first-year experience through their capstone experience.

He is a founding member of the HIPs in the States national working group and conference planning committee. His particular passion is professional development for faculty and staff and championing HIPs as a vital component of the student experience.

Ken O'Donnell is vice provost and professor of communication at California State University Dominguez Hills. He has been an energetic proponent of high-impact practices since working at the California State University Office of the Chancellor, where he led development of a multicampus taxonomy for organizing HIPs and identifying their key qualities and successfully won several million dollars in public and philanthropic funding to support HIPs implementation and assessment across California. He came late to higher education, after writing and producing independent movies. He learned about HIPs before they went by the name, teaching undergraduates in the film school at Chapman University, leveraging the power of group and experiential learning in real-world settings.

Carleen Vande Zande is the associate vice president for academic programs and faculty advancement at the University of Wisconsin System Administration. She is also a tenured professor of educational leadership at the University of Wisconsin-Oshkosh. She has facilitated HIPs development activities at the campus and system levels for several years and is interested in ways to integrate HIPs into student success strategies as well as incorporating HIPs into university level assessment. She has had an outsized effect on the way educators in the Wisconsin System think and work, as demonstrated by the high number of Wisconsin-based entries to this volume. She advises the National Association of System Heads and other groups looking to replicate her work.

Contributors

Ryan P. Barone is assistant vice president for student success and an assistant professor for the School of Education at Colorado State University.

Denise Bartell is associate vice provost for student success at the University of Toledo. Her work focuses on taking a holistic, equity-minded, assets-focused approach to supporting student success through the development and assessment of HIPs for faculty and students.

Caroline Boswell is the faculty development specialist in the Delphi Center for Teaching and Learning at the University of Louisville. She contributes to the Quality Enhancement Project, Find Your Fit, designed to enhance the experience of "exploratory" students and she provides educational development opportunities that support institution-wide strategic priorities.

Pam Bowers is an associate vice president for planning, assessment, and innovation at University of South Carolina. She contributes to an initiative at the UofSC to improve the quality of institutional data on student engagement and learning in HIPs and the cocurriculum. The goals of the initiative include informing data-driven improvement, producing better evidence of student learning, and advancing diversity, equity, and inclusion regarding these practices.

Regina Branton is a professor in the Department of Political Science at University of North Texas. Her research and teaching focus on political behaviors, elections, and institutions and the implications of race/ethnicity and gender. She is also a statistician and methodologist.

Glenda Breaux is the senior director of planning, research and evaluation at Community College of Baltimore County. Her work with HIPs at CCBC involves analyzing student outcome data to evaluate the effects of participating in HIP infusion projects.

Jennifer Gruening Burge is the director of institutional effectiveness at Bradley University. She has been involved with HIPs through assessment work on campus. Burge helped analyze the NSSE results and supported the processes to implement the Bradley Core Curriculum and required experiential learning tags.

Angela Byrd is an applications programmer analyst at Western Kentucky University. As a staff member in Western Kentucky University's Office of Institutional Research, she conducts and analyzes research projects related to the effects of HIPs on student outcomes. Her research helps to inform and support strategic planning at WKU.

Theresa Castor is a professor of communication at the University of Wisconsin-Parkside. She has engaged in a variety of HIPs activities such as supervising and promoting internships, designing and implementing community-based learning courses, mentoring undergraduate researchers, and teaching in as well as developing study abroad programs. She has also done work to broaden the implementation and impact of HIPs as department chair, faculty director of internships for her campus, and member of her campus's HIPs leadership team.

Alma Clayton-Pedersen is CEO of Emeritus Consulting Group (ECG), LLC. ECG uses organizational development principles to assist nonprofit, public, and education entities in enhancing their efficacy for the public good. Previously she served as a vice president at the Association of American Colleges & Universities (AAC&U) and currently is a distinguished fellow. She led the team that crafted the initial concept of inclusive excellence and work of the Making Excellence Inclusive initiative.

Brian Danielson is the director of the Center for Teaching and Learning at Slippery Rock University. In this role he designs, develops, and coordinates faculty professional development in the area of HIPs. His role is also to coordinate and sponsor the HIP faculty learning communities at SRU.

Dallas M. Dolan is an assistant dean of faculty training and development at Community College of Baltimore County. She is the chairperson of the HIP infusion committee at the CCBC. Over the past 6 years she has worked to engage faculty at the college in utilizing HIPs to promote student engagement and student success, and is particularly interested in the use of HIPs to close achievement gaps among minoritized groups.

Lara Ducate is the faculty executive director of the Center for Integrative and Experiential Learning at University of South Carolina. As a faculty member, Ducate regularly engages her students in study abroad and service-learning. In her role as the faculty executive director of the Center for Integrative and Experiential Learning, she encourages faculty and staff to engage their students in HIPs as a component of integrative and experiential learning.

Jocelyn Evans is a professor and associate dean at University of West Florida. She teaches in the UWF Kugelman Honors Program and serves as an administrative leader and campus liaison for HIPs. She has published scholarship and hosted faculty development workshops on building interdisciplinary faculty teams to scale up undergraduate research and increase access of lower division students. In 2021, she coedited a special issue on undergraduate research as high impact practice for publication in *The Journal of the Scholarship of Teaching and Learning*.

Sara Z. Evans is an assistant professor at Kennesaw State University. Her main research interest in HIPs is by working with student groups of varying sizes and class levels to engage in undergraduate research. She has facilitated faculty professional development workshops as well as attended and presented at conferences focused on the scholarship of teaching and learning in HIPs since 2015. In 2021, she coedited a special issue on undergraduate research as high impact practice for publication in *The Journal of the Scholarship of Teaching and Learning.*

Peter Felten is executive director of the Center for Engaged Learning, assistant provost for teaching and learning, and professor of history at Elon University. He works with colleagues on institution-wide teaching and learning initiatives, and on the scholarship of teaching and learning. Peter has published six books about undergraduate education, including (with Leo Lambert) *Relationship-Rich Education: How Human Connections Drive Success in College* (Johns Hopkins University Press, 2020).

Ashley Finley is the vice president for research and senior advisor to the president at the AAC&U. In this role, she oversees AAC&U's research agenda through the coordination of projects and reports on pressing issues in higher education. She also provides guidance on strategic initiatives. Her recent HIP publications include *A Comprehensive Approach to Assessment of High-Impact Practices* (University of Illinois and Indiana University, National Institute for Learning Outcomes Assessment NILOA, 2019).

Steven S. Graunke is the director of institutional research and assessment at the Office of Institutional Research and Decision Support at IUPUI. In his role, Steven has conducted analyses of the effectiveness of learning communities, study abroad, community engagement, ePortfolios, and other HIPs. He has presented on the direct assessment of learning outcomes in HIPs at several conferences.

Heather A. Haeger is the research director of the STEM Learning Center and an assistant professor in educational policy studies and practice at the University of Arizona. She conducts research on educational equity in HIPs and the transition to graduate education. Her research is used to inform programmatic interventions aimed at engaging traditionally underserved populations in HIPs.

Thomas W. Hahn is the director of research and assessment in the IEL at IUPUI. His current responsibilities include conducting assessment and research on civic engagement programs and undergraduate research. He also serves as chair of the IUPUI Experiential and Applied Learning Subcommittee.

Ronald E. Hallett is a professor in the LaFetra College of Education at the University of LaVerne. His research focuses on how to increase educational access and success for at-promise students, with a particular focus on low-income, racially minoritized, housing-insecure, and first-generation college students. His work demonstrates how HIPs can be used to create validating experiences for these subgroups of students.

Michele J. Hansen is the assistant vice chancellor in the Office of Institutional Research and Decision Support (IRDS) at IUPUI. She is responsible for conducting investigations on the effectiveness of HIPs and facilitating improvements based on results. She has spent the last decade working with campus leaders and faculty to ensure fidelity of HIPs so that they are done well and result in increased higher order thinking, retention, engagement, completion, and satisfaction rates of students.

Shaun Harper is provost professor of education and business at the University of Southern California (USC). He also is one of 26 university professors at USC, the Clifford and Betty Allen Chair in Urban Leadership, and founder and executive director of the USC Race and Equity Center. He served as the 2020–2021 American Educational Research Association president and the 2016–2017 Association for the Study of Higher Education president, and was inducted into the National Academy of Education in 2021.

Jason Hilton is the director of the Honors College, the chapter president of Slippery Rock University Association of Pennsylvania State College & University Faculties, and a professor of education at Slippery Rock University (SRU). At SRU, he assisted in creating HIP faculty learning communities (FLCs), including designing how they operate and connecting the successful completion to the university curriculum process. Additionally, Hilton often teaches courses that are HIP-designated, including a diversity-designated course and a writing-intensive-designated course.

Myrna Hoover is the director of the Career Center at Florida State University and has served in the field of career services for 36 years. She leads a team of Career Center professionals committed to student success. Through their initiatives, programs, and services students at Florida State University are provided high-impact opportunities through career advising and counseling, job shadowing, internships, mentorship, competency development, and instructional courses in experiential learning and career planning.

Matthew T. Hora is an associate professor of adult and higher education and a director of the Center for Research on College-Workforce Transitions at the University of Wisconsin-Madison. In this work he leads mixed-methods applied research projects and brings applied insights from cultural anthropology, relational sociology, and the learning sciences to study how educators and employers can improve the design of internships as learning spaces, how to make experiential learning accessible for all college students, and the cross-cultural aspects of skills acquisition and socialization into the professions.

James Hunt is a director of institutional research at Florida State University. Through his previous work in student affairs assessment and now as a director of institutional research, he has spent nearly a decade collecting data and tracking student participation in various HIPs, including efforts to understand the effects of HIPs as well as looking at patterns of participation among underrepresented student populations.

Caroline J. Ketcham is a professor and chair of exercise science and codirector of Elon BrainCARE Research Institute at Elon University. She has been engaged in HIP research, including comentoring undergraduate research for student and faculty development, student-athlete access and engagement, and capstone experiences. She has been recognized for her high-quality teaching, scholarship, and mentoring with college and university awards.

Adrianna Kezar is the Wilbur Kieffer endowed professor and dean's professor of leadership and director of the Pullias Center at the University of Southern California. She has worked on several projects related to HIPs, including the California State University STEM collaboratives that connected and aligned three HIPs for students' 1st-year transition.

Jennifer Kilbourne is the dean of curriculum and assessment at Community College of Baltimore County, a large multicampus institution. Her work focuses on implementation of best practices in general education outcomes assessment, student learning outcomes assessment, guided pathways, and HIP infusion models.

Cindy Ann Kilgo is an associate professor of higher education and student affairs and interim codirector of the National Survey of Student Engagement at Indiana University. Their research has evolved from examining to interrogating HIPs. Specifically, their focus is on the role of identity and environment for minoritized student populations participating in HIPs.

Joseph A. Kitchen is an assistant research professor in the Pullias Center at the University of Southern California. His work with HIPs has primarily involved research and evaluation examining whether, how, and why

HIPs implemented as part of a comprehensive college transition program promote the success of low-income, first-generation, and racially minoritized students.

George D. Kuh is Chancellor's professor emeritus of higher education at Indiana University and the founding director of its Center for Postsecondary Research, the widely used National Survey of Student Engagement, and the National Institute for Learning Outcomes Assessment. He has written extensively about HIPs, student engagement, and institutional improvement.

Heidi Leming is the vice chancellor for student success at Tennessee Board of Regents. She serves as the system-level coordinator for scaling and implementation of HIPs at the 40 institutions governed by the Tennessee Board of Regents (TBR). Under her leadership, the TBR System has received several grants focused on scaling and embedding HIPs into academic pathways and the TBR was the first system to code student participation in the student information system.

Wendy Lin was the assistant director for the Office of Institutional Research and Decision Support at IUPUI, where she conducted high-level statistical analyses to help inform decision-making in areas of enrollment management, HIPs, and factors relating to student success. She is currently a manager of clinical data and data and analytics at Eli Lilly and Company.

William Loker is a professor of anthropology at California State University, Chico. As dean of undergraduate education (2004–2018), he helped foster, implement, assess, and disseminate HIPs, especially for 1st-year students and in the general education program at CSU-Chico.

Kevin McCarthy is the director of analytics and decision support at Slippery Rock University. He works with the faculty and academic affairs leaders to track and understand HIP course-taking patterns among students. Through careful analysis of the data, he also assists them in assessing the impact of HIP course enrollment on student outcomes.

Kelly McConnaughay is a professor of biology at Bradley University. She served as Bradley's general education coordinator from 2008 to 2015 and as cochair of the general education revision process from 2012 to 2015. As the first director of the new Bradley Core Curriculum (2016–2019), she oversaw the development and implementation of Bradley's required Core Practices, the HIPs required of all undergraduate students at the university.

Tia McNair is the vice president for diversity, equity, and student success and executive director for the Truth, Racial Healing and Transformation (TRHT) Campus Centers at AAC&U. She has more than 25 years of experience leading equity and student success efforts. She is the lead author of *Becoming a Student-Ready College: A New Culture of Leadership for Student Success* (2016) and *From Equity Talk to Equity Walk: Expanding Practitioner Knowledge for Racial Justice in Higher Education* (2020). McNair also directs AAC&U's Summer Institutes on High-Impact Practices and Student Success, and TRHT Campus Centers.

Jessie L. Moore is the director of the Center for Engaged Learning and a professor of English at Elon University. She leads planning, implementation, and assessment of Elon University's international, multi-institutional, and multidisciplinary research seminars on HIPs and other engaged learning topics. Her recent publications focus on mentored undergraduate research, writing-intensive experiences across and beyond the curriculum, and multi-institutional research on HIPs.

Meena C. Naik is currently at Jobs for the Future, where she focuses her work on promoting a skills-based ecosystem for learners and workers. She previously led efforts for skills credentialing and high-impact practices at the University of North Texas. Her work is grounded in supporting student success, persistence, skills-based credentialing and transferability, and enhancing equitable social and economic mobility pipelines.

Jon C. Neidy is the assistant vice president of student affairs and executive director of Smith Career Center at Bradley University. As a facilitative, learning-focused, and data-driven educator, he is committed to creating opportunities for all students to engage in and benefit from HIPs and experiential learning. He believes these opportunities empower students for immediate and sustained success and serve as a foundation for lifelong learning.

A. Sonia Ninon is the director of assessment and planning in the Division of Student Affairs at IUPUI. She is working with colleagues to identify cocurricular experiences that have attributes of HIPs and measure their impact on student learning outcomes, sense of belonging, retention, and graduation. They already examined the impact of living in one of the residential-based learning communities (RBLCs) at IUPUI on students' academic performance (term and cumulative GPAs) and retention.

Taé Nosaka is an associate executive director at Colorado State University. She has been designing, building, and scaling up equity initiatives at Colorado

State University for over 20 years, with the goal of closing opportunity gaps for structurally underserved students. In her role, she is responsible for integrating HIPs into the design, implementation, and assessment of intentionally diverse communities.

Heather Novak is the director of Institutional Research, Planning, and Effectiveness at Colorado State University.

Joe O'Shea is associate provost and dean of undergraduate studies at Florida State University. As dean, his work with HIPs involves developing new HIP programs, scaling programs across the diverse student body, and driving assessment to deliver a world-class learning experience for every student.

Kirsten Pagan is a student engagement analyst at Binghamton University. She is chiefly responsible for maintaining Binghamton University's robust cocurricular engagement platform, which doubles as the institution's database for HIPs. Additionally, she provides annual summary reports of HIPs participation for graduating seniors as well as providing answers to ad hoc research questions such as "Is there a natural sequence among HIPs for those who participate?"

Scott Peecksen is a senior evaluation and research consultant and data analyst for the U.S. Department of Education and University of North Texas (UNT). He has directed large-scale quasi-experimental designs to evaluate UNT's Student Success Initiative that integrated high-impact practices and marketable skills assessments into existing course and cocurricular experiences for underserved and general student populations as an outcomes assessment.

Rosemary J. Perez is an associate professor of higher education at the University of Michigan. When she was a student affairs practitioner working in residential life, she oversaw several living and learning communities, including one centered on intercultural learning. Her research has examined undergraduate students' experiences in and the effects of diversity/global learning programs and common intellectual experiences.

Rasha M. Qudisat is a measurement and evaluation expert, and program director of diversity and inclusion for Utah Valley University. Until 2019, she was the director of undergraduate research and creative works. She has codeveloped a methodology to measure the level and type of engaged learning of courses and methods to measure HIPs outcomes. She has conducted studies of HIPs' collective impact on students' persistence and academic performance.

Mike Simmons is currently the strategic projects director for the American Association of Collegiate Registrars and Admissions Officers (AACRAO). Simmons is also the CEO of the Mike Simmons Group and formerly an assistant vice president of Academic Affairs Curricular Innovation and Academic Partnerships at University of North Texas. His work with HIPs spans 20 years of direct support for faculty, course development, instructional design, and research. Implementing HIPs at scale, measuring impact on learning outcomes, and advancing the important relationship between HIPs and job skill attainment have been areas of focus, culminating with the recent implementation of a marketable skills comprehensive learner record based on HIPs.

Adrienne Viramontes is an associate professor of communication at the University of Wisconsin-Parkside. As a phenomenologist, she focuses on the experience of first-generation college students and first-generation faculty of color in the classroom. She examines how class-based experience and working-class ways of knowing/communicating shape and inform equity-minded, student-centered access to higher education.

Monica Walker is the dean of the School of Writing, Literacy, and Languages at Community College of Baltimore County. She provides strategic leadership and vision to guide the implementation of HIP infusion projects in general education courses, facilitates college-wide faculty development on HIPs, and serves as the cochair for the CCBC High Impact Practices Steering Committee.

Adam N. Wear is the director of the Curriculum and Partnership Initiatives at the University of North Texas. He has been working to integrate HIPs through a variety of course and cocurricular experiences in his work with UNT Career Connect, the UNT core curriculum, and UNT's Dual Credit Program. He is also interested in how students understand and communicate the skills gained through participating in HIPs.

Anthony G. Weaver is an associate dean of the School of Communications and professor of sport management at Elon University. He has been instrumental in the development of several capstone experiences at Elon, including the integration of these experiences into the School of Communications curriculum. He has also been a leader in HIPs for the student-athlete, including mentoring undergraduate research projects, coordinating and supervising internships, and developing leadership opportunities.

Frederick H. White is a professor of Russian and integrated studies at Utah Valley University. Until 2018, he was the associate vice president of engaged learning and administered the Office of Engaged Learning at Utah Valley University, which promoted and supported institutional strategies for academic engagement and collaborative learning opportunities to connect students' professional and civic lives with their educational aspirations.

Bradley Wilson recently retired from the position of associate provost of academic affairs and integrated learning at Slippery Rock University. He led HIP-related initiatives at SRU.

Thia Wolf is a professor emerita of English at California State University, Chico. As director of the First-Year Experience Program and as faculty in English at CSU, Chico, she designed courses, student-centered events, and programs drawing from communities of practice theory and research. Communities of practice require the use of authentic practices, regard for prior and ongoing development of knowledge of each participant, and social approaches to learning.

Kimberly Yousey-Elsener is the director of student affairs assessment and solutions for engagement at Binghamton University. She has been using data to create and enhance HIPs opportunities for students at various institutions. In addition, she has been studying the impact of participation in HIPs on student success for over a decade.

VOLUME TABLE INDEX

This index maps salient HIP topics, including student populations, HIP type, research and assessment method, level of implementation, institution type, and faculty development emphasis, addressed in each chapter. The intent is to help readers quickly find chapters and content that aligns with their HIP interests and to encourage exploration of new topics to advance their HIP practice and research.

INDEX

ability, student, asset-based mindset regarding, 51
academic advisors, 129
academic engagement, measurement of, 255
achievement gaps, at Community College of Baltimore County (CCBC), 151–152, 157, 161
Achieving the Dream (ATD) Engaging Adjunct Faculty in the Student Success Movement, 152
advisors, Engagement role of (University of South Carolina), 170
advising, proactive, 35–36
African American students
  academic motivation of, 136
  Centennial Scholars Program, 289
  at Community College of Baltimore County (CCBC), 157
  as first-generation students (FGS), 136
  HIP benefits to, 238
  retention of, 159–160, 162
  success rates of, 160–161, 162
  TLC results regarding, 98
agency, within capstone, 125, 127, 131
aggregation, 45–46
alumni, 131, 278
ambiance, classroom, within community-based learning (CBL), 141
Anthropology-English course (California State University, Chico), 83, 86–87
application, within capstone and HIP practice, 125, 127, 131, 273
applied learning experience program (SUNY system), 277
Asian American and Pacific Islander (AAPI) students, 287–288
aspirational cultural capital, 19
assessment
  of broad skills, 26
  within capstone projects, 126, 130–131
  of critical reflection, 106
  equity within, 24–27
  within experiential learning (EL), 195–196
  of HIPs, 153–154
  of outcomes, 233–235
  SEGO (Utah Valley University), 252–257
  of student experience, 106
  within Utah Valley University (UVU), 252
asset-based approach, 32, 35, 50–51
assignments, 85, 103
at-promise, defined, 30
at-promise students, 32
autobiographical writing, 34
average treatment effect for the treated (ATT), 67, 263

backstopping, 84
Beckman Scholars Program, 216
belonging, modes of, 86
B-Engaged (Binghamton University), 212
Beyond the Classroom Matters (BTCM) program (University of South Carolina), 165–170
bias, sensitivity analysis and, 268

Binghamton University
barriers within, 216
B-Engaged, 212
career development programs within, 214
Center for Civic Engagement (CCE), 209, 215
data collection within, 211–212
Education Abroad, 209–210
equity gap identification within, 211–212
External Scholarships and Undergraduate Research Center, 209
financial resources within, 213–214
Fleishman Center for Career Development, 209
future steps within, 216–218
High-Impact Practices Innovation Council (HIPIC), 210, 211–212, 213–214
HIP participation data within, 212–216
nonparticipants within, 213–214
Roadmap to Premier at, 209, 211
sequence of HIPs within, 214–216
Boston College, 130–131
Bradley University
challenges within, 184–186
collaboration within, 185
cultural change implementation within, 179–184
curriculum changes within, 180, 181–183
data-supported equity evidence within, 176–178
experiential learning (EL) within, 175–178, 179–186
graduation requirements within, 181
overview of, 175
pedagogy changes within, 183–184
Strategic Plan of, 180–181
student success goal within, 180
successes within, 184–186
Undergraduate Learning Experience, 176–177
broad skills, assessment regarding, 26

California State University, Chico, 82–83, 84, 85–89
Capital Community College, 278
capstone courses and experiences
assessment within, 126, 130–131
compensatory effect of, 125
components of, 125
data tracking and analysis within, 129–130
defined, 124
faculty development within, 127–128
promise within, 131–132
qualities of, 125
recommendations regarding, 125–131
shared goals and pathways articulation within, 125–127
statistics regarding, 126
Career Center (Florida State University), 191–192
careers
competency of, 193, 194, 230
development of, 214
outcomes of, 210
Centennial Scholars Program (North Carolina Central University), 289
Center for Civic Engagement (CCE) (Binghamton University), 209, 215
Center for Service and Learning (IUPUI), 94, 264
classroom, community building within, 278
classroom ambiance, within community-based learning (CBL), 141
coarsened-exact matching (CEM), 242
Coca-Cola, 194
cocurricular transcript (CCT), 211

collective reading, within Gateways to Phoenix Success (GPS), 53
College Internship Study, 115–116
College System of Tennessee, 219, 223, 224, 228–229. *See also* Tennessee Board of Regents (TBR) System
Colorado State University (CSU), 62, 65–73
communication, within capstone projects, 126, 128–129
communities of practice framework, 83
Community, Belonging, and Inclusion Priority Strategy (Tennessee Board of Regents), 219, 220
community-based learning (CBL)
  classroom ambiance within, 141
  curriculum for, 144
  departmental implementation of, 144
  designs of, 138–139
  encouragement within, 140–141
  for first-generation students (FGS), 135–136
  negative results regarding, 142–143
  open discussion within, 141
  at UW-Parkside, 139
Community College of Baltimore County (CCBC)
  achievement gaps at, 151–152, 157
  data collection and analysis within, 156–157
  demographics of, 151
  fidelity in implementation at, 155–156
  HIPs within, 152–163
  Infusion Steering Committee, 154
  internships at, 168–169
  overview of, 151
  pathways model within, 152
  research questions within, 156
  retention at, 157, 159–160, 162
  success rates at, 160–161, 162
community cultural wealth framework, 3
community-engaged learning (CEL), 215
community engagement, 264–265
Community for Excellence Scholar Program, 63
community of practice approach, 89–90
compensation, within internships, 115, 117, 120
Completion Agenda (Tennessee Board of Regents), 219
comprehensive college transition program (CCTP), 30, 31. *See also specific programs*
Connect Activities (University of North Texas), 240
control group, 234, 241–242
corequisite remediation model (Tennessee Board of Regents), 221
course-based undergraduate research experiences (CUREs), 102–110
courses, HIPs within, 152, 158–159
critical reflection, assessment of, 106
cross-stakeholder teams, 21
cultural capital, 19–20
culturally engaging campus model (CECE), 44
culturally relevant pedagogy (CRP), 50–51, 58
culturally responsive institutional research, 97
cultural wealth model, 19–20
curriculum, 144, 180, 181–183, 192–193, 199–208

dashboard, HIPs (Utah Valley University), 253, 256
data collection
  analysis within, 104–105
  within Binghamton University, 211–212
  within capstone projects, 129–130
  within Community College of Baltimore County (CCBC), 156–157
  within propensity score matching (PSM), 268–269

significance of, 164
of student engagement, 165–170
student management within, 103–105
within Tennessee Board of Regents (TBR) System, 223
Deakin University, 128
deficit mindset, 51, 55, 59
departments, HIPs within, 144–145
describe-examine-articulate learning (DEAL) model, 106
design, HIP, equity-centered approach to, 18–21
Digital Legacy Stories Project (UW-Parkside), 139
diversity, experiences within, 88, 93
diversity/global learning, through HIPs, 42
DVP-Praxis Ltd., 228

Education Abroad (Binghamton University), 209–210
Ellucian Banner designation, 203
Elon University, 21–22, 129–130
employment, 137, 278
encouragement, within community-based learning (CBL), 141
engaged learning, 94–95, 253, 257–259
engagement indicator scores, for TLCs-SLs, 99
Engagements (University of South Carolina), 165, 166, 167, 169–170, 171–172
ePortfolio (University of North Texas), 239, 240, 244, 245–246
equality, 287
equity
for Asian American and Pacific Islander (AAPI) students, 287–288
within assessment, 24–27
authentic, 72–73
challenges of, 286
data-supported, 44, 96–97, 176–178, 190–196, 269–270
defined, 19
gap identification regarding, 211–212
within HIP implementation, 21–24
pursuit of, 287
racial, 286–287
equity-centered approach of HIP design, 17–21, 24–27
equity-minded practitioners, 19
equity orientation (EO), 54–55
equity-oriented participation, 277
Experience Recognition Program (ERP) (Florida State University), 192–193
experiential learning (EL)
barriers regarding, 191–192
benefits of, 188
within Bradley University, 175–176
challenges and successes regarding, 184–186
cultural change implementation regarding, 179–184
within curriculum, 192–193
data-supported equity evidence regarding, 176–178
defined, 183
demographics and statistics regarding, 189
financial assistance for, 193–195
within Florida State University, 192–193
strategy development regarding, 196–197
tracking, evaluation, and reflection within, 195–196
Experiential Learning Opportunities (University of South Carolina), 167
experimental group, 234, 241–242
exploratory factor analysis (EFA) replication procedure, 253
External Scholarships and Undergraduate Research Center (Binghamton University), 209

faculty
attitude of, 141
capstone project role of, 126, 127–128, 129–130
within community-based learning (CBL), 141
within data collection process, 104
encouragement from, 140–141
equity orientation of, 54–55
within Gateways to Phoenix Success (GPS), 51–59
within HIP curriculum, 200
HIP design role of, 20–21
HIP feedback from, 167–168
HIP knowledge of, 22
internship role of, 169
as mentors, 84, 88
professional development for, 22–23, 58, 59, 127–128, 206
validation practices of, 33–34, 38
faculty-led curriculum (FLC), 201–203, 206, 208
faculty-student relationship, 43, 51, 52–53
familial cultural capital, 20
Federal Bureau of Investigation (FBI), 194
feedback, 25, 88, 107–110, 167–168
fidelity, 77–79, 94, 155–156, 279–280
financial aid, 213–214
first-generation students (FGS)
challenges of, 188
community-based learning (CBL) and, 138–139, 140–143
data regarding (University of South Carolina), 171
employment of, 137
HIP scaffolding for, 137–138
overview of, 135–137
research methods regarding, 139–143
first-time, full-time (FTFT) students, 66–72, 226–227
first-time-in-college (FTIC) students, 189
first-year experience program, 277
First-Year Experience (FYE) program (California State University, Chico), 83
first-year research programs, 216–217
first-year seminar (FYS), 36–37, 40, 223
Five Pillars of Student Engagement (Utah Valley University), 250–252
fixed mindset, characteristics of, 51
Fleishman Center for Career Development (Binghamton University), 209
Florida State University (FSU)
Career Center at, 191–192
cocurricular pathways within, 191
data-supported equity evidence within, 190–196
Experience Recognition Program (ERP), 192–193
experiential learning (EL) within, 190–196
Formative Experience within, 189–190
FSUshadow, 194
Garnet and Gold Scholar Society (GGSS), 196
institutional strategy of, 190
InternFSU, 194
pedagogies and practice within, 189–190
ProfessioNole Pathways, 191, 192, 193
Student Employee of the Year Award (SEOTY), 196
work-based learning programs at, 194
focus group data, regarding internships, 117–118
Formative Experience (Florida State University), 189–190
FSUshadow (Florida State University), 194

Garnet and Gold Scholar Society (GGSS) (Florida State University), 196
Gateways to Phoenix Success (GPS) (UW-Green Bay), 50–59
general education, HIPs within, 152–153, 158–159, 162–163
global learning, 207
goals, for capstones, 125–127
good data, 164
grade point average (GPA), 43–44, 98, 243–244, 245, 258
Graduate Senior Survey (GSS), 190
graduation rates
- of California State University, Chico, 82–83
- of College System of Tennessee, 223
- of Gateways to Phoenix Success (GPS), 57
- of Key Communities (Key) (Colorado State University), 71
- of Slippery Rock University (SRU), 204–206
- of Utah Valley University, 257–258

group projects, 106

Hendrix College, 277
hidden bias, sensitivity analysis and, 268
Higher Education Research Institute (HERI), 38
High-Impact Practices (HIP)
- benefits of, 238, 276
- capacity building within, 22–23
- challenges within, 2, 78
- data-supported equity regarding, 96–97
- defined, 1
- delivering on the promise of, 2–5, 11–12
- dimensions of, 7, 153
- examples of, 1, 3–4
- expectations regarding, 2
- features of, 274–276, 278
- feedback within, 25
- implementation equity within, 21–24
- implementation fidelity of, 279–280
- implications for practice of, 143–145
- implicit bias within, 3
- influence of, 1
- interaction within, 25
- knowledge increase regarding, 22
- learning outcomes within, 207
- next generation, 280–281
- overview of, 285–289
- participation opportunities within, 92–93
- quality dimensions of, 25–26
- quality indicators of, 87–89
- raising awareness of existing, 21–22
- reflection within, 25
- restrictions regarding, 21
- scaling of, 147–149, 222–225, 229–230, 240, 244, 276–279
- self-discipline within, 4
- sustaining of, 23–24

High-Impact Practices Innovation Council (HIPIC) (Binghamton University), 210, 211–212, 213–214
HIP Quality assessment tool (NSSE), 26
"HIPs for All" goal, 4–5
Hispanic students, HIP benefits to, 238
Homeless Assistance Leadership Organization Project (UW-Parkside), 139

identity, recordkeeping regarding, 47
implicit bias, within HIPs, 3
Indiana University-Purdue University Indianapolis (IUPUI), 93–100, 264, 266
inequality, within internships, 119
Infusion Steering Committee (CCBC), 154
Institute for Engaged Learning (IEL) (IUPUI), 96–97

institutional review board (IRB), 103
integration, 125, 127, 131, 274
interaction, within HIP practice, 25
intercultural competency, 259
interdisciplinary teams, 21
InternFSU (Florida State University), 194
Internship Council, 195
internships
  access-related issues regarding, 114–115
  alternative forms of, 119
  availability within, 117–118
  challenges regarding, 113–114, 115, 116, 118–120
  College Internship Study, 115–116
  at Community College of Baltimore County (CCBC), 168–169
  compensation within, 115, 117, 120
  at Florida State University (FSU), 190–196
  focus group data regarding, 117–118
  location of, 118
  for low GPA students, 43–44
  micro, 120
  on-campus, 194, 196
  online, 119–120
  paid *versus* unpaid, 190
  privilege and inequality within, 119
  remote, 119–120
  research regarding, 114–115
  resources for, 193–195
  scheduling within, 117
  strategy development regarding, 196–197
  types of, 114

Key Communities (Key) (Colorado State University), 65–73
Kurtinitis, Sandra, 151

Latinx students, 88, 136
learning experiences, design process of, 19
learning outcomes, within HIPs, 207
lesbian, gay, bisexual, and queer (LGBQ+), 43
linguistic cultural capital, 19
living-learning communities, 265–266
living-learning programs (LLPs), 265–266
logistic regression, 263
Lumina NASH TS3 HIPs grant, 225
Luther College, 277

mentoring
  within California State University, Chico, 84
  faculty within, 84
  within a major, 102–103
  peers within, 84
  ProfessioNole Pathways, 192
  quality indicators of, 88
  teaching assistants (TAs) within, 84
  within undergraduate research, 81
Miami University, 201
microaggressions, 286
micro-internship, 120
minoritized students
  data-supported equity regarding, 44
  within Gateways to Phoenix Success (GPS), 56
  HIP datasets regarding, 41–44
  HIP implementation for, 46–48
  identity recordkeeping for, 47
  within Key Communities (Key) (Colorado State University), 66, 68
  quality of research regarding, 45–46
  See also specific nationalities
modes of belonging, 86
Momentum Year approach (Tennessee Board of Regents), 221–222

National Study of Lesbian, Gay, Bisexual, Transgender, and Queer Student Success (LGBTQSS), 42
National Study of Living-Learning Programs, 265–266

National Survey of Student Engagement (NSSE), 26, 81, 99, 276, 280, 285
navigational cultural capital, 20
nonparticipant project (NPP), 216
North Carolina Central University (NCCU), 289

Office for Community-Engaged Learning (OCEL) (Slippery Rock University), 201
Office of Diversity, Equity and Community Engagement (ODECE) (University of Colorado Boulder), 23
Office of Engaged Learning (OEL) (Utah Valley University), 250, 258, 260
Office of Institutional Research and Decision Support (IRDS) (IUPUI), 97
Office of Teaching and Learning (OTL) (Utah Valley University), 256
online internships, 119–120
open discussion, within community-based learning (CBL), 141
outcomes, 24–25, 233–235

pathways, for capstones, 125–127
peer mentors, 84, 88
Pell Grant, 189
practitioners, equity-minded, 19
presentations, 105
privilege, 119, 288–289
proactive advising, 35–36
proactive support, 34
professional development, 22–23, 58, 59, 127–128, 206
ProfessioNole Pathways (Florida State University), 191, 192, 193
propensity score matching (PSM)
  data collection within, 268–269
  data-supported equity regarding, 269–270
  methodology regarding, 263–264
  overview of, 262, 268–269
  pedagogies and practices regarding, 264–267
  quality of research within, 267–268
  residential-based learning communities and, 265–266
  service/community engagement and, 264–267
  study abroad and, 266–267
  undergraduate research and, 265, 270
  use of, 66–72, 263
public reading, of autobiographical writing, 34

quality assurance tool (Tennessee Board of Regents), 224
Quality Enhancement Plan (QEP) (University of North Texas), 247
quantitative questionnaire, 107–108

race, diversity interactions by, 42–43
racial equity, 286–287
randomized experimental studies, 262–263
the Record (Experiential and Applied Learning Record) (IUPUI), 96–97
reflection, 25, 106, 195–196, 273
registrar, capstone project role of, 129–130
remote internships, 119–120
research, undergraduate
  applied nature of, 89
  course-based undergraduate research experiences (CUREs) within, 102–110
  data collection and management within, 103–105
  feedback within, 88, 107–110
  mentoring within, 81, 84
  outcome measurement of, 105–110
  overview of, 102
  practice of, 85–86

propensity score matching (PSM) of, 265, 270
purpose of, 81
quality indicators of, 87–89
research partners within, 86
scaffolding of assignments within, 85
within Slippery Rock University (SRU), 208
student experience assessment within, 106
research partners, 86
research questions, development of, 267–268
residential-based learning communities, 265–266
resistance cultural capital, 20
retention
within College System of Tennessee, 226–227
within Community College of Baltimore County (CCBC), 157, 159–160, 162
within Gateways to Phoenix Success (GPS), 56, 57
HIPs and, 237–239
within Indiana University (IU), 266
within Key Communities (Key) (Colorado State University), 71, 73
from service-learning (SL), 100
study abroad and, 266–267
from TLCs, 100
within University of North Texas (UNT), 243–244, 246
RIBS framework, 21, 23–24, 27
Roadmap to Premier (Binghamton University), 209, 211
rubrics, 26–27, 240, 247

Sam H. Jones Scholarship (SHJ), 264
scaffolding, 85, 103, 137–138
scaling, of HIPs
overview of, 147–149, 276–279
within Tennessee Board of Regents (TBR) System, 222–225, 229–230
within University of North Texas (UNT), 240, 244
SEGO (Utah Valley University), 252–257, 259–260
self-discipline, within HIPs, 4
sensitivity analysis, 268
sequence, of HIPs, 214–216
service/community engagement, 264–265
service-learning (SL)
benefits of, 93
defined, 94
demographics of, 98
engagement indicator scores regarding, 99
literature regarding, 93–94
overview of, 93, 99–100
retention from, 100
statistics of, 227
study regarding, 97–99
at Utah Valley University (UVU), 257
shadowing, career, 194
shared academic courses (SAC), 33–34
short-term career exposure, 194
signature work, 125
Slippery Rock University (SRU)
assessment results within, 203–206
FLC model at, 201–203, 206, 208
institutional profile and context of, 199–200
Office for Community-Engaged Learning (OCEL), 201
professional development at, 206
undergraduate research within, 208
social capital, 20
Sodexo, 194
Southern Association of Colleges and Schools Commission on Colleges (SACSCOC), 171

staff, professional development for, 22–23
stakeholders, 27, 247
Strategic Plan (Bradley University), 180–181
strengths-based approach, 32, 35, 36–37, 38
Strengths Finder (Gallup), 37
structural equation model (SEM), 254–255
student ability, 51, 55, 59
student departure, theory of, 237–238
Student Employee of the Year Award (SEOTY) (Florida State University), 196
student engagement, 126, 129–130, 165–170
student experience, assessment of, 106
student-instructor relations, 43, 51, 52–53
students, implicit theories regarding, 18
Students of Color, 45–46, 286, 287. *See also specific nationalities*
student success
  within Bradley University, 180
  within Community College of Baltimore County (CCBC), 160–161, 162
  defined, 178
  factors regarding, 220, 281
  within Tennessee Board of Regents (TBR) System, 228–229
  within Utah Valley University (UVU), 257–259
study abroad
  academic development and, 43
  career earnings and, 40
  propensity score matching (PSM) of, 266–267
  statistics regarding, 224, 257
  student outcome measurement of, 234
  at Western Kentucky University (WKU), 266–267
summer bridge programs, 191
SUNY system, 277, 278
supporting evidence, gathering of, 105–106

taxonomies, HIP, 221–222
teaching assistants (TAs), as mentors, 84
Tennessee Board of Regents (TBR) System
  Community, Belonging, and Inclusion Priority Strategy of, 219, 220
  Completion Agenda of, 219
  corequisite remediation model of, 221
  early evidence within, 225–227
  events and milestones of, 220
  future directions within, 230–231
  goal of, 224–225
  HIP scaling approach of, 222–225, 229–230
  HIP statistics within, 224
  HIP taxonomies of, 221–222
  Momentum Year approach of, 221–222
  student participation in HIP statistics within, 226–227
  student success effects within, 228–229
  warranty card within, 230
Tennessee Transfer Pathways (TTP), 221
themed learning community (TLC)
  benefits of, 94
  data-supported equity regarding, 96–97
  demographics of, 98
  elements of, 93
  engagement indicator scores regarding, 99
  overview of, 99–100
  pedagogies and practices within, 94–95
  purpose of, 93–94

retention from, 100
study regarding, 97–99
themes within, 93
theory of student departure, 237–238
Thompson Scholars Learning Community (TSLC), 31–37, 38
Title V, 278
transfer students
experiential learning for, 181, 189
first-year research programs for, 217
as nonparticipants, 213
pathways for, 221, 225
resources for, 191
TRIO, 32
21st Century Citizen course (UW-Green Bay), 52, 53

U-Courses (California State University, Chico), 82, 83, 85–87
Undergraduate Learning Experience (Bradley University), 176–177
undergraduate research
applied nature of, 89
course-based undergraduate research experiences (CUREs) within, 102–110
data collection and management within, 103–105
feedback within, 88, 107–110
mentoring within, 81, 84
outcome measurement of, 105–110
overview of, 102
practice of, 85–86
propensity score matching (PSM) of, 265, 270
purpose of, 81
quality indicators of, 87–89
research partners within, 86
scaffolding of assignments within, 85
within Slippery Rock University (SRU), 208
student experience assessment within, 106
University of Calgary, 128
University of Colorado Boulder, 23
University of Nebraska, 31
University of North Carolina at Pembroke, 127–128
University of North Texas (UNT)
analysis plan within, 242–243
discussion and implications within, 245–246
ePortfolio of, 239, 240, 244, 245–246
equitable impact and success within, 241
GPA statistics within, 243–244, 245
HIP model within, 238–239
HIP scaling within, 240, 244
methodology and samples within, 241–244
recommendations regarding, 246–247
results within, 244–245
retention statistics within, 243–244, 246
UNTConnect, 239, 240, 241, 244–245, 247
University of South Carolina (UofSC)
advisor role within, 170
Beyond the Classroom Matters (BTCM) program within, 165–170
data analysis within, 170–172
Engagements within, 165, 166, 167, 169–170, 171–172
Experiential Learning Opportunities within, 167
feedback within, 167–168
future directions within, 173–174
HIPs within, 165–174
implementation workflow within, 167–170
University of Wisconsin- Parkside, 136–145
UNTConnect (University of North Texas), 239, 240, 241, 244–245, 247

Utah Valley University (UVU)
baseline measurement within, 252
centralized model within, 250–252
Five Pillars of Student Engagement, 250–252
GPA statistics within, 258
graduation rate at, 257–258
Office of Engaged Learning (OEL), 250, 258, 260
Office of Teaching and Learning (OTL), 256
SEGO within, 252–257, 259–260
structural equation model (SEM), 254–255
student success within, 257–259
study abroad within, 257
UW-Green Bay, Gateways to Phoenix Success (GPS), 50–59

validation
challenges of, 38
defined, 31
faculty role within, 33–34
within first-year seminar (FYS), 36–37
within HIPs, 32–33
measurement of, 38
within proactive advising, 35–36
scalability of, 38
within shared academic courses (SAC), 33–34
strengths-based approach to, 38
VALUE rubrics (AACU), 26, 240, 247
vision statement, 25

Wabash National Study of Liberal Arts Education (WNS), 41–42, 45
warranty card (Tennessee Board of Regents System), 230
Western Kentucky University (WKU), 266–267
white students, 125, 157, 159–161, 162
white-washing, 45
work-based learning, 194, 227
writing-intensive courses, 175

Made in United States
Orlando, FL
06 May 2024

46559072R00180